Cats of Any Color

cats

Gene Lees

of
Any

color

Jazz Black and White

DA CAPO PRESS

A CIP catalog record for this book is available
from the Library of Congress.

First Da Capo Press edition, December 2000
ISBN 0-306-80950-8

Published by Da Capo Press
A Member of the Perseus Books Group
http://www.dacapopress.com

1 2 3 4 5 6 7 8 9—04 03 02 01 00

To the memory of Dizzy Gillespie.

I miss you, Birks.

I thought you would be there forever,

like the Matterhorn, and the Aurora Borealis,

and Polaris.

Acknowledgments

The essays in this book first appeared, some of them in somewhat different form, in the *Jazzletter*, PO Box 240, Ojai, CA 93024-0240. This is the fourth collection of pieces from the *Jazzletter* to be published by Oxford University Press.

I am grateful to many persons for information, counsel, and suggestions, Grover Sales and Cliff Hopkinson high on the list. I thank Sheldon Meyer, senior vice president of Oxford, for his faith in this work, as well as Joellyn Ausanka and Leona Capeless, also of Oxford. I especially thank Charles Sweningsen. Chuck is the best copy editor I ever knew. A former *Down Beat* editor on the staff of the *Chicago Sun-Times*, he edited the copy and read proof of every issue of *Down Beat* while I was the magazine's editor. Retired now, he did me the honor of dragging himself away from the ski slopes long enough to do similar work on this book, and it has benefited from his keen eye and unfailing taste.

Finally I thank the readers of the *Jazzletter*, who for more than thirteen years have supported it and made my researches possible—a remarkable body of scholars in all fields, journalists, doctors, and above all musicians.

G. L.

Contents

Introduction to
the Da Capo Edition

Often it will be found that someone speaks a third language with the accent of the second. My Spanish, for example, has a French accent. Gene Kelly spoke French with a slight Italian accent. He grew up in an Italian neighborhood in Philadelphia.

Over the years, I have also observed that anyone who has had two professions practices the second with the disciplines and outlook of the first. You can see this in movie-makers. Directors who were first actors elicit fine work from their performers—for example, Richard Attenborough. Consider the miraculous performance he got from Robert Downey, Jr. as the English Charles Chaplin. Or the performances Robert Redford gets from actors, as in *Ordinary People* and *A River Runs Through It*. Or Sydney Pollack and Mark Rydell, both of whom had been actors, in any number of pictures.

Alfred Hitchcock, who early manifested a skill in things mechanical, went to work for a telegraph company, then broke into the film industry as a title-card illustrator. His pictures were always visual, mechanical, and short on great acting, no matter the idolatry toward his pictures fashionable in film circles. He was quoted as saying that actors should be treated like cattle, and his movies look like filmed storyboards. David Lean began as a film editor, and though his films—*The Bridge on the River Kwai*, for example—reflect prodigious gifts for working with actors, they also reveal his first training in that they are magnificently, meticulously photographed and edited.

I was trained as an artist, but my first profession was journalism. I had been a newspaper reporter, editor, and foreign correspondent for ten years before I became the editor of *Down Beat* in April, 1959, and a thirst for factuality would stay with me. I looked the magazine over and sent a memo to staff members and contributors saying that its first duty was to be a good magazine, literate and readable. If it did not fulfill that obligation, it could not serve its subject matter well. I also urged a concern for factuality, in contrast to the opinion-mongering that comprised much, even most, of jazz criticism, and still does. To say something is exciting or boring or touching or disturbing is only to confess what excites, bores, touches, or disturbs *you*. It is not a fact about the work of art in question, it is a fact about *the critic*, a projection of his or her own character and experience.

I did what everyone did at *Down Beat*: I wrote record reviews. Projecting your opinions in print is the fastest way in the world to alienate the victims of your inescapable subjectivity. In any case, unless you are like Addison DeWitt in *All About Eve* and enjoy causing pain, writing criticism ain't your thing. So I fired myself as a record reviewer soon after joining the magazine. I have written very, very little jazz criticism, which is why I was in early years discomfited to see myself referred to as a jazz critic, later embarrassed, and finally resigned to it.

My education in jazz came not from magazines and books but from studies of composition, piano (with Tony Aless, among others), and guitar—and from long, rich conversations in such places as Jim and Andy's bar in New York with Phil Woods, Gerry Mulligan, Ben Webster, Coleman Hawkins, Hank d'Amico, Will Bradley, Jimmy McPartland, Lockjaw Davis, Dizzy Gillespie, Clark Terry, J.J. Johnson, and many more. I found that jazz history, as it was generally accepted, was to a large extent a fiction that has been agreed upon, as Voltaire said of all history. It dawned on me that, since such founding figures as Louis Armstrong and Earl Hines were still with us, I had met nearly all the great jazz musicians who had ever lived, and knew some of them, such as Bill Evans and Woody Herman, intimately. At the same time, because of my activities as a lyricist, I met and in some cases came to know many of the major songwriters who had inspired and influenced me, including Howard Dietz, Arthur Schwartz, Harold Arlen, Johnny Green, Hoagie Carmichael, Mitchell Parrish, Harry Warren, and particularly Johnny Mercer, someone else who became a close friend.

After leaving *Down Beat* toward the end of 1961, I settled in New York and devoted myself primarily to songwriting. I spent the early 1970s in Toronto, then settled in 1974 in Southern California, where I have remained ever since, the climate being one of its blandishments. By the end of the 1970s, my songs had been recorded by Mabel Mercer, Frank Sinatra, Tony Bennett, Sarah Vaughan (my dear, dear friend!), Ella Fitzgerald,

Nancy Wilson, Joe Williams, Carmen McRae, Peggy Lee (another dear friend), and so many others that my royalties, at least in theory, made it possible for me to retire, and I tried. I soon found that I missed my friends, among them all the jazz musicians I had come to know since 1959.

On a morning in May, 1981, I sent a questionnaire to several hundred persons, asking whether I should start a letter—not a *news*letter, giving record reviews, nightclub listings, and current news, but a letter on matters of interest to all of us. I specified that it would contain no advertising. Within a week, I had a mailbox full of letters urging me to do it, some of them containing checks. I realized that I was committed. Broadcaster Fred Hall and composer-pianist-arranger Roger Kellaway gave the *Jazzletter* its name. I still remember the list of early subscribers. It included Phil Woods, Gerry Mulligan, Dizzy Gillespie, Clark Terry, Shelly Manne, Benny Carter, Jimmy Rowles, John Lewis, Art Farmer, Kenny Wheeler, Kenny Drew, Sahib Shihab, Rob McConnell, Henry Mancini, Johnny Mandel, Julius La Rosa, Jackie and Roy Kral, Robert Farnon, and Audrey Morris, such record-company executives as Charles Lourie, Bruce Lundvall, and Ken Glancy, and a number of critics and jazz historians, including Whitney Balliett, Doug Ramsey, Grover Sales, James Lincoln Collier, Philip Elwood, and the late Leonard Feather, as well as academics.

The *Jazzletter* addressed a list of subscribers almost all of whom I knew personally. It was written for musicians, dealing with matters that concern musicians—jazz musicians to a large extent but not exclusively. I did not design it to exclude laymen, and indeed whenever technical discussions proved necessary, tried to make them as clear and brief as possible. But in general, the publication assumed a measure of knowledge in its readers. I asked guitarist and composer Mundell Lowe what he thought the limits of *Jazzletter* subject matter should be. He said, "Anything that is of interest to *us*."

And what was of acute interest to jazz musicians was the history of the music and its makers, whether one of the older players and the era he or she had lived through, or younger ones, anxious to know about the times they did not know. And given that I faced no limits in length, I was able to write extended pieces that simply would not be practical in most magazines for structural reasons. I soon found that I was recording the life stories, derived from extended interviews, of musicians who might deserve book-length biographies but were unlikely to get them, the nature of publishing being what it is. I found myself writing what I came to think of as mini-biographies.

In time, Oxford University Press published four anthologies of these essays, each of them gathered loosely around a central theme. *Cats of Any Color* was the fourth of these collections. Cassell has published a fifth, *Arranging the Score,* Yale University Press is publishing a sixth, and a seventh is pending. I know of no other publication that has produced a comparable quantity of anthologized material. Two of the books received the ASCAP–Deems Taylor Award.

My awareness of the racial problem of the United States predates my moving here in 1955 from Canada. Canada may be a vague entity to the north of which Americans know little, but Canadians are acutely aware of events in the United States. The Toronto-Hamilton-Niagara area in which I grew up is within a day's driving of eighty percent of the population of the North American continent, and Canadians received all the American radio, and later television networks, saw all the American movies, read the American magazines and American novelists, and bought records by American bands and singers, all of whom included the major Canadian cities on their touring itineraries. I saw Duke Ellington and Jimmie Lunceford when I was thirteen. Because so many of my heroes were black musicians, as I grew older I read as many works by black writers as I could get my hands on.

Over the years of interviewing musicians, black and white, I made it a point *not* to raise the subject of race, not because I wasn't interested in this dimension of American life but precisely because I was, and did not wish to lead the subject. If one of them raised it, fine; but I was not going to be the one to do so. It came up often with white musicians, and almost invariably with black musicians. How could it be otherwise? It is the central problem of the United States, and the more I lived in the jazz world the more I was made aware of it, having friends insulted or endangered for no other reason than color. Dizzy Gillespie and Clark Terry, among others, told me some harrowing stories.

After the third collection of *Jazzletter* essays, Sheldon Mayer, Oxford's senior editor (unfortunately now retired) began talking to me about a fourth book. Musing on how often the subject had come up in my interviews, I thought that a collection in which racial abrasion played an important part might make an interesting documentation of this phenomenon as it affected jazz and jazz musicians. This collection was the result.

The first essay relates my shock on encountering some of the reality of racism during my residence in Louisville, Kentucky. The second, on the great scholar Dominique de Lemma, now teaching at Lawrence University in Wisconsin, reviews some of the pre-jazz history of African influence on American music and, equally importantly, on that of Europe before the United States was even founded.

The next essay, centering on Dave Brubeck, deals with the first ethnic group in America to encounter the ruthlessness of the European invader, the so-called Indians. Some of Dave Brubeck's ancestors were of a people that came close to obliteration, and Dave is only one of many jazz musicians with Indian ancestry, from Benny Golson and Art Farmer to Jim Hall and even Duke Ellington. One of the major influences in jazz, Frank Trumbauer, was Indian.

The next segment, on the career of singer Ernie Andrews, touches on the horrors of being black in white show business, and above all, being black under the redneck Los Angeles police department, which has been frightening citizens both black and white since a time long before the Rodney King incident and the scandals of the 1999 investigation of corruption, still going on as I write this.

The next piece is on Horace Silver, who is of mixed stock: Indian, like Brubeck, but also African and Portuguese. His father came from the Cape Verde Islands, once the place of the holding pens for blacks about to be sent off into the hopelessness of America. Red Rodney is one of the most interesting trumpet players—a brilliant soloist—who was, in effect, one of the "white boys" Dizzy Gillespie and Charlie Parker supposedly tried to keep off the bandstands in Harlem when bebop was evolving. In fact they nurtured and encouraged and taught him, as they did so many others.

Benny Golson was not allowed to play the saxophone during his time as a student at Howard University, because it was a "jazz" instrument. The prejudice against jazz was nowhere more severe than among middle- and upper-class black Americans, so many of whom were (and sometimes still are) more proud of Leontyne Price than of Sarah Vaughan, if indeed they weren't actually embarrassed by Sarah. That is one—just one—of the stinging tragedies of American racism, for its recipients to reject their own massive cultural contributions.

Many black American jazz musicians moved to Europe to escape the racism of their native country, among them Bill Coleman, Kenny Clarke, Johnny Griffin, Ben Webster, Kenny Drew, Ernie Wilins, Edmund Thigpen, Sahib Shihab, and Arthur Farmer. When Sahib and I were living together in Geneva, Switzerland, working on an album we eventually made with Sarah

Vaughan, and he told me he was homesick for the U.S. (he had been living for some years in Copenhagen), I said, "Then why don't you come home?"

He shook his head; we were in our little kitchen, having dinner. "I'm not gonna go back there and just be some nigger," he said.

Red Mitchell was not black. Yet racism was one of the reasons he left the United States to live in Stockholm. In due course he was to see incipient racism where he thought it could never be, and returned after many years to the United States. Red Mitchell was one of the most influential of all jazz players; this is not noted in the history books.

After that there are three short pieces—on Cedar Walton, which touches on the intimidation that racism can cause; on Kenny Washington, a marvelous drummer and jazz historian, which in part deals with a young black musician and all that he gained from a white mentor and hero; and on Jack De Johnette, who attests to the scope of the influence of pianist Bill Evans and even the trio he led.

Does it come as a complete surprise that some blacks have retaliatory feelings towards whites? Clark Terry told me that his first wife could not even talk to white persons. When she was a young girl, hooded white men came into her home and took her equally young cousin out to the porch and hanged him. But Clark Terry will reminisce about whites who saved his life, and he, like Dizzy Gillespie, will not draw racial judgments. So too Milton Hinton, who in his childhood in Vicksburg, Mississippi, saw hideous things, and heard narratives of more. These are great men, magnificent human beings.

But there has long been an anti-white sentiment among certain jazz musicians. They for the most part have been the lesser ones. Certainly this was never true of the truly great ones: not Duke Ellington, Louis Armstrong, Bud Powell, Charlie Parker, Dizzy Gillespie, Clark Terry, Count Basie, Lockjaw Davis, Philly Joe Jones, Sy Oliver, Ben Webster, Coleman Hawkins, and so many more.

In the final section of *Cats of Any Color*, after documenting some of the effects of white racism on jazz musicians, I dealt with the phenomenon of anti-white sentiment among some black jazz musicians, and, incidentally, not a few white critics, especially in France. Various reviewers considered this politically incorrect. Chip DeFaa wrote (for the British publication *Crescendo & Jazz Music*) that the book's last section "began garnering attention as galleys circulated, well before the book's official publication date." And some of the reviews gave the impression that the writers had leaped to the last section and the mention of Wynton Marsalis without first (if ever) reading the discussions of white racism that preceded it.

"New Book Hits Sour Note Calling Marsalis Racist," the headline read, in a severe attack on the book by Larry Gabriel in the *Detroit Free Press*. He neither disproved nor refuted even one of the facts I had cited, nor the statements made by both Stanley Crouch and Wynton Marsalis. A headline in the *Winnipeg Free Press* read: "Author Says Marsalis is Racist." Show me where. But I did delineate his practices and quote him extensively.

And that is the point, I think. I simply did a newspaperman's research and wrote the results. Little has changed in the jazz program of Lincoln Center since the book was published, except that it will soon expand into a multi-million-dollar jazz palace at Columbia Circle, of which Marsalis is in charge. Many, many jazz musicians think the effect of Jazz at Lincoln Center has been destructive to the art.

The book received many reviews in praise. The one that meant the most to me was by Bob Cranshaw, which appeared in *Allegro*, the newspaper of 802, the New York local of the musicians' union. Cranshaw is himself a musician, a bassist, and indeed one of the truly fine ones. I would like to quote it, because Bob is black and because he knows the world of jazz very well indeed, including that of New York City. He wrote:

"In *Cats of Any Color*, Gene Lees deals with the explosive issues that are increasingly dividing jazz in a judicious, balanced manner. Lees's sensitivity and beautifully written plea to recognize jazz not as the sole property of any one group but as an art form that celebrates the human spirit is bound to stir up controversy and strong emotion in all who read it.

"Please, get this book and read it."

Gene Lees
October 2000

Cats of Any Color

These people who make the restrictions, they don't know nothing about music. It's no crime for cats of any color to get together and blow. Race-conscious jazz musicians? Nobody could be who really knew their horns and loved the music.

—*Louis Armstrong*

I am prior to borders.

—*Antonio Carlos Jobim*

The Prez
of Louisville

The first black man I ever knew was named Charlie Dorsey. He worked in a paper mill and wrote poetry, free verse that he published at his own expense in slim little volumes he gave to his friends. I remember holding one of these books, words in black ink on white paper and encased in a red paper cover, with a sense that I was caressing a treasure. I had never known an author of words that were actually in print, and I was in awe of books. It mattered little that he had paid to publish the book himself; what mattered was that he gave it to me.

I held Charlie Dorsey in a kind of reverence, and that was even before he saved my life. But then I thought all black people were gods. This was because most of my idols were black, men named Benny Carter, Nat Cole, Duke Ellington, Jimmie Lunceford, Joe Thomas, Ray Nance, Count Basie, Lester Young, Coleman Hawkins, Teddy Wilson, Arnett Cobb. Dozens of them. One young friend of mine, who played trumpet and shared my awe of them, said that whenever he saw a Negro (the requisite polite term in those days), he wanted to get his autograph, even if the man was a railway porter. Such indeed was our conditioning. There were a few white heroes, too: Woody Herman, Buddy Rich, Cappy Lewis, Mel Powell, Bunny Berigan, Artie Shaw. I even had a few heroes who weren't musicians, John Steinbeck, Thomas Wolfe, William Saroyan, and William Faulkner among them. But one thing all—or almost all—my heroes had in common, black or white, musicians or otherwise: they were Americans. And I wasn't.

This awareness went back even deeper into my childhood. To anyone growing up in Canada fifty years ago, it appeared that Canadians had never accomplished anything. Superman, Batman, The Green Lantern, The Spirit, Dick Tracy, Red Ryder, Flash Gordon, Tailspin Tommie and Smilin' Jack, and for that matter, Frank Merriwell and Tom Swift, were Americans. Our afternoon and evening radio-series heroes were Jack Armstrong the All-

American Boy, Don Winslow of the U.S. Navy, The Shadow, The Green Hornet, Mr. District Attorney, and The Lone Ranger, Americans to a man. So too the comedians who made us laugh and the singers who sang our love songs, all of them American.

So while Robert Taylor resisted the wicked Japs in *Bataan* and John Wayne beat them back in *Sands of Iwo Jima*, we remained insensitive to the tragedy of Dieppe. When Cecil B. DeMille gave a nod to our existence in *Northwest Mounted Police*, an American cowboy, Gary Cooper, had to come up to Canada to show the hapless redcoats how to lasso a Gatling gun and save the day. Come to that, so completely did American entertainment appropriate our Mounties that I thought *Renfrew of the Mounted*, one of the radio serial heroes, *was* an American. I can remember being vaguely surprised to find out that the Mounties were Canadian.

Small wonder that so many of us had an identity problem, one symptom of which was that we approached whatever Canadian art or entertainment there was with a conditioned condescension, imposing our own doubts upon it. That problem left me permanently sympathetic to the black-identity problem in the United States. When all the heroines presented to your young people are in the mold of Jean Harlow and Marilyn Monroe, how can a young black girl see herself as beautiful? When all the blacks in movies were porters or doormen or housemaids (Billie Holiday appeared in one as a maid), how can a young black boy aspire to be a test pilot? Or an astronaut? Or cardiologist?

And how much worse was it for American Indians, whose achievements in jazz (Frank Trumbauer's among them) and other fields of the arts have simply been ignored. Not only were they offered no heroes by the inescapable mass media, their ancestors were portrayed almost universally in movies and on television as murderous savages endlessly victimizing white women and children. The reverse is more true. In 1800 there were 300,000 Indians in California. In 1900 there were only 20,000.

I never have understood those who pull back from difference, or worse, hate it, some of them with a lethal dedication. I loved it and in time fled into it, any kind of difference I could find: French, Jewish, Italian, Latin American, Oriental, black.

My parents had a lot to do with my attitudes. My father went to work in a Lancashire cotton mill when he was twelve and in a coal mine at fourteen. He practiced violin fingerings on the handle of a shovel and eventually became a musician. Only late in his life did he tell me that for a time he had played in little bands on Rhine river boats, which explained why he spoke fluent German.

I do not remember either of my parents ever saying they loved me, and neither do my brother and two sisters. My parents had many faults, but they had two virtues: though neither of them had much formal education, they were highly literate persons; and they were devoid of any kind of ethnic prejudice. My mother, however, was afflicted with that peculiarly English sense of class. She was born in London—she was technically a Cockney, although she had been in Canada from the time she was three and had no trace of English accent—and she despised my father's Lancashire relatives. I was made very conscious of their accent and I can slip into it instantly. I was made to feel that they were her social inferiors. I do not know how much damage she did with this—if they were such trash, what did this make me? And yet I loved their culture, the songs of George Formby and Gracie Fields, *Mr. Woo's a Window Cleaner Now* and *The Biggest Aspidistra in the World*, that entire English music-hall tradition, much of which became part of me by osmosis when my father would take me with him in the car and sing songs. As I got to know them I would sing them too. I learned an enormous amount of Gilbert and Sullivan from him. And I never hear Jerome Kern's *They Didn't Believe Me* and *I've Told Every Little Star* without thinking of him; I learned both songs from him in the car. He loathed *Rhapsody in Blue*, he was intensely anti-American, and never wavered in this hostility until he died. I must refine that: he liked Americans and hated the United States for such things as the Haymarket Riot, the Scottsboro trial, the shooting of automobile workers in Detroit, the depredations of J. Edgar Hoover, McCarthyism, the House Un-American Activities Committee, the execution of the Rosenbergs, and the Cold War, which he insisted was primarily the creation and fault of the U.S. Yet he greatly admired certain specific Americans, and I was named after one of them: Eugene Debs. My mother was a Lincoln buff.

I went to work as a bag boy in a supermarket when I was twelve and in a paper mill when I was fourteen. I worked in one mill or another from then until I was eighteen. I worked in them weekends and summers all through my high school years. I liked the paper mills. I liked the sense of camaraderie with the men. And I liked having my own money and decent clothes. My mother never cared much what her kids wore, and I was usually rather shabbily dressed. I blame this on Communism. Her father was a Communist, a friend incidentally of Jack London and Horace Traubel, Walt Whitman's biographer. My grandfather too was highly literate, though most of his reading was pertinent to The Cause. My mother had absorbed his attitudes, and there is one thing you must know about orthodox Communists: they have no real sense of pleasure. They are austere people, and they see art only as purposive. It is supposed to be "doing" something, "improving" society. If it doesn't do that, it is worthless. Such people measure all art according to a tenet of social utility. Therefore my grandfather's authors of preference were the likes of Upton Sinclair, Jack London, and Charles Dickens. He used to say that all art is propaganda. I never knew whether he meant it was or was supposed to be, nor whether the phrase was original with him. I read it years later in an interview with Abbey Lincoln, who shared the sentiment. Certainly it is the viewpoint behind all that proletarian art of the Stalinist period in Russia and Italian heroic public architecture under Mussolini.

I know of only one writer about jazz who has the same view of this reflexive imposition of the political viewpoint on aesthetic interpretation that I do, James Lincoln Collier, and he has been excoriated by other critics for it. Collier, like me, has good leftist family credentials, and he can read and see right through the interpretive presupposition this philosophy produces. Collier is absolutely correct in his view that writers of the left, the late John Hammond among them, have falsified jazz history.

How anyone can think the art of Louis Armstrong—or Benny Carter or Count Basie or Coleman Hawkins or John Coltrane—is the cry of pain of a downtrodden people is beyond me, for jazz is the most sensual and joyous music I know. Of course there is pain in it; it would be shallow, and false to the human experience, like the poems of Edgar Guest and the piano of Eddy Duchin, if there were not. But there is joy, exuberant and luxuriant, in it as well. Coltrane said to me once, "Why do they say my playing is angry? I'm not angry." And he wasn't, either; he was a very gentle man. It is precisely the range of its expressivity that makes jazz the magnificent art that it is and, according to my lights, the most significant music in the world from approximately 1920 to the present. And I was listening to it from a time before I can remember, certainly before I knew what to call it. My mother's brother, my Uncle Harry, who was a trombone player, probably turned me on to it first. He was everything my mother wasn't, a meticulous and dapper dresser and a lover of pleasure. He hated my grandfather and hated Communism. He hipped me to Basie. He played in and wrote charts for a band led by someone named Len Allen, and I would listen to their radio broadcasts. Every once in a while they would dedicate a song to me. That was my true introduction to dance bands. I could recognize the sound of any instrument by the time I was three.

And so I grew up in a town called St. Catharines, Ontario, a narrow and bigoted little city not far from Niagara Falls and Buffalo. I collected my jazz records and made friends with the young local musicians, several of whom—including a drummer named Rodney North and a trumpet player named Kenny Wheeler—are still friends of mine. And I worked in paper mills, to get money for my clothes and my records and, eventually, a small black portable Remington typewriter. I taught myself to touch type.

There was always work for school kids in the mills in summer, for that was when the logs came in on the boats. One of the mills was that of the Ontario Paper Co,, on the east bank of the Welland Canal. The company was a subsidiary of the *Chicago Tribune*, and once when I was working on a paper machine the *Tribune*'s owner, Colonel McCormick, came through on a tour of inspection. I remember him tall and white haired, wearing, I think, a white suit—another regal American. My father hated him because of the *Tribune*'s isolationist stand during the war years, when my dad's country was getting bombed. The young men in the graduating class the year I entered high school were gone, almost all of them dead in the Battle of Britain.

But McCormick in fact treated his Canadian employees extremely well. He was one of the pioneers of reforestation. The money in the mill was good, and I liked the Ontario.

I grew up along the Welland Canal, and I am creature of the Great Lakes. The ships would tie up at the Ontario dock and a great crane would drop its claw, at the end of a cable, into the holds. The fingers would close and the crane would lift the claw, pulp logs protruding from its fingers, and drop them on a conveyor. The job of the yard workers, including me, was to see that they didn't jam. The chain that moved them ran along the bottom of a V-shaped wooden track, dragging the logs to a second conveyor, this one rising at about a 30-degree angle. The logs would drop off the end of it, gradually building into a great conical mountain of wood, which later would be fed into the mill, reduced by sulfuric acid into the long white fibers called sulphite or ground into a porridge called groundwood. These are combined in huge roaring machines to make newsprint. The sulphite holds the paper together; the groundwood forms its surface.

Yard work at the Ontario was hard, but handling pulp logs made me strong. I liked to work nights—it left the days free for going to the beach with the first girl I ever loved—and I remember standing on that top conveyor, a pike pole in hand to break up any log jams that might occur, as the sky turned gradually green and then the trees and the mountains of pulpwood stood in blackest silhouette against a red sunup occurring a few miles over there in New York State. The rows of lights in the yard would grow weak and then would be extinguished for the day.

But my favorite hour was midnight. We took our lunch break then. All the young guys would scarf down sandwiches brought in brown paper bags or lunch pails. Then we'd go swimming in the canal. Great floodlights illumined the ship and the waters around it. We'd climb way the hell up on the ship, the bridge or higher, and then dive, screaming, into the warm water. After so long a plunge, you'd go deep, and the water was gorgeously green in the flickering shafts of descending lamplight, and you'd rise to the surface by the side of the ship, climb up on the dock and then up on the ship and do it all over again. Sometimes a big rust-red laker would plow slowly along the canal, going up to Chicago or Milwaukee or Cleveland or down to the St. Lawrence River and Montreal and ports on the far side of the world. I yearned to go with them. These lakers were awesome when viewed from water level with your head sticking above the surface. You made sure to stay well out of their wash, of course. The Great Lakes were not yet polluted, and the water was very clean.

I suppose what we did, swimming and diving in that night-time canal traffic, was dangerous. But it sure was fun.

It occurred to me once that I must be one of the few writers who has been in on the process from unloading the logs to making the paper to writing the words that go on it. I know of another: Charlie Dorsey.

There was little visible prejudice against blacks in that part of Canada. That was because there were few blacks. I don't remember that there was even one in my high school. There were a few in the area, a very few, including several young musicians who were friends of Kenny Wheeler's. Kenny was terribly shy, and so was I. In that he has never changed. Kenny turned me on to Sauter-Finegan, Sarah Vaughan, and Miles Davis. He was the first person I knew to appreciate Miles. I did not foresee that Kenny would himself join the ranks of the great jazz musicians. Or that I would write songs for Sarah.

I suppose Charlie Dorsey was around forty, and I surmise that he must have been one of the first persons with whom I ever discussed writing. Somewhere in the shadows that lie just beyond the edge of consciousness, I have an idea that he encouraged me to take it up.

The Alliance paper mill was not on the bank of the Welland Canal. It got its pulpwood by railway. Charlie and I would work together, relieving these boxcars of their logs, cut to a uniform length. You had a big hook in your right hand, what they call a baling hook on the New York waterfront. You'd dig it into one end of a log, raise the end, pick up the log with your free hand, and toss it out the door onto a conveyor belt. One became very skilled with one of those hooks. We held informal contests to see who could throw a log the farthest. I could pitch a pulp log a good twenty feet, maybe more. I loved being with Charlie. He was wise and warm and funny and he teased me a lot.

As at the Ontario, the yard at the Alliance contained those conical mountains of logs, so characteristic of paper mills, together with smaller cones of brilliantly yellow sulphur, used to make the sulfuric acid that breaks down the fibers of the wood. One of our jobs was to move the wood from this huge pile onto other conveyors that carried them into the plant. When you had worked on the cone for a while, it would become undercut. The wood at times was hanging over your head. When it reached the danger point, you'd use a long pike pole to pull on the overhang until it collapsed.

I was working beneath that overhang one day when it began to give way. Charlie was behind me. He saw what was happening. His action was reflexive, instant, and perfect. He reached out with that wood hook, stabbed it into me, and yanked me back just as the logs came crashing down. I didn't feel the pain at first; I suppose I was too elated to be alive.

I couldn't sit for a week or so. The hook had left quite a wound. But I wasn't dead.

I left that town as soon as I could get out of it and never saw Charlie Dorsey again. Later I made enquiries, but nobody could tell me anything about him. He surely is dead by now.

The second and third black men I ever knew personally were Oscar Peterson and Ray Brown, whom I met when I was a young reporter in the city where I was born, Hamilton, Ontario. A barber refused to cut Oscar's hair, and I was assigned to the story. I interviewed him, but we did not become close friends until years later, in Chicago.

At that time, whereas one American in ten was black, only one Canadian in 740 was black. And so I didn't get to know anyone else black for two or three more years. In Montreal—I had gone there because it was French-speaking, and I was already well along on my journey into difference—I became friends with a young pianist, singer, and songwriter named Cedric Phillips, who was from Barbados. We became very close and Cedric gave me my first real insight, aside from the music I already loved, into black culture.

Cedric worked in cocktail lounges, and when he was off, we'd go to the rooms where jazz was played. And there were a lot of them. Montreal was a swinging city in those days. It has lost much of its color, because of the linguistic racism that has been written into law. English is virtually a forbidden language there, and the city is slowly atrophying of its own isolation, the vain attempt to save a language that cannot be preserved.

But Montreal was a wonderful place when I lived there, with jazz—not to mention a whole cabaret world in French—in fairly good supply. The city was wildly bilingual in those days. And whereas I had always absorbed the lyrics sung by Frank Sinatra, Peggy Lee, Jo Stafford, and other American idols, I was now absorbing those I heard on the records of Edith Piaf, Maurice Chevalier, Yves Montand, and Gilbert Becaud. Becaud came to Montreal to do a concert, and I interviewed him. I still admire his songs.

I was a reporter in those days for the *Montreal Star*, a newspaper that had a good reputation it didn't deserve. Quebec was corrupt, Montreal was corrupt, and the city's newspapers were corrupt, none more so than the *Star*. It had your standard hard-drinking Irish city editor, a man named Ted Murphy, and a bilingual reporting staff.

One of my best friends at the *Montreal Star* was Alain Braun, whose parents died at Auschwitz. Alain had survived a terrifying childhood odyssey all over France, hiding from the Germans, dragging his little brother Gad with him. (Gad became a prominent New York advertising executive.) Al had a peculiar lingering effect of those years: he had missed the year of school when you learn the order of the alphabet, and thus, not knowing the sequence of the letters, had trouble using a telephone directory.

This did not impair his extraordinary gift of words. With the end of the war, when he was seventeen, he got a visa to Canada, and spent the next six months sitting all day, day after day, in movie houses, learning English. Within six months he wrote it so well that he got a job on a small newspaper and then moved to the *Star* when he was only eighteen. Alain Braun was one of the most brilliant men I ever knew. He was rather small, with an aquiline nose, very tough, and skilled at judo. Our friendship left me with a haunted, internalized vision of life—and death—in Europe under the Nazis.

I covered strikes and plane crashes and fires and murders. I was sent to Europe on assignment. I worked out of the *Herald Tribune* office, writing stories on the Royal Canadian Air Force, among other things. I met a beautiful girl named Micheline in the bank where I went to pick up my expenses and persuaded her to attend a Beethoven concert with me. We fell in love by moonlight in a restaurant on a barge on the Seine, with the Eiffel Tower reflected in the water. I thought it was too unreal to last, which intuition proved correct.

I flew home again with the air force. Planes didn't simply jump the Atlantic in those days. The usual procedure for the air force was to refuel in Iceland. It was the time of the midnight sun, and all night I watched the red sun crawl along the horizon.

One of the reasons I left Canada, I can see in retrospect, is that it simply was too small—not in terms of area, of course, but in terms of population. If you wanted to practice any of the arts that require a reasonably large audience, it was almost impossible to stay there. That is why so much of its talent went to England, as in the cases of Robert Farnon and Kenny Wheeler, and even more to the United States.

I was hired to become classical music critic of the *Louisville Times*. And there I experienced a series of culture shocks.

I was issued my residence visa and left Montreal. I took a train to Windsor, Ontario, and crossed by bus to Detroit, where I turned in my residence papers to U.S. Immigration on April 29, 1955. I was told that my green card would be issued by mail shortly. I remember buying a pair of shoes while I waited for my train to Louisville. The clerk asked my name. I told him. And he instantly addressed me not as Mr. Lees but as Gene. They didn't do that in Canada, though this casual American intimacy since has become customary there too.

I had visited the United States often, of course, and during the war I bought most of my records in Niagara Falls, and smuggled them across the border. That's how I got the early Nat Cole, Bobby Sherwood, and Stan Kenton records on Capitol. But this was different: now I was going to live here. Now I had to become a part of it, and my antennae were extended.

I was somewhat affronted by the presumption of that shoe clerk. But in time I came to realize that Americans were far friendlier than Canadians. Warmer. Or they were then, much more so than they are now. Forty-five years of postwar avarice and vicious competition have seemingly made them colder.

The train trundled through the night. In the morning I was in Louisville. I descended from the train in the Louisville & Nashville station. And I felt an almost physical shock when my eye caught sight of the station's lavatories. They had signs on the doors. Colored. White. I never had seen such a thing. I cannot say there was no racial prejudice in Canada. Ask Oscar Peterson (now the chancellor of York University) or Ed Thigpen (who lived in Toronto for a while) or Sonny Greenwich or Oliver Jones. But, as Oscar told Ray Brown when Ray chided him about the haircut incident, "At least in my country, the law was on my side." And it was. What I was looking at in Louisville was official, sanctioned, accepted, enforced segregation.

I took a room at the YMCA and checked in at the paper. It was a few days before the Kentucky Derby. I was pressed into duty to write color stories about it. And then I was sent to the Derby itself, to write more color material. I found myself in the press box sitting beside a small, handsome man with a mustache and a stained tie. His suit was rumpled. But I'd have known that face anywhere. He was on assignment, I learned later, to cover the Derby for a New York magazine. One of the older reporters said to me, "Gene, this is Bill Faulkner." Another of my gods. And since there was nothing much for us to do until post time except sip mint juleps (a drink for which I acquired an instant dislike) and sit there, I had the incredible experience of talking to Faulkner about writing. I wish we'd had cassette recorders then.

But my greatest Louisville shocks lay ahead.

I soon was immersed in the jazz world of the city. I pressed the paper's editor to let me write about it as well as classical music, believing it to be just as important as the modern "classical" music being commissioned and performed by the Louisville Orchestra.

Louisville was a fairly progressive city, certainly when compared with others of the South. The famous Supreme Court ruling banning segregated schooling had just come down. Louisville was ready for it and implemented school desegregation within months. But private business was not affected by the ruling, and you simply did not see anyone black in any of the restaurants there. A concert package came through, presenting Nat Cole and Count Basie. I met them both. Nat invited me to have lunch with him. I remember that he sent for room service and we ate in his hotel room. The significance of that didn't strike me until many years later.

Almost from the moment I hit Louisville, I began doing something that just wasn't done in the South: going to black nightclubs to listen to music. And going to black homes.

There was a prosperous black middle class in Louisville, with its own separate culture. One of the social groups presented Leontyne Price in recital, and I was invited to a reception for her at one of the black homes, and from that point on I was often in educated black middle-class society. I found many of those people charming, but on the subject of jazz, quite unaware. Indeed, some of them spoke of it, if they spoke of it at all, with ill-concealed condescension. Jazz is the cry of protest of the black American? Not to a lot of those I met in Louisville: they didn't even like the stuff.

I do not wish to suggest that I was the only "liberal" on the paper. A passionate opposition to segregation was endemic on the reporting staff. Even the Southerners among the reporters were militant about it. One of them, Bill Peeples, a reporter from Georgia, almost started a strike when he found out that black employees (all of them in lower-echelon jobs) were not allowed to eat in the paper's cafeteria.

I liked Barry Bingham, the handsome owner of the *Louisville Times* and its sister paper, the *Courier-Journal*. And I liked his cool and aristocratic wife, Mary. Bingham was a Democrat, and a friend of Adlai Stevenson's. The official editorial stance of both papers was staunchly liberal and pro-integration.

A joke went around on the paper. Barry is sitting in his garden and swats at an itch, muttering, "These damn chiggers."

"Please, Barry," Mary says. "You have to say Chegroes."

There was more truth to that joke than I knew. Two books have been written about the Binghams of Louisville. One of them contains a chilling revelation. A black gardener was working at their home. The Bingham children were swimming in the pool. The gardener's young son was with him. The Bingham kids invited him to come in for a swim.

When Mary Bingham saw him there, she was horrified and ordered the boy out.

And she drained the pool.

It struck me as peculiarly American that I could be on friendly terms with the owner of the newspaper and with one of the black janitors who cleaned the building at night. His name was John Woods. And the reason I became friends with him was that he was a very good guitarist. He couldn't get enough work in music to live on, but he could play. And he and I would sometimes go up to my little efficiency apartment to listen to records. I would have to enter with my key through the front door, go to the back of the building, let him in a rear door and go with him up the fire escape.

I learned something from John, something about the inherent poeticism of the South, which I have concluded is the consequence of the marvelous and mad love of language of the Irish and a decorative, allusive indirection of expression that is a heritage of Africa. John, who had a solid Southern accent, was talking about a girl he'd been in love with. He told me she was very passionate. He said that when he was making love to her, "she like to clawed de paper off de wall." My God, I thought, that's poetry. And then he topped it. He said, "An' when I pulled it out, she groaned like I took a knife out of a wound." From then on I used to hang out with John not just to hear him play guitar but to hear him talk as well. Wow. Did he have a feel for language.

Not that it did him any good. In that society, he was just a janitor. What would he have become had he ever had access to the implements of education?

I hadn't had much "formal" education either. But at least I hadn't been debarred from the public library. And at least I had the company of my friends among the reporters, two of whom had been Rhodes scholars. And I met all the famous composers whose work was performed by the orchestra. I met Gregor Piatigorsky. I met the Budapest String Quartet, even saw Piatigorsky "jam" with them one night, playing a Schubert quintet.

I had lunch with him the next day. He was a huge man; the cello looked like a toy in his hands. I knew he had known Ravel. I adored Ravel and was curious about the man: the biographies never mentioned a sex life. Usually this was a clue that the subject was homosexual. No book would flatly say so in those days. And so I asked Piatigorsky about Ravel's sex life. In that thick Russian accent, he said, "I do not go around peeking in bedroom windows."

Later, in Paris, I came to know a number of Ravel's friends, and my best conclusion is that he lived an almost sexless existence. Sad. And lonely.

I became friends in Louisville with Larry Parks, who was playing the translator in a touring company of *Teahouse of the August Moon*. His Hollywood career had been destroyed by his admission that he had once been a member of the Communist Party, and he was trying to rebuild his career on the stage. I studied piano and harmony with a Louisville pianist named Don Murray, one of those first-rate jazz players you find all over this country whom nobody ever has heard of elsewhere. He died a few years ago of alcoholism. I met Terry Gibbs, when he came through Louisville, and Don DeMicheal, a local vibes player and drummer whom I encouraged to write.

I met all sorts of celebrities, actors and composers and jazz musicians among them. Some of them I liked, some I didn't. And I met a black local tenor player whose nickname was Prez, because that's who he played like.

I had learned a few things about black society, including poor black society. One of its devices is a certain evasiveness, a certain skilled obfuscation when dealing with the distrusted white man. Can you blame them? This entailed a certain calculated vagueness and sometimes a hiding in nicknames. I'm sure it is the legacy of slavery.

All the black musicians called him Prez, and I never pressed him to know his full name. Odd, but I didn't. John Woods introduced me to him. Once the two of them were at my apartment. The paper had just taken some photos of me for use in ads about my column, which had made me something of a local figure. There was a stack of prints on a coffee table. Prez asked me if he could have one. Though the request struck me as odd, coming from someone I scarcely knew, I gave him one.

Time passed. One Saturday night I was in some club or other, listening to the Louisville Prez. After the gig I invited him back to my place for a drink. He put his tenor in the back seat of my car, and we made the usual trip up the fire escape. We listened to records for a while, and then I drove him home, across the Ohio River to Jeffersonville, Indiana. He mentioned that he had an afternoon gig the next day. He gave me directions and I dropped him off in a poorly lighted neighborhood. Then I went home.

In the morning, I saw his tenor still resting on the back seat of my car. And I knew he had a gig. I didn't know what to do. I drove over to Jeffersonville, not even knowing his address. I felt my way around, soon finding myself in a neighborhood of dirt streets and unpainted clapboard houses, the wood gray with age and weather. There wasn't a white person to be seen anywhere.

I began to ask about Prez. And you have to picture this. A young white man, six feet tall, in a black neighborhood, asking black strangers if they knew someone who bore the nickname Prez. You know what they thought I was: fuzz.

I encountered silences and shakes of the head. Finally, desperate, I told an elderly woman that he was a musician. I opened the horn case and said: "That's his saxophone. He needs it today. I have to get it back to him. And all I can tell you is that he goes by the name Prez."

Slowly she took my measure, her face absent of anger or hostility, but full of distrust. And then she made up her mind. She pointed to a house. She said, "He lives there. Second floor."

I thanked her profusely and got out of the car, carrying the horn. I mounted a flight of stairs so creaky I thought they might collapse under me. I knocked on a door at the top.

And the Louisville Prez opened the door. He looked startled to see me. I told him I had his horn. Quite shyly, he invited me in. I had never seen such poverty. The "apartment" was unpainted, and sparsely furnished, and very dark. Lying on a bed was a naked, smiling little baby. Prez introduced me to his young wife, who seemed in shock to see a white man in her home. And above all one who was not a cop, not a collector, not someone wishing her ill. I shook her hand; she held mine gravely. I suppose it is entirely possible that she had never touched a white hand.

And then I saw something that gave me the worst shock of those years in

Louisville. There pinned to the wall, in all this darkness and poverty and pain, was my photo.

Its very presence there said, "I have a white friend."

Not long after that, I was awarded a Reid Fellowship, $5000, a fair amount of money in 1958. It would allow me to live and study in Europe for a year.

I had come to know a black woman probably in her fifties. She was a cleaning woman at the paper. I was often there at nights, writing. She was an elegant and very beautiful woman, with gray hair, gorgeous features, and somewhat lined handsome orange skin. I used to chat with her of evenings; in the course of three years we had become quite friendly.

On my last night before leaving for Paris with my young French wife and our infant son, I was cleaning out my desk. I bade good-bye to my friend, giving her a hug and kissing her on the cheek. She stiffened and drew back; white people didn't do that. And I realized that even she accepted the separation.

I stayed in Paris a little over a year. Al Braun, who had taught me in Montreal to speak French and instilled in me a lifelong love of the language, came over to join me. My friendship with him, the hellish and highly personal vision he left me of how far unleashed racism can go, further heightened a hatred of it that my parents had planted and Charlie Dorsey and then Oscar Peterson and Cedric Phillips had advanced. Al got a job in the Paris bureau of United Press International, and later founded a highly successful photography agency. He still is in Paris. An atheist in his youth, he is now a practicing Orthodox Jew. I think of him fondly and often. I hear from him every Christmas.

I returned to America and within a few weeks became editor of *Down Beat*. Soon I had all sorts of black friends and acquaintances, none of them poor, all of them successful, and most of them musicians: Miles Davis, Dizzy Gillespie, Blue Mitchell, Donald Byrd, Art and Addison Farmer, Jo Jones and Philly Joe Jones, Benny Golson, John Coltrane, Ahmad Jamal, Oscar Peterson, Ray Brown, Ed Thigpen, Sahib Shihab. And a lot of white friends, too. I met Dave Brubeck and Paul Desmond then, and Phil Woods, Bill Evans, Gerry Mulligan, Scott LaFaro, Woody Herman, Zoot Sims. It was a very long list. One day it struck me that since Louis Armstrong was still alive, I had met, and in many cases knew well, most of the great jazz musicians who had ever lived.

The years slip irrevocably away. I'm a long way from diving off the boats into the green waters of the Welland Canal. Sometimes I think of people who touched me in ways they never knew.

Cedric Phillips from Barbados, whose playing was ended by a stroke a few years ago. But he's still my friend, as is Oscar Peterson, whose hair that barber wouldn't cut. John Woods, the janitor and guitar player. The lady who cleaned the newspaper's floors whose name I no longer remember. Charlie Dorsey showing me his precious poems and sinking a wood hook into me to save my life.

And the Prez of Louisville. I held back the tears that day, looking at my picture on the wall.

November 1992

Dr. de Lerma,
I Presume

In the summer of 1990, the president of Chicago's Columbia College appointed Sam Floyd academic dean. Floyd wanted to retain his position as director of its Center for Black Music Research. To hold both jobs, he would have to select someone to work with him as assistant director.

Almost all the early writing on jazz—and to this day, most of it—is by whites. Sam Floyd is one of a growing group of black researchers in the field. Tall, bearded, handsome, Floyd, then fifty-two, had a reputation as a responsible scholar, and he was concerned for the integrity of his department.

"I wanted somebody with impeccable credentials whom I knew I could work with," he said. He chose Dr. Dominique René de Lerma. "Having known Dominique for years and years," Floyd said, "and considering him one of my very best friends, I thought of him immediately."

Few people in the Chicago jazz community knew who de Lerma was.

There are persons we encounter along the way who have serious influence on our thinking. Dominique de Lerma had an influence on mine.

I have become increasingly suspicious of the credo of jazz:

I believe in Jazz as America's only begotten Art Form. Jazz is a folk music of protest against inequity, born in New Orleans to uneducated descendants of slaves. They made it up out of their own rhythmic tradition and the harmonic and melodic materials they found in Protestant hymns. It went up the river to Chicago, where Jelly Roll Morton was its Prophet, King Oliver its Baptist, and Louis Armstrong its Messiah, and a group of white boys called the Austin High Gang became its Apostles. They went among wolves. This religion was despised in the land of its birth until the Epistles of John the Hammond forewarned the Europeans, who became the first true Jazzians, and took up the burden of evangelizing the Philistine Americans to what had been wrought in their midst when their unrecognized saints went marching in.

There are several things amiss in that version of the genesis of jazz, not least among them that the first European music the African slaves would have encountered in New Orleans was Catholic—not Protestant—French and Spanish—not English. It also implies that the music's inventors were deaf to all the secular music that was part of the New Orleans culture in the nineteenth century, including opera, symphonies, and chamber music. It overlooks parallel developments in music under way in other American cities. And it ignores the crowded nightclubs, best-selling records, national network radio broadcasts, serious academic consideration in many quarters, and enthusiasm of college students for this music during the years of its early evolution. Above all, it overlooks that most—not some, most—of the early makers of jazz were educated men, sometimes well educated.

I have never seen a study of the educational backgrounds of major jazz musicians. There is little useful information on the subject in the dictionaries and encyclopedias of jazz. If you look up Milt Hinton in Chilton, you'll read only that he "learnt brass and string bass whilst at high school in Chicago." That it was Wendell Phillips High School is not specified. Thus the inspiration of Captain Walter Dyett goes unnoticed. *The New Grove Dictionary of Jazz* almost never gives such details. And so the influence of certain key high schools, Wendell Phillips in Chicago, Jefferson in Los Angles (alma mater of Art Farmer and Addison Farmer, Edmund Thigpen, Dexter Gordon, Big Jay McNeeley, and Frank Morgan), Cass Tech in Detroit (Donald Byrd, Pepper Adams, Frank Rosolino), and the High School of Performing Arts (Thelonious Monk) in New York simply is ignored, contributing to an impression that jazzmen are autodidacts and that the music came about by a sort of parthenogenesis. I often ask jazz musicians about their early musical education. And, meanwhile, I have made note of the training of earlier jazz players, becoming increasingly aware of the place of European "classical" music in their studies. I was always uneasy with the simplistic myth of the music's origins. Dominique de Lerma made me actively skeptical of it.

I met Dominique in Toronto near the mid-1970s. I was asked to interview him on one of the educational television channels. The interview went pleasantly enough, but it was the conversation that followed that had the impact on me. Dr. de Lerma was an ethnomusicologist (although he is not comfortable with the term), who made me more aware of black participation in nonjazz music in New Orleans and elsewhere. From then on, I kept an eye open for the education of black musicians, noting that Will Marion Cook, who was an influence on Duke Ellington, had studied at the National Conservatory under Antonin Dvořák and later was a violin student of Josef

Joachim in Berlin and that his father was a law professor; I noted that Fletcher Henderson was trained in European classical piano and had a degree in chemistry and mathematics from Atlanta University, and that his brother Horace and Benny Carter went to Wilberforce; that Jimmie Lunceford was a student in the Denver high school music system directed by Paul Whiteman's father, then went on to get a bachelor's degree in music at Fisk and study at the City College of New York; that Don Redman, son of a respected music teacher, graduated with a degree in music from Storer College and attended the Chicago and New England conservatories; that Claude Hopkins studied music (and medicine) at Howard University, where his parents were on the faculty. And on and on . . . . The more I looked at it, as the years went on, the more jazz appeared to be distinctly a product of the middle class, not of the downtrodden poor.

Though quite fair-skinned, Dominique de Lerma looked as if he might have African antecedents. He spoke beautifully in round vowels and pensive cadence. I did not ask about his personal life; his name is Spanish. That day in Toronto passed, Dominique left, and I didn't see him again for sixteen years.

Two or three years ago, Billy Taylor and I were discussing the influence of university training on jazz musicians. I asked Billy if he knew anything of a man named Dominique de Lerma. "Yes," Billy said, "I know him very well."

"Where in the world is he?"

"Teaching at Morgan State University and Peabody," Billy said.

A little after that, I was visiting my friend Hale Smith, composer, distinguished music educator, and closet scat singer, at his home on Long Island. Hale attended the Cleveland Institute of Music when Jim Hall was there. Later he taught composition, orchestration, "and life," as he put it, at the University of Connecticut, from which institution he is now retired. Because of his academic connections, I asked Hale if he knew Dominique de Lerma. "Sure," Hale said. "Dominique is one of the three greatest scholars in black American music, the other two being Sam Floyd and Eileen Southern."

"Got a phone number?" I asked.

Billy Taylor and Hale felt that people in the jazz world knew far too little about Dominique de Lerma. I phoned Dr. de Lerma. He was astounded that I remembered him. I was astounded that he remembered me. And I arranged to meet him in Baltimore. A few weeks later he booked a room for me near Morgan State. Morgan State is a substantially black university. When I checked in, I got into conversation with a black clerk, a notably pretty girl who was studying voice there. She knew much about European music but little about jazz. She also knew Dominique. When I mentioned his name, she smiled broadly. I learned he was adored by his students.

Dominique arrived. He had a pointed black Van Dyke beard, and that dense black hair I remembered had not turned gray. The greeting was warm, and over dinner in the hotel's restaurant, we talked as if our conversation in Toronto had occurred yesterday. This time I asked him about his family.

"I was born in Miami, Florida, on the Feast of the Immaculate Conception, December 8, 1928," Dominique said. "My family background is black Spanish, integrated before coming to this country—Afro-Spanish in Spain. In the sixteenth century, in Spain, Portugal, and Italy, there were whole black populations, which probably accounts to some extent for the Italians. Think of Othello. The Moor of Venice. And there were groups from Africa in unexpected places like Mexico. Over a period of time, they became assimilated."

"Well," I said, "we tend to think that travel began with Columbus. They found a Roman galley on the bottom of Guanabara Bay, at Rio de Janeiro, and Irish monks crossed the Atlantic in curraghs before the Vikings did. Where in Africa did your people come from. Do you know?"

"I don't know specifically. It was somewhere in the vicinity of Benin or the Ivory Coast. There apparently was a large migration in the sixteenth century, which was not the first, to Europe. It was Moslem, no question about that. My family coat of arms has the cross and the moon together. My grandfather was ambassador to Mexico. I never knew him. At some point in his life, he moved to California. And that's how the family got to the United States."

"There was African migration to France too," I said. "Alexandre Dumas was black. The Mediterranean is not that big a pond."

"And Gibraltar is very close to Africa," Dominique said. "I'm certain that Africans with boats didn't sit there waiting for the great white father to come and discover the Dark Continent. Already, by the year 1000, there was trade with the southeast Pacific, which is how the xylophone got to Africa— along with elephantiasis. There was an African community actually living on Java by the year 1000. There was a black community in China.

"There is an awful lot of supposition that can take place in music and you're not entirely sure whether some of the rhythms that you find, say, in late Renaissance music, come about because of innovations in notation or African influence. You're encouraged to think African when you encounter something like the moresca, which was very popular in the late sixteenth century. It is that dance, in fact, that concludes Monteverdi's *Orfeo*. The moresca, as everybody knows, was an African dance that was taken to Naples at earlier times. It spread all over Europe, particularly Italy, and even to England, where it was known not as the moresca but as the Morris dance."

The moresca, a pantomimic dance that turned up in Europe at least as far back as 1530, was done in Moorish costume with little bells attached to the legs. The dancers blackened their faces—three centuries before the rise of minstrel shows in the United States. It was the most popular dance in Renaissance ballets and mummeries, and forms of it survive to this day in Spain, Corsica, and Guatemala, and in England as the Morris dance, which underwent a revival around 1900.

"The moresca," Dominique said, "originally had to do with fertility. The English decided to remove the element of fertility, but they forgot to take down the Maypole.

"One of the problems of African history is that it is based on oral history. And we can't speak about historical periods, or some kind of political unification. We can't say that during the reign of so-and-so something happened. I guess the approach has got to be different. And there have to be an awful lot of assumptions, which could be a little dangerous, especially if you're working with the kind of fervor of Joel Augustus Rogers, the guy who in the 1930s wrote a number of books trying to prove that everybody important in history had an African background, including Beethoven.

"He was a fascinating person with a lot of wisdom, but his details are not always very accurate. There isn't any question about Beethoven. I checked the genealogy back to the fifteenth century, and the family line was not even Belgian or Dutch. It was all Flemish. When I first heard the story, I remembered the time when the area was called the Spanish Netherlands, and I thought there might have been some importation of darker skin. There very possibly was, but it didn't affect Beethoven's family."

"How did you get interested in these things?"

"My father spent his life as a dilettante," Dominique said. "That included music, but it included anything that might have appealed to him. There was a piano in the house and a record player. I grew up with whatever records happened to be around. Probably the first composer I was aware of was Schubert. When I went to take piano lessons—I really wanted to play piano awfully much—I arrived with the thirty-two Beethoven sonatas under my arm. And I had the feeling that the teacher never even knew Beethoven wrote any sonatas. That pretty well ended our relationship right there, which accounts for the fabulous piano technique I have today.

"If I was not going to make it as a pianist, somehow or other the violin attracted me, but it did not attract my father, so he suggested I look into the oboe, which I did.

"I feel that sometimes people who become musicians are built for certain instruments. I got an oboe in November. Within one month, I had a professional engagement, three concerts a week. I played the Miami Opera Guild. I didn't even have my first lesson until the following summer. But throughout all of this, I kept thinking the instrument I was built for was the cello. And I've never played it. The idea of string quartets excited me very much. I felt culturally deprived, because I had friends who played stringed instruments. I was very happy one time when they did not have a cellist around, and I played the cello part on the piano. That was not satisfactory, because my piano playing is not that good. So I decided the closest thing I could do was the bassoon. So I picked up the bassoon, and I was just fantastic with it. I played it for only a year. I really miss that instrument, much, much more than the oboe or the English horn. It's such a fantastic instrument. It's not a bass, it's a baritone and a tenor and everything. I feel so funny to be at the bottom of the harmony, instead of the top.

"I was going to school at the University of Miami. I finished my music courses there and got disgusted and went to Curtis and got disgusted and went to Tanglewood. That's when I realized I really did not want a career as a performer. I wanted something that was more conceptual. So I went back to Miami as a history major. Then I majored in art history and French. I started Italian. I was thinking about anthropology and geology, and by this time I was on the faculty, teaching oboe and music history. I got a call from the dean, who said, 'You're teaching on the faculty?' I said, 'Yes.' He said, 'But you don't even have a bachelor's degree.' I said, 'No.' He said, 'Why?' I said, 'I don't want to stand in line.' He said, 'If you want a contract next year, get your degree. Stand in line.'

"So I did. But I knew that was not where I had to stop. I had a chance to go to Florence to play in an orchestra that a friend of mine had, Newell Jenkins, who is now in New York. Newell was doing early eighteenth-century Italian music. I had done the world premiere of the Vincenzo Bellini oboe concerto, a concerto Bellini wrote when he was fifteen or sixteen. Not very good. But since then lots of people have played it. Newell had conducted it, and so he asked me if I would join him in Florence. I was all set to go when I began thinking what I really ought to do is go for a master's degree. I went to Indiana University, primarily to work with Paul Nettl, professor of music and father of Bruno Nettl, ethnomusicologist at the University of Illinois. He said, 'Don't settle for the master's degree—

that's like a high school diploma, go for the doctorate.' So I got my doctorate without a master's.

"I got a call to join the faculty of Indiana, because the head of the music department was on leave for a year and a half, so I did that. Then I went to the University of Oklahoma for a year. I was called back to Indiana University, where I stayed thirteen years as music librarian, not knowing anything about music libraries. I went there in '63 and left in '75.

"With the death of Martin Luther King, I realized I could do one of two things. I could utilize whatever skills I had developed by this time, or I could get matches and bricks and join the folks in town. Not that there was that much of a town in Bloomington, and the waves always got there a year or two late. That's when I decided I had better give serious attention to black music research. I knew there was more to it than we were told. And I just sort of took off from that point.

"I was married during my student days at Indiana. My wife died of cancer. We had a son who died in the early 1980s. So it was a matter of my leading a rather monastic existence, which is fine because of what the field required of me and what the people really required of me—responding, answering questions, and fulfilling needs that simply were not being addressed elsewhere. It's been a lot of pressure and a lot of responsibility, but I feel really as if I am in a religious order. I've taken vows, and one of the vows is that whatever happens, I've got to get my work done."

I asked what year he had been up to Toronto.

"You and I met in 1974," he said. "That was about five years into the research."

We finished dinner and went up to my room, a pleasant one with a balcony overlooking an evening garden full of Maryland foliage, exuberant with springtime. In the elevator we had begun talking about the influence of popular music on "classical" music and of classical music in turn on popular music—and on jazz.

Dominique said, "There was no distinction between popular music and nonpopular music during Mozart's time. Do you know how to tell the difference between a minuet that Mozart wrote to be danced and one of the minuets in the symphonies? The dance minuet doesn't have violas. Period. That's it."

I said, "In the nineteenth century, concert music moved farther away from dance forms and dispensed with improvisation. Prior to the Romantic era, soloists in concertos were expected to improvise their cadenzas."

"Absolutely true," Dominique said. "Maybe it's not the nineteenth century that should be blamed but musicology. Some pianists never really lost the idea of improvisation in the nineteenth century. The concept of personal involvement encourages improvisation, some sort of elaboration, and that's a good Romantic thought. But we also had with the nineteenth century an awareness of earlier music and a concern about being accurate and sticking to the printed page. And you get these myths—people like Toscanini, who never did anything other than what the composer wrote. Which is absolute foolishness, because he *did*. It's just that his p.r. people said he didn't. And on the other side of the fence there is someone like Stokowski, who, however inaccurate he might have been historically, was never afraid to be a musician. This is something that has bothered me for a long, long time. I have not seen Toscanini as a musician.

"We're not talking about improvisation, but in Stokowski we're getting into the same kind of re-viewing, reliving, reworking something which already had happened with Gustav Mahler as a conductor, with Fritz Reiner as a conductor, with Bruno Walter as a conductor. It happens."

"Was there," I asked, "a point in your life when the traditional view of jazz history didn't add up?"

"Yes. Because of the kind of information people needed, my first attention was directed to the composers. As I got into this, I realized that it's impossible to understand black culture without understanding all of the idioms, as best you can. And certainly jazz cannot be eliminated, nor can blues, or gospel, or even non-American expressions. It's such a huge world that it's probably too much for one person to manage. And then it's all the more frightening when people refer to you as an ethnomusicologist, which means you should know this much about every other culture that exists on Earth. And I'm not about to undertake that.

"But with the kind of orientation I had to questions that were being asked, I began to see patterns with regard to the composers that I could discuss and think about. Things did not make sense to me when I started to look at jazz through other people's words.

"One of the problems with black music is that it's entertaining and therefore that's where people stop. Once people are amused, they don't go any further, which is selling the culture very short. And there's a sociological reason for this also: The black musician performs, does not analyze, does not write the histories, does not do the reflection. Or if there is a reflection, it is done in so intuitive a manner that it's almost like an atavistic memory.

"I mean, nobody ever told Louis Armstrong how African it would be to use your instrument like a voice, or if you tried to develop a sonority in your voice that matched that of the trumpet. These things simply happened. It's not a matter of a philosophic stance.

"So as a result, there's an awful lot of writing that people are exposed to—certainly that which is most accessible—dealing with jazz that is not really very important. Things which are not really critical and don't relate to the culture. But one other thing: there's something you said in the elevator about the attitude people had to American history, to black music or any other aspect of American history."

"You mean, when I mentioned Harold Arlen."

"Exactly."

"I said he told me that he and Gershwin and the others were well aware that what they were creating was art music. But it was always treated as popular music and therefore taken lightly. For that matter, there's been a condescension even toward American classical composers."

"Sure," Dominique said. "When Dvořák came to the United States in 1893, the question thrown at this visiting celebrity from Europe—whether he was a celebrity or not, it was enough that he was from Europe—was, 'Maestro, do you think this country will ever produce any good music?'

"And his answer was in essence, 'Of course not. Not until you stop writing music that pretends that you're German and ignores the fact that you're American.'

"They replied in essence, 'Well, we all come from Europe, and we're thinking of our roots, and Germany is the intellectual center.'

"And he said, 'There are other roots. The spirituals, for example.' Well of course it had never even dawned on them to look at these ignorant people as being the source for American music. Dvořák said that as soon as you begin to write music like Americans, you will write American music.

"Which meant, the blacker you get the more American you will get. And he was absolutely right."

"He was," I said. "But when Louis Moreau Gottschalk brought these African influences into serious composition, John Sullivan Dwight castigated him for it in one of the Boston papers."

"Right," Dominique said. "In 1981, I terminated my membership in the American Musicological Society, which I had joined thirty years earlier, not because I felt there was anything wrong with the society but there was something wrong with calling it the American Musicological Society when it had shown no interest up to this point in anything American. And please understand me: I am not an Americanist. I mean, the thing that really got all these musicologists excited would be the publication of a transcription of a Maltese manuscript from the Medieval period. But if you mentioned anything American, anything jazz, anything black, it was out of the question.

"Now, in about 1987 or '88, I joined Hale Smith for a meeting that the American Musicological Society had in New Hampshire, a committee for the publication of American music. And I was there specifically to be a watchdog to see that black interests were going to be included, if in fact AMS was going to publish a monumental edition of American musical history, very much like the *Denkmäler deutscher Tonkunst*. I don't know how many volumes that is; it came out at the end of the nineteenth century, critical editions by German composers, not well known ones, but obscure people. There's also one for Austria and Bavaria.

"So when the American Musicological Society was going to do this, I thought, 'Sure, they're going to come out with some Elliot Carter string quartets.' But what they were talking about at last was bringing out for the first time the full orchestral score of *Porgy and Bess*. And on the agenda was one volume of boogie-woogie piano. When I mentioned Will Marion Cook's *In Dahomey*, which I think is a fabulous work from 1902, I was surprised to find that there were fifteen or twenty representatives—academics—who admitted they knew who Will Marion Cook was, they knew *In Dahomey*, and they knew that it had never been published in a full score. A full score did not exist. It was a piano-vocal score. And they could start singing tunes from it.

"These people were coming out of the woodwork. They had been hiding before.

"Shortly before this, I had a surprise when Sam Floyd was at Fisk University. He had a conference. Someone read a paper on three Miles Davis versions of *My Funny Valentine*. And I knew the guy's name—Howard Brofksy, an eighteenth-century specialist from Brooklyn College. Afterwards we had a drink, and I said, 'How did you get out of the eighteenth century?'

"He said, 'I worked my way through college playing jazz. But it was not considered legitimate. So as soon as I got my degree, I put it out of my mind, and only got up enough courage in the past few years to go back to it.' He had never heard John Coltrane. But after having had the kinds of experience Howard had had in other music, he was ready to assimilate and evaluate things much, much faster than if he had grown up with it.

"You've objected in your writings to the story that the black jazz musician is born with it and doesn't have to practice. Coltrane is a good case in point of real, hard practice. People are surprised when they find out that one of the most worn volumes in Coltrane's library was Slonimsky's *Thesaurus of Scales and Musical Patterns*. But that message that you've complained about gets through to our kids, and they feel that they don't have to practice because they're black. Or it's: 'I'm black so I'm qualified to teach black music.'"

"Or," I suggested, "they get discouraged when it doesn't come easy. They think, 'I'm supposed to be able to play this trumpet in twenty minutes,' and when they can't, they quit."

"Exactly!" Dominique said emphatically. "You're not kidding. That, seriously, is the attitude. They don't have to practice. Somehow it's going to work. They don't realize the biographical details behind figures who had to do the practice. They need to know what Miles Davis has to say about Ravel.

"There was a house of pleasure in St. Louis run by Babe Connors. She had, among other offerings, a rather rich musical life. The pianist who played there attracted Paderewski's attention. And he frequented the place just to hear the pianist.

"So when we speak about the contacts that Jelly Roll Morton might have had with opera in New Orleans—and there's no question that he had, because he knew the material—I wonder what contact performers and composers who visited this country had with black music. For example, when Ravel came, he wanted to go and hear Jimmie Noone in Chicago. Immediately. When Milhaud came to the United States in 1921, he wanted to go to a jazz club in Harlem. That was before he wrote *La Création du Monde*. These were the kinds of contacts Europe had with black music."

"I think that's well verified," I said. "Gene Krupa was working in a club in Chicago and saw Ravel in the audience. Joe Venuti said Ravel came to visit him and Gershwin."

"Now," Dominique said, "I wonder if Ravel when he was in France took advantage of the chance to hear Jim Europe's band."

"I would think it's almost impossible that he didn't. Look at Debussy going to the Javanese exhibit at the Paris Exhibition of 1889. And the French were interested in the Russians—and anything they saw as exotic."

Dominique said, "Dvořák *seems* to have known the spirituals before he came to the United States."

"Will Marion Cook studied with Dvořák. And consider the case of Milton Hinton, who might not have been a jazz bassist had he been allowed into a symphony orchestra as a violinist."

"Not to denigrate jazz in any way," Dominique said, "but that kind of prejudiced exclusion created a lot of jazz musicians and enriched jazz. In the case of Dvořák, the Fisk Jubilee Singers gave their first concert in the United States in 1871. Subsequently they toured Europe. Fisk University brought me in to look over in their special collections all the materials of the singers. They have the originals, programs, mementos, a scrapbook, for example. At that time it was customary in Europe for the audience to give the singers little photographs of themselves, as well as autographs, all of which went into the book. On one page, I found autographs of Moody and Sanky, who were American white gospel writers. They attended the concert in Scotland, I think it was. And there were letters. There was a proposal from a guy in Nashville to his girlfriend who was touring Europe with the company. His letters are not there, but her responses are. She turned him down. There is this wonderful, elegant language of these liberal-arts-educated black students in the nineteenth century: very, very proper. There's a whole drama here that has not been told, despite the publications that came out very soon after the tour.

"I think that whole history has to be looked at very carefully, with day-by-day documentation. Where were the singers, in what city? And is there a point—not just Fisk, but the Hampton Singers were there—when the chronology overlaps, and we can find that Dvořák might have been, I don't know, in Leipzig or Dresden, when a black chorus was there and had first contact with the spirituals? That same kind of comparative relationship might pinpoint specifically what Debussy or Ravel or any of the other composers who were so strongly attracted to American music actually heard. *Golliwog's Cakewalk* of Debussy is a charming, lovely, terribly French piece, but it is really not ragtime, which the cakewalk is. Then if you look at the ragtime music Sousa's band had played in Paris just a few years before he wrote this, it is white ragtime. But it's not Scott Joplin. It's not this additive rhythm that really distinguishes ragtime. How much authentic black music did Debussy get a chance to meet before his death?

"As far as Ravel is concerned, you were speaking about Gottschalk absorbing all kinds of influences."

"All of them," I said. "European, Caribbean, Cuban, Brazilian. He traveled so much. I've always said, with all due respect to John Lewis, whom I admire immensely, if you're going to say who is the founder of a Third Stream in American music, I'd have to say it's Gottschalk. Putting habaneras in a symphony orchestra and things of that kind. . . ."

"And how is that tradition retained?" Dominique asked.

"It isn't followed immediately."

"That's the problem," Dominique said.

I noted that Robert Offergeld, a brilliant scholar who did years of research on Gottschalk and published the first extensive catalogue of his work, had documented the critical assaults on the composer. As the Mozart music bears K. numbers, the Gottschalk music now carries R.O. numbers, for Robert Offergeld. Offergeld was music editor of *Stereo Review* when he hired me in 1962 to write for the magazine and soon became one of my life's major mentors. Dominique said he wanted to meet Offergeld; I said I'd arrange it. Instead I spent the last week of Bob's life holding his hand as his emphysema drained away the last of his energy in Lenox Hill Hospital in New York. So Dominique never met him. What I knew of Gottschalk came not from books Bob didn't live to write but from Bob himself. I said, "Gottschalk's stuff was extremely difficult to play, very challenging. And even if you bothered to master it, all it would get you was bad reviews. From the time Gottschalk died in 1869, there is a long lag. From the time he died until John Lewis and Gunther Schuller and their colleagues, there's about a hundred-year gap. I think the movie composers enormously advanced the integration of European concert tradition and American influences, including jazz. Guys like Henry Mancini, Johnny Mandel, Oliver Nelson, Benny Carter. I was talking about you to Benny recently. How you'd made me more aware of the black classical participation. Benny said, 'It doesn't matter that it was black. The question is: Is it any good?'"

"That," Dominique said, "is the complete reversal of the attitude of twenty years ago, when T. J. Anderson said, 'It doesn't matter whether it's good, what's important is that it was written by a black composer.' I ask my students: What is black? Do you know black when you see it? And they have all kinds of misconceptions."

"Are these students mostly black?"

Dominique chuckled. "If they're not at the beginning of the semester, they are by the time it's over. Just as if I were teaching a course on Mozart, by the time we got to the end of the semester they would all be eighteenth-century Rationalists.

"Let's admit the fact that black is not really all that pure. When you think of Willie the Lion Smith, he was a cantor. The Jewish element is there. I know a lot of people who ignore the Indian background or the Jewish background or something else and consider black is black and that's all there is to it. Consider somebody like Roque Cordero, who is a fantastic twelve-tone composer born in 1917 in Panama. He was originally offended when we included him on the black composers series with Columbia. He said, 'Why do you call me a black composer? I'm Panamanian. Panamanian means black, Indian, and Spanish.'

"I said, 'Roque, William Grant Still was born in Woodville, Mississippi, and he was black, Indian, and Spanish. But also Welsh and Irish. And he is not regarded as an American composer but as a black composer.'

"And what do you know, one thing that my students eventually come up with is that as black nationalists, they have been co-operating with the white racists.

"It's been rare that I have found people who on their own are willing to acknowledge the diversification that exists within the black society. I went to dinner with a retired judge and his lawyer son in St. Louis, sat down at the table ready to eat my chicken, watermelon, and everything like that. The conversation at the table was already in progress. A lady said, 'Oh yes, honey, we've already traced down all the black folks in the family. Now we're gonna start on the white folks.' It was said without any shame.

"We have a choreographer here in Baltimore who is absolutely fabulous. In all contexts she is called black. But her great-great-grandfather was Jefferson Davis. Now the thing is, when you say black, what you really are saying—and excuse me, I really don't mean to be a flag-waver, I'm not waving the flag for anything—but what you're talking is American. Black is American. I think there's a great deal of shaking up of philosophies and attitudes that needs to be done. An awful lot of the militant viewpoint is exactly what the white racists want it to be. The separate attitudes. Only blacks can do this. Just keep it segregated and you don't have to worry about it.

"But it's a misconception, and it perpetuates the mythology that if you're black you automatically can do such-and-such in music. Which is not so."

"Some of the people who co-operated most passionately in this," I said, "have been white writers. Their work suggests that these black musicians were so bloody dumb that they were unaware of what else was going on in the culture. It implies a ghettoization of the intellect."

"There were restrictions, no question," Dominique said. "But the minute any barrier is opened, as in New York City and in New Orleans at a certain time, there's no doubt that the musicians took advantage of it. If they were able to get to the opera, get to this concert, get to talk with this person, to move in that society, they did it. The Harlem Renaissance was a flourishing of enormous black talent with white, Jewish, liberal support all the way down the line."

"Where and when does the black participation begin in America in what we imprecisely call classical music?" I asked.

"The earliest figure in the western hemisphere whose music I can get my hands on was a contemporary of Monteverdi. Her name—and it was a lady—was Teodora Gines. She was born within one generation after Columbus landed on the island of Hispaniola. She was very influential on the music of the Caribbean. How much earlier we can go, I don't know, because we're dealing with a culture that's got to be acculturated. Because as soon as you put down notation, this is not an African thing to do. But we have it already by 1600.

"As far as the United States is concerned, I don't think it was ever really necessary in the past to go to a conservatory to get a degree before you could become a composer. The opportunity for gifted or interested blacks to associate with musicians, to come in contact with contemporary musical thought, really did not exist very strongly, certainly not in the South. We don't know the name of a single composer of the spirituals. I know of only one composer who was born into slavery, and that was Blind Tom, born in 1849, who stayed in slavery after the Emancipation. Here was this guy, who had an ear every bit as good as Mozart's or Mendelssohn's, who never really was properly exposed to the music of his time. I mean, maybe he played Beethoven or Bach or Chopin, I'm not sure, but the people he really was pushed on were the Fakers. Look at the music he wrote: *The Rainstorm, The Sewing Machine*, things of this sort, little descriptive pieces to cater to Confederate society, that was not awfully musically literate in the first place. The people who liked to listen to little tunes in the parlor that did not have any musical substance but reminded them of something nonmusical, waterfalls or sunsets or something.

"And his owner had no interest in providing him with the kind of exposure and contact that Mozart had when Mozart was little. He died unhappy because he knew he'd been exploited. He got 10 percent of his income, and never really developed his talent.

"There was not in this country any interest or need in developing serious, nonutilitarian composers in the nineteenth century. With the social limitations on black musicians, it's a matter of counting the doors that got opened and when they got opened and who opened them. For example, minstrelsy, after the Civil War, with somebody like James Bland. But minstrelsy is not going to produce normally, you would think, an art song that would make it to the recital hall today if that is in fact what people in the past lived for. We do have Marilyn Horne singing *I Dream of Jeanie with the Light Brown Hair* with harp. And we could also have James Bland—for example, the state song of Virginia, *Carry Me Back to Old Virginny,* by James Bland. But now some revisionists decide that it would probably be better not to use any of the Jim Bland tune because it refers to the darkies and magnolias, and it's nostalgic for slavery. They made it the state song knowing that Jim Bland was black."

"Was he tomming when he wrote it?" I asked.

"He was being free when he wrote it. He could not have done this before. Now at last he could write songs about the darkies. We can't evaluate those times by looking backwards. We have to look forward as it was in their minds. Never had they known freedom—and then to be granted it. And if they had a good slave owner, and had never known anything but slave owning, they were appreciative of it. So maybe the magnolias really were rather nice on some plantations.

"With minstrelsy ending toward the end of the century, if you wanted to be a great composer, you had the opportunity of writing coon songs, like Ernest Hogan. The question comes up: What would have happened if Leontyne Price had been around a hundred years ago? Instead of one of the arias that she sings for encores, maybe at the end of a minstrel show the audience would be clamoring for her to sing Ernest Hogan's *All Coons Look Alike to Me*. And that would have been the high spot of the evening for Leontyne Price.

"But in the midst of this atmosphere came Will Marion Cook, who had very serious academic training at Oberlin, and in Germany with Josef Joachim. Cook regarded himself as being a pretty good violinist. He gave a recital. The critics said he was the best Negro violinist in the country. Cook went to a critic's desk and said, 'You wrote this review, saying I am the best Negro violinist in the country?' The critic said, 'Yes.' Cook said, 'I'm the best violinist in the country,' took out his violin, smashed it on the critic's desk, and never touched the instrument again. It's a true story. It was reported to me by Maurice Peress, who worked with Duke Ellington, was conductor of the orchestra in Kansas City, and now is teaching at New York University. He re-created the James Reese Europe concert at Carnegie Hall. He's done some very good research.

"But then Will Marion Cook opened the doors for musical theater in New York, which had not been open to blacks before. That was in the first decade of the century. But we still don't have the composer who wants to write a symphony. We don't have any black musicians who knew Charles Ives, who was writing symphonies at the time. Then in the teens, there were a variety of problems, with Jim Europe being the prime figure. But he spent part of his time in Europe and then died in 1919. And then in the 1920s, we got the Harlem Renaissance and suddenly here flourishes all this talent that had been in the wings, waiting for opportunities.

"William Grant Still might be symptomatic. Somebody who worked for W. C. Handy, who played in a Broadway show *Shuffle Along*, who wrote music for the Old Gold show and Artie Shaw, and all this time was thinking that what he'd like to do was write a symphony. He had ambitions that went beyond the stereotype. So he opened a door.

"At the same time, there are some other people who did not break out of the stereotype, like James P. Johnson, one of the most enjoyable pianists I have heard in my life, an absolute genius, and an awfully good composer;

sophisticated, urbane. And he wanted to follow a path very much like Still. I think a lot of Harlem Renaissance people might have had these ambitions. He wanted to write piano concertos. But he made his money in shows on Broadway, and playing piano, and things of that sort, and by the time he had leisure, he'd already had a stroke. He did try his hand at some works for piano and orchestra—not awfully good. There needed to be some experience in working with extended forms, as Duke Ellington found out also.

"The same thing with writing an opera. I think Gershwin in *Porgy and Bess* became an American Puccini. *Porgy and Bess* is a very moving experience. It is awfully valid."

I said, "Todd Duncan, who created the role of Porgy, was interviewed on television. He took exception with those black musicians who objected to it on grounds that it was written by white guys. He said it was not popular music, it was opera and should be judged by that. The logical extension of that is that Verdi shouldn't have written *Aïda* because he wasn't Egyptian and Puccini shouldn't have written *Madama Butterfly* because he was neither American nor Japanese. And by further extension that no black American should ever write an opera about, say, Elizabeth and Essex."

Dominique said, "I am giving a talk next month at a university in northern Wisconsin. When I talked with the dean, he said, 'Now you have to understand that there are no blacks in our area.' I said, 'You're talking Scandinavian and German Lutherans.'

"He said, 'That's exactly it.'

"I said, 'I understand. So there won't be any blacks in the audience. Tell me, in your course work, do you deal with Bellini, Rossini, Verdi, and Puccini?'

"He said, 'Yes.'

"I said, 'Do you have any Italians there?'

"He said, 'No. Aha, I see what you mean.'

"When we're dealing with the subject of black, whether in music or not, there are two possibilities for approaching the subject, which need to be admitted right from the very beginning. One is political and one is parallel. And if it's political, you admit it's political and you fight the battle that way. If it's a matter that there are not enough black teachers in a school, that's a political thing. It certainly is not parallel. Just because your skin is black doesn't mean you know anything about jazz.

"I visited another school last year. The jazz teacher, who worked very, very hard to get the course going and is doing an awfully good job, is not eligible for a position at another school because he's white.

"I said, 'I don't understand.'

"He said, 'Because jazz is black music.'

"I said, 'So? If you were a specialist in Bach, does that mean you have to be an eighteenth-century musician who was born in Saxony? You can't find very many people who were born in the eighteenth century who have Ph.D.s and are eligible to teach in a college today.' That's a parallel situation. If you know the material, you know the material, that's all.

"The Negro String Quartet, sometimes called the American String Quartet, was there in New York early in the century. One of the players is still alive in New York, Marion Cumbo. There was a string quartet in Atlanta around the same time."

I said, "How do you account for the bass player with Buddy Bolden in 1906 holding his hand on the neck of the bass in the correct symphony fingering position?"

Dominique said, "What needs to be done very badly is iconographic studies. If we admit that black musicians perform rather than write about their performance, that observers don't always see anything—the camera sees more than gets written about. For example, the early pictures of Duke Ellington's band, when Sonny Greer is there with an enormous array of percussion instruments that you never hear on the recordings, cymbals and tympani and tam-tams. Maybe it was posed for Zildjian cymbals. . . ."

"No, it was there on the bandstand. I saw that band when I was very young, and he really did have all those things."

"Did you ever see them get used?"

"Nope."

And both of us laughed.

"What are you doing now?" I asked at last.

And Dominique, with the wry self-deprecation I was getting used to, said:

"I'm teaching two courses that I'm not qualified to do. One is solfège. This is at the freshman and sophomore level. The students don't know how to listen to music, so how can they listen to music? They don't know what to listen for.

"I also have an undergraduate music history course. We have spent the entire semester on Saint-Georges, Haydn, and Mozart. And I have a seminar on the music of black composers at Peabody. It's designed as a practical course for people going into careers as performers. It's on Ulysses Kay, William Grant Still, Antonio Carlos Gomes, Jose Mauricio Nunes Garcia, T. J. Anderson, Hale Smith, Primus Fountain."

But he was thinking of making a change, he said. He'd had attractive offers from a couple of universities. A few months later, I got a card from him, saying he had taken a new post as assistant director of the black music studies program at Columbia College in Chicago. "I hope we can get together again soon," he wrote on it. And I wrote back: "How about next Wednesday at the Blackstone?" The Blackstone Hotel is just down Michigan Avenue from Columbia College. The Blackstone and Columbia alike overlook the magnificent spread of Grant Park and, beyond it, Lake Michigan.

And so I saw him again. He was enthusiastic about his new post. He said the college had just hired an expert librarian to catalogue the materials it was acquiring. I asked him if he would like to have my research materials as well as the taped interviews that went into the Oscar Peterson biography.

"Yes!"

"And my computer disks?"

"Absolutely!"

"How about the materials on white musicians?"

"Absolutely. For one thing, how can you understand the career of Marian Anderson if you don't know Bach?"

Dominique found an apartment and settled in. He said, with a sense of wonder, "If I look straight out of my apartment window, I can see the whole panorama of Chicago. But if I look *down*, I'm looking at the exact spot where King Oliver and Louis Armstrong got off the train!"

A few months later, Dominique gave a speech at the University of Chicago in which he dealt with aspects of this matter. Dominique continued to tell black students that if they deny the other tributaries of their bloodstream, if they ignore the English or Irish or French or whatever else they may also be, they are complicit in their own ghettoization, offering a suppliant acquiescence to the white racists who want them kept in their "place."

Dominique said in his speech:

"While there are few problems determining who is Italian or who lived during the Renaissance, defining who is black poses a greater problem. . . . The identification of black Americans and their culture is initially rooted in American sociology. When William Grant Still . . . [For those unfamiliar with Still's work, we should note that he was a "classical" composer who studied with Varèse; he was also an arranger who wrote for bands, including that of Artie Shaw. The chart on *Frenesi* is his.] . . . was born in Mississippi, his birth certificate identified his race; when Roque Cordero was born in Panama, his birth certificate identified his nationality. Yet both of these composers share African, Indian, and Spanish blood. Cordero's nationality acknowledges all three, while Still's recognizes only one, and totally ignores his Anglo background. Let us not forget then that Willie the Lion Smith was a cantor, that John Tchicai is Danish . . . and that the history of music in France can readily include the Chevalier de Saint-Georges.

"The black American currently reacts in the same simplistic manner. In his 1949 autobiography *A Man Called White*, Walter Francis White wrote: 'I am Negro. My skin is white, my eyes are blue, my hair is blond.' The irony of such a comment would be transformed into irrationality in a Panamanian setting, but American thinking accepts it, with far more than passive black co-operation. The matter is compounded if a non-black marries a person of African ancestry, which union produces a child who is then regarded as black. And to a far greater extent than appears in print, miscegenation has quite often included Native Americans, whose identified contributions are far fewer and whose culture is often thought even farther outside of the mainstream . . .

"In this post-Reagan wake, a symptom of the times is the emphasis now being given to matters outside of black music to account for as many of its characteristics as rhetoric and speculation will allow. . . . Yet black national-ist stances will not consider other acculturated factors, such as the contribu-tion to jazz history of Jewish and Native American musicians—although we can maintain that jazz is first and foremost a black music."

July 1991

In the fall of 1993, Dr. de Lerma was appointed visiting professor of music at the Conservatory of Music, Lawrence University, Appleton, Wisconsin.

The Man on the Buffalo Nickel: Dave Brubeck

We must act with vindictive earnestness against the Sioux, even to their extermination, men, women, and children.

—*William Tecumseh Sherman to President U.S. Grant*

This war of civilization . . . admits of but one solution . . . the extermination of the red man.

—Rocky Mountain News, *July 24, 1865*

Singer Kay Starr is three-quarters Indian—including Choctaw and Cherokee—and one-quarter Irish. "The American people would like us to just disappear," Kay told me. "And we have almost done it." John Lewis is part Cherokee and part Comanche. Joe Williams is part Seminole; so was Bobby Scott. Art Farmer and Lena Horne are part Blackfoot. Benny Golson and Ed Thigpen both have Indian background. "You could see it my father's face," Ed told me. His father was Ben Thigpen, who played drums with Andy Kirk. Earle Warren was part Cherokee, and so is Jim Hall. Doc Cheatham's maternal grandparents were full Cherokee; his father's father was Choctaw. Kid Ory's wife said that he was Cherokee. Big Chief Russell Moore was pure-blooded Pima, born on a reservation. Joe Mondragon was Apache, possibly full-blooded, and often teased about it: once when he was looking for a light for a cigarette Shelly Manne offered him two drumsticks. Oscar Pettiford, Trummy Young, Mildred Bailey, and Lee Wiley were part Indian. So are Horace Silver and Sweets Edison, and there was Indian in

Duke Ellington's family. Indeed, Ellington's sister, Ruth, told Dave Brubeck, "All the credit's gone to the African for the wonderful rhythm in jazz, but I think a lot of it should go to the American Indian."

Carl Fischer, the Los Angeles pianist and Frankie Laine's friend and accompanist, who wrote the melody of *We'll Be Together Again*, was full-blooded Indian. "That," Dave Brubeck said when I mentioned it to him, "is one of the most beautiful ballads ever written." Fischer also wrote *You've Changed* and *It Started All Over Again*, and he wrote an orchestral suite called *Reflections of an Indian Boy*, recorded on Columbia and long since out of print. It is a haunting thing, full of a sense of the West, the best thing of its kind since MacDowell orchestrated a group of Indian themes.

One of the major influences in jazz was Frank Trumbauer, who helped shape the playing of Lester Young and Benny Carter. Benny told me that himself, and Lester Young attested to it so often that there can be no question about it. Woody Herman said Trumbauer influenced him, and was sure that Johnny Hodges would say the same thing. Thus Trumbauer's influence can be found in Phil Woods, whose avowed influences are "Benny Carter, Johnny Hodges, and Charlie Parker, in that order," and in those whose work comes out of Phil's.

John Chilton wrote of Trumbauer's "pithy sense of understatement and dry, delicate tone." Put that together with this: Trumbauer's wife, Mitzi, made the wry observation, "Frank was an Indian, you know, and would never say one word where none would do."

Archaeologists have established that the Chumash—it is a misnomer, like the term American Indian, but it is in general use—were living in California by 8000 B.C. They were a clever, friendly, civilized people whose technology by 2000 B.C. was in advance of that of the barbarians in the forests of northern Europe. They had an elaborate fishing and trading economy, and their terrain, which extended up the coast from Malibu for about 200 miles, almost to the Monterey County border, was huge. They were also a very musical people. The Franciscan friar Juan Crespi, who accompanied the Portola expedition of 1602, wrote in his diary that "the Indians were quite kind but . . . they played weird flutes all night and kept us awake." In common with other Indians of California, they utilized something like the Finnish sauna, rooms built into the ground with a fire in the middle. The Spanish called these sweat houses *temescals*. When they had worked up a good sweat, the Chumash would dive into the sea, even as the Finns roll in snow. A friar on a later expedition wrote, "The women cover themselves with deer skins hanging from the waist, with a cape of otter skins over the shoulders . . . and are pretty, and they have pendants in the ears." The Spaniards consistently remarked on the kindness and gentility of the Chumash. The Chumash welcomed, fed, and guided them.

The Chumash lived continuously in California for 9000 years. The Spanish brought them to the edge of extinction in just sixty years, and destroyed their culture forever. There are no pure-blooded Chumash left.

The gringos impressed some of the surviving Indians into a system of peonage somewhat like that of the Spanish period, but much harsher. An Indian had no resort to the courts, and could—legally—be shot for breaking the white man's code with such offenses as demanding his wages. (It should also be noted that railways of California often paid off the Chinese laborers who built them by executing them.) The Indian male, of course, was much more liable to this summary termination. Women, after all, have a certain utility to men. A scholar at the University of California estimated that 12,000 Indian women became the concubines of American settlers. The resulting mixed-breed populace was considered to be Indian, as anyone with a traceable amount of "black" blood was considered Negro in the South. They retreated into a sullen hatred of the white man that persists in many of them to this day. And of course this hatred of the white man is endemic in the ninety-six reservations still extant in California.

The first gold-mining and the first wine-making were done with Indian labor. J. Ross Brown, Inspector of Indian Affairs, wrote, "If ever an Indian was fully and honestly paid for his labor on the Pacific coast, it was not my luck to hear of it." Where they could not be used, they were eliminated: 50,000 Indians were slaughtered in two years of the Gold Rush. That's not counting the Mexican peon population, the "greasers" whose sobriquet derived from the hide-and-tallow trade in which many of them worked.

In 1850 a mob of 2000 Americans destroyed the Mexican mining town of Sonora in a week of unimpeded rioting and lynching. The indiscriminate lynching of Mexicans went so far that in July of 1851, a Mexican woman three months' pregnant was hanged. In 1853 there were more homicides in California than in all the rest of the United States put together, and the figure rose to one a day in Los Angeles in 1854. In the five years from 1849 to 1854, the population of California spent $6,000,000 on bowie knives and pistols, and during that period there were 2,400 murders, 1,400 suicides, and 10,000 other "miserable deaths," which historian Carey McWilliams took to mean Mexican deaths. A peaceful, even docile, Mexican peasantry was stirred to a hatred of the Anglos that continues to this day.

California takes a back seat to no other state, probably even no other nation, for its record of relentless racism. It has been a killing ground comparable perhaps to Cambodia under Pol Pot, with entire populations simply exterminated. Dave Brubeck told me a story: "Outside of Yreka, at the foot of Mount Shasta, they gave a feast for the Indians. The old ones said to the younger ones, 'You better not go.' A few of the older guys didn't go. And they poisoned the food, and there was just a trail of dead Indians, hundreds. There were just unbelievable things that were done."

The Yuki, who lived in north central California, numbered 6,880 in 1850. By 1864, the number was down to 300, and by 1973 to one. The Modoc, once a powerful and important people, didn't fare quite that badly: there are still a few of them on a reservation at Klamath, near the California-Oregon border.

"Don't teach him that nonsense," Elizabeth Ivey Brubeck would say to her husband, Peter Brubeck, whenever he would try to tell Dave to be proud of his heritage. Her own father came from Cornwall, England, and there was either Polish or Russian background on her mother's side—she was never sure. Peter's father came from Indiana. There was some German in the family history, which is whence the name derives. And the "nonsense" she didn't want filling her son's head was that there was Modoc Indian in the line as well.

"There's maybe a fourth Modoc," Dave told me.

"My dad was born in 1884 near Pyramid Lake, which is an Indian reservation." Pyramid Lake is in Nevada, close to the California border and thirty miles north-northwest of Reno. "That lake still belongs to the Indians. He was born maybe twenty miles from the lake at a place called Amedee, where there's no one living, in Honey Lake Valley. At the time there was an eighty-mile-long lake. It's dried up. There were steamboats on it. It's gone. Some lakes disappear. He was raised there.

"I wanted to see where my dad was born, so I took Iola and the kids and we drove up there. When we got there we found a historic California marker, and I think it said, 'This is the site of the last Indian uprising in California.'

"My mother's attitude was, 'Don't tell him that nonsense.' And my father toward the end of his life told his grandson to be proud of what you are."

Peter and Elizabeth Ivey Brubeck had three sons, all of whom became musicians. Henry, the eldest, eventually was head of music in the Santa Barbara public and high school system. He is dead. Howard became dean of humanities at Palomar College. Dave, the youngest, was born December 6, 1920, in his mother's home town, Concord, California, which is a little north of Oakland, but the family moved to Ione, about 115 miles east of San Francisco.

Dave was a working cowboy by the time he was thirteen. "My dad," he said, "was a cattleman and a top rodeo roper, maybe the top in California some years. He was the Salinas Rodeo and Livermore champion in roping. He wanted a son that would follow him. I was the youngest of the sons, so I was his last chance. He would come down to San Simeon and buy cattle from the Hearst stock."

Dave was referring to the huge ranch of newspaper magnate William Randolph Hearst, which occupies magnificent hilly land overlooking the Pacific. Hearst stocked it with exotic animals from all over the world, including dangerous wild European boar which turned native and are still hunted in that part of the country. It is north of the Tehachapi range, which divides California into its north-south regions, and the magnificent Big Sur country starts just a little north of San Simeon. The huge, preposterous, and gloomy Hearst castle stands atop a long rise, overlooking the sea. Among its other architectural indulgences is a full Roman bath, which was photographed in the film *Spartacus*. Hearst raised some of the finest blooded cattle in the West.

"My dad covered the western states, buying cattle for a big company called the Moffet Meat Company," Dave said. "And like myself, he was always on the road. He wanted to settle down. So the company gave him a 45,000-acre ranch to manage, if you can imagine how large that is. In some places it was twenty-five miles across. He moved there and took me and my mother when I was twelve. The other boys stayed in Concord, where we were born, Howard to finish high school. Henry at this time was playing with Del Courtney and Gil Evans. Gil had a band out of Stockton.

"Jimmy Maxwell was one of the trumpet players in that band. Jimmy and I were talking about it one time, and he mentioned the persecution of the Japanese during the war. They confiscated their lands and sold them cheap. Jimmy's father had a Japanese friend. He bought the guy's land. When the neighbor came back after the war, Jimmy's father sold him the land back for a dollar.

"But I didn't know Gil in California. I didn't meet him until I went to hear the session he did with Miles Davis, and he had arranged *The Duke*." *The Duke* is one of Dave's best-known compositions. Gil's magnificent arrangement of it is in the landmark *Miles Ahead* album.

"Gil said, 'Brubeck. Did you have a brother who played drums?' I said, 'Yeah, Henry.' He said, 'I never put that together. He was a great drummer, and he played with me in Stockton!'

"So Henry stayed in Stockton to play drums with Gil, and we moved to the ranch in Ione. It's in the foothills of the Sierra Nevadas.

"On our ranch there was a reservation for Indians. There was maybe the last sweat house in California, where the Miwoks used to come. Many of my friends were Miwok Indians. Mother's piano assistant when she moved to Ione was Ramona Burris, an Indian girl. I'm still in touch with her. She recently sent me some Indian songs that I wanted from this great friend of mine, Al Walloupe, a cowboy. Full Miwok. He was my father's top cowhand. I always tried to ride with him.

"We moved from Stockton to Ione when I was in the eighth grade and went through high school there. I could ride horses from the time I can remember."

"Could you rope?" I asked. "Do all that?"

"Oh sure!" Dave said.

"Did you work the ranch."

"Sure. Oh sure."

"How did you get into music"

"My mother started all of us in music. She was a classical pianist. She studied piano with Tobias Matthay in England." Matthay, an English pianist born in London in 1858, gradually gave up his concert career to teach, first at the Royal Academy of Music and then at his own school. He developed what is now known as the Matthay System of playing, and students from all over England, the Continent, and America, then went home to spread his method, which tended to produce a glorious warm tone. He died in 1945. He taught an approach to piano at variance to the German school of playing. It emphasized a particular approach to touch and tone, a way of pulling on the key rather than hitting it hammer-like from above. It is an approach that Margaret Chaloff, Serge Chaloff's mother, imparted to a whole generation of jazz pianists, including Mike Renzi, Steve Kuhn, and Dave Mackay. It produces the radiant golden tone that Bill Evans brought into jazz, now manifest in countless pianists, including Herbie Hancock, Keith Jarrett, Alan Broadbent, and Chick Corea.

"This was after all three sons were born," Dave said. "My mother was one of these people with tremendous drive. After three children, she went to college and she was in class with her oldest son, Henry. They went to summer sessions in Moscow, Idaho, until he could get a master's and she was just trying to get a college degree. In 1926 she went to London to study with Matthay. I was six, and she boarded Howard and me out.

"She also studied with Dame Myra Hess. And that's why she quit. There were some kids walking along the street in London. My mother looked at them. Myra Hess said, 'You're staring at those children. Do you have children?' And she said, 'Yes. I have three sons.' And Myra said, 'Why don't you go home to them? That's where you belong.' Whether it was a kind way of saying you'll never make it as a great classical pianist, or that's a wonderful life to live, I don't know.

"You see, Dame Myra Hess was always panicked about playing. She said walking from the curtain to the piano was always terrible for her. She said there's a river of ice between you and the audience until you break through to them. She hated all that. So she told my mother, If you've got three children, just go home and be with your family.

"So she came back and taught for years, taught so many people who are in the music business. She insisted that I go to college. My dad didn't ever want me to leave the ranch.

"When I first started playing at four or five, I only wanted to compose. For some reason my mother didn't discover I couldn't read music until it was too late to correct all the wonderfully wrong habits I had, which was to listen and learn that way. I fooled her. I'd stare at the music and play it well enough so she didn't know. They weren't hard, they were kids' pieces.

"When I went to college I switched from pre-med to music the second year, 'cause the head of zoology said, 'Brubeck, your mind's not here. It's across the lawn in the conservatory. Go over there, will you?' It was then College of the Pacific, it's now University of the Pacific in Stockton."

It was during these period that Dave met Iola, his wife-to-be. Her family had been in California since 1835, shortly after the Mission period of its history. She too was a student at College of the Pacific, a drama and speech major.

Dave said, "At this point I transferred to the music department, but I couldn't read. And my mother had this reputation as sending great students. My brother Henry, eleven years older than I, had graduated as a violin and percussion major, and was a teacher. Howard is four and half years older than I.

"So I went over to the conservatory. I was pretty sure I could hide the fact that I couldn't read a note. Everything went well. You had to take a string instrument, a brass instrument, a reed instrument. And when you're learning these instruments, it's the scales and stuff that even somebody like myself could slip by a teacher. But you still had to take keyboard. So I waited till my senior year."

"You mean," I said, incredulous, "you faked it through college without reading?'"

"Yeah, harmony, ear training."

"That's *really* what they mean by faking," I said.

"Yeah," Dave said, laughing. "You know it. Like, in ear training, I'd usually be asleep, 'cause I'd been working in some joint the night before until two in the morning. There are stories about the teacher saying, 'Well, can anybody play this progression and tell me what I've just played?' Then he'd say, 'Well, if nobody can, then wake up Brubeck.'

"In my own way, I could do it. He'd say, 'What chord is this?' and I'd say, 'That's the first chord in *Don't Worry 'Bout Me.*' Then he'd say, 'Well explain that, Mr. Brubeck.' I'd go play that chord. He'd say, 'Well can't you say that that's a flat ninth?'

"I didn't know it was a flat ninth. But that's the way I got through.

"I had to take organ. I thought, 'If I take organ, it'll be harder for them to know I can't read music yet.' So the first lesson, I left the damn electric organ on after my last practice. The teacher was furious. It was on all night, and he said, 'You could burn up an organ this way.' He kicked me out and gave me an F. I still had a whole semester. In a way I'd taken keyboard and gotten an F, but I'd still done it.

"But then they insisted that I take keyboard. I got a wonderful piano teacher who figured out I couldn't read in about five minutes. She went to the dean and said, 'Brubeck can't read *anything.*'

"The dean said to me, 'You were going to graduate this year. I can't let you graduate. You're a disgrace to the conservatory.'

"So I said, 'It doesn't make any difference to me. I don't care whether I graduate or not. All I want to do is play jazz. And I agree with you.'

"The word got around to the counterpoint teacher and the ear-training and harmony teacher that I'd been disgraced and flunked. The counterpoint teacher went to the dean and said, 'You're making a mistake. Brubeck has written the best counterpoint I've ever had in this class.'"

"But how did you do it?" I asked.

"I struggled," Dave said, "but I could do it."

I said, "I've known a number of arrangers and composers who can write better than they can read."

"There's a lot of guys that way," Dave said. "Maybe even Duke. I've been in some situations where I thought Duke had some of my problems."

"Reading and writing music are different skills."

"Yes," Dave said. "So the ear training, harmony, and composition teachers went to my defense and said, 'You know, you're making a big mistake.' So the dean called me back in and he said, 'You can graduate with the class, but you have to promise you'll never teach.'

"So I made that promise and I graduated. Then I went into the army for four years."

"Since your father wanted you to stay on the ranch with him, how did he take it when you switched to music? Was there a break with him?"

"I thought there would be, but he took it pretty well. He said, 'Well we'll always be partners.' He kept track of how many cattle I had. He gave me four Holstein cows for $80—that's $20 a piece—when I graduated from grammar school. He kept those separate in his herds. I could always come back to the ranch. My herd had grown, and he always wanted me back. And many years I wished I were there, when it was rough. We would go home once in a while, wouldn't we, Iola? When we just couldn't make it."

Iola is an Indian name, but Iola is not Indian. Dave said, "In one tribe it means A Cloud at Dawn. And in the other tribe we've looked up, Never Discouraged.

"I went into the army in 1942—for 46 months, to be exact. Iola and I were married in Carson City, Nevada. I was on a three-day pass. I went into a band, and then for D-Day they sent us all to infantry. I went overseas as a rifleman. We went right across England, we didn't even stop, from the boat to the train to the boat, and then across to the Le Havre area, to Omaha Beach. It was three months after the landing. We went up to Verdun. I was a replacement in Third Army, under Patton.

"I was almost in combat every day. I was on the other side of the German lines twice, trying to get back. You didn't know where anybody was. We were always at the front and the front would move on you. I spent the Battle of the Bulge in a cellar, being told by Axis Sally we should all come out with our hands up.

"When we saw that movie *Patton*, when you see all the trucks moving up, I said, 'They forgot one thing. The one truck going the wrong way. Me.' All the guys at the sentry point had been killed the night before. Germans in American uniforms killed every guy right there. So when they came up to us, they took the pins out of hand grenades and held them out. They walked right up to the truck. If you shot one of them, he'd blow up and you with him. They weren't believing my story.

"I was one day away from fighting.

"Then I got a band."

By pure luck, Dave was tapped to play in a unit that was traveling in the European theater of operations to entertain battle-weary troops. The reassignment may well have saved his life.

As I was writing the foregoing, an eerie coincidence occurred. I was wondering what outfit Dave had been in. I took a break and went down to browse in Bart's in downtown—if you can call it that—Ojai, the small California town where I live. The name is Chumash for "nest." Bart's is a very good used-book store. On some obscure impulse, I went back to the office to say hello to Gary Schlichter, the owner, whom I hadn't seen for a while. He said, "I've got something to show you," and handed me a copy of Spengler's *Decline of the West*. "Look inside it," Gary said.

I opened the book. I was dumbstruck as I stared at the printed signature of a 24-year-old GI who had inscribed it on this flyleaf nearly fifty years before: *David W. Brubeck 140th Infantry Regiment A Company*. And in the book was a photograph of Dave at the age of four, taken at the Franciscan Mission at Carmel, according to the writing on the back.

I rushed home to call Dave. He was astounded. "Where did your friend get the book?" he asked.

"I haven't the slightest idea," I said.

"I carried that book all through the war!" Dave said in astonishment. "I carried that and a Bible in my knapsack! With all the other stuff you're carrying, any extra weight has to be something important. I couldn't be more thrilled that you found it. I never knew what happened to it."

The next day, September 21, was Dave and Iola's wedding anniversary. Gary Schlichter gave me the book to send to them as our joint anniversary gift. Gary said, "How many soldiers were reading Spengler in the middle of war?"

Dave said, "My memory is that we were outside Verdun. If the train had turned left at Verdun, we'd have gone to Omar Bradley's army. If we'd turned right, we'd go to the front with Patton's. We turned right. We were in boxcars for three days. Stand up or sit on your pack, that was the amount of room. We were as if we were in cattle cars. So we wound up there and Red Cross girls came up to do a show and they asked for a piano player. I was sitting on my helmet and I volunteered to play piano. The colonel said, 'This guy shouldn't go to the front.'

"In the morning we were supposed to do this horrendous thing. . . ." Dave stopped speaking. Tears appeared on his face. And he released one deep, shuddering sob. We were in his hotel room in Santa Monica. He was to play the Hollywood Bowl that evening. I looked beyond him, through the curtains and across that strip of green park with palm trees that runs along the seaward edge of the Santa Monica palisades. Children on the grass, playing. Beyond that the sea, shining in the sun. Iola was sitting behind us on a bed.

"We don't have to talk, Dave," I said. He was silent for a long time. Then he resumed, struggling to control his voice:

"There was about a foot of mud. We were sleeping on reeds, three guys in a pup tent. The tent was supposed to hold two, but if you took in a third guy you could put his shelter half on the ground under you. They brought up some huge cannon on the railroad and started blasting, to try to blast the Germans out of an emplacement on a hill. It shook the ground. Everybody just ran out in that mud. It was the damnedest sight you'd ever want to see.

"The Germans were shelling down. The only way they could get them out was take the replacements and send them in there to climb up there and dump oil into the bunkers. And that's how those German guns were silenced. Those guys had to go right up a mountain at point blank range and dump the oil and light it. That's where I think I was going. Some guys I never heard from again were in on that, where I should have been that day.

"And they called three of us out to start a band. We got pulled right out of that formation. Most of my guys had purple hearts. They'd been shot at the front. If they said they were musicians, they sent them over to me, and I would keep them in the band.

"I spent the rest of the war in that band. I integrated that band. It was the first integrated unit in World War II that I've ever known about. The trombonist was Jonathan Dick Flowers, who was black, and we had an emcee who was black, but his name was White. We had all kinds of guys who had been shot and had come back. So we could play at the front very well, because my guys all wore their Purple Hearts. I asked them to.

"I remember we'd be playing a show and the Germans would come in to strafe, and they'd try to shoot the planes down. Then we were in the Maginot Line, underground. Like *Star Wars*, with the trains underground.

"The Radio City Music Hall Rockettes were touring Europe and they needed a band, and they chose us." He started to laugh. "So we got from sleeping in haystacks and barns and on the ground to this unbelievable luxury in hotels."

Mustered out of service in New Jersey at war's end, Dave headed west immediately to join his young wife. He studied composition with Darius Milhaud at Mills College in Oakland on the GI Bill. For a time Dave and Iola lived with Milhaud. The first of the six Brubeck children arrived at that time—David Darius, born June 14, 1947, in San Francisco.

Dave thought of himself as a composer who played piano, not as a pianist. He still could not read well, but Milhaud saw his potential as a composer, and encouraged him to apply his studies immediately. As a vehicle for counterpoint exercises, Dave formed the Dave Brubeck Octet, whose members included clarinetist Bill Smith. Paul Desmond, a saxophone and clarinet player, and drummer Cal Tjader, both students at San Francisco

State College, used to come over to sit in. This was the beginning of Dave's professional association with Desmond, and almost the end of it.

"In '46, '47, when I was studying at Mills with Milhaud, I was in a trio called the Three Ds—Dave, Darryl, and Don. Paul would come in and sit in every night. Paul had a chance for a gig. He hired the bass player and Frances Lynn, the singer. All of a sudden I was in a group that wasn't a group any more. Paul had hired them away to work in a Quonset hut kind of place called the Band Box, near Stanford. Paul wrote a song for us to sing."

"Oh yeah," I said. "Paul told me about that. I had a lot of trouble picturing you and Paul singing. I remember saying, 'You and Dave *singing*?'"

And to prove he was telling the truth Dave broke into song, rhythmically chanting a lunatic lyric that was typically Desmond:

> It's the Band Box,
> that's the joint for you.
> Get high when you're happy
> and blind when you're blue.
> The whisky is old
> but the music is new
> at the Band Box.
>
> If the state you arrive in'
> encourages jivin',
> relax on the sofa
> with a chick you can go fa'
> That's where the proletariat
> make merry at—
> at the Band Box.

"We all sang it," Dave said.

"You were a quintet?" I asked.

"No. We had no drummer," Dave said. "Paul's favorite situation."

"He really hated drummers," I said, "except Connie Kay and one or two others. He just wanted them to stay out of his way."

Dave said, "Joe and Paul and Gene and I were really friends, regardless of any differences that came up between us. I remember Paul saying to Joe Morello, 'You're the world's greatest drummer, but sometimes you play too much.' When Paul was at home dying Joe sent one of his drum students to stay with him.

"Do you know the story about Mingus going to see him? We'd known Charlie since the early days in San Francisco, and he and Paul were good friends. Mingus and I were too. We were really close for years. Paul had to leave his apartment door unlocked, because he was too weak to answer it. Charlie let himself in while Paul was asleep and stood by the bed. Paul woke up and saw him standing there in a black cape and a black hat, and Paul said for a moment he thought it was the angel of death.

"Charlie said to me, 'Dave, when I'm dying, will you come to my bed-side?' And I said I would. But he died in Mexico, and I couldn't be there. I felt bad about it."

Iola said, "I have a new Desmond story—at least, new to me. Paul saw a picture in a newspaper showing Aristotle Onassis in front of the Hollywood home of Buster Keaton, looking at it with an eye to buying it. Paul's comment was, 'Hmm. Aristotle contemplating the home of Buster.'"

After a pause she said, "We all miss him, don't we."

We laughed for a while, as Paul's friends always do when his memory is evoked, and then Dave resumed the story.

"I went along with Paul on that job. I had been making a hundred a week and Paul offered me forty-two a week. An offer I couldn't refuse. But I enjoyed Paul's playing. I didn't know how the hell I was going to live on the money.

"And then Paul got a job at Feather River, the Feather River Inn. You know why he liked Feather River? Because he could go over to Reno to gamble.

"I thought, He's gonna leave me. I'm stuck. I can't go back to the other job. There's very little work. I said, 'Paul, okay, I'm going to bring Bill Smith in on clarinet because the guy at the Band Box will keep me on.' He said, 'No! It's my job!' He wouldn't let me take the job, he got furious. He said, 'I found this job, it's my job when I come back!' He was going to Feather River for three months."

Feather River is about eighty miles north by northeast from San Francisco, and twenty or so due north of Sacramento. It was in those days, and for that matter still is, extremely bucolic and quiet, horse and cattle country yellow-brown under the fierce summer sun and brilliant green when the rains of winter come.

No one who really knew Paul would gainsay his borderline solipsism. Yet for all his selfishness, he could be kind and he was gentle, and he was very, very funny. Iola said, laughing: "Paul could charm you out of anything." But at the time of that Feather River booking, he didn't charm Dave.

Paul didn't even come back to the gig: he went on the road with the

Alvino Rey band. Dave, meantime, had lost the Band Box and had a family to feed. He said, "I told Iola, 'I *never* want to see Paul Desmond again. I don't know how we're going to make it.' Scale at that time was forty-two a week. I got a job for scale and room and board at Clear Lake, and we lived in a corrugated tin room about the size of these two beds and with no windows. Just a door. So we got sacks and dipped them in tubs of water and ran a fan. We had to get out of there all day. It was miserable.

"And then Jimmy Lyons called me and said, 'I've got a job for you, if you want it, at the Burma Lounge.' It was right in the center of Oakland. We went in there with the trio and everything was going great. That's how the trio started."

The late Jimmy Lyons at that time was a San Francisco disc jockey, one of the most influential spokesmen for jazz in that city. Later Jimmy founded and directed the Monterey Jazz Festival. It was Jimmy who in 1977 flew out over the Pacific and scattered Paul's ashes, in accordance with Paul's wishes.

"I owe so much to Jimmy Lyons," Dave said. "He got me a once-a-week shot on NBC. I was on with the trio, Cal, Ronny and I, for three, maybe six, months. And being it was NBC, you could hear us clear out into the Pacific, and all up and down the coast. It was a very strong signal. And when the sailors would come in, and they were always coming into San Francisco, they'd look for where I was playing. That really helped me in my club work, this constant flow of sailors every week. We developed a very good following, and we were at the Blackhawk for maybe six months of every year. It was a good home base for us.

"I said to Iola, 'If Paul Desmond comes back, don't let him in the door.' He'd heard the trio on the radio while he was in New York with Alvino Rey. So he knocked at the door. I was on the back porch, hanging out diapers. Iola always liked Paul."

"He looked so forlorn," Iola said, "that I went to the back porch and told Dave, 'You just have to see him.'

"Paul's charm," she added, smiling and shaking her head. "And he was full of promises to Dave. He said, 'If you'll just let me play with you, I'll baby-sit. I'll wash your car.'" The memory trailed off in laughter.

"So he broke down my resistance," Dave said. "And of course it was a good thing. We worked well together. Seventeen years. Longer. Right to the end. His last concert was with me.

"The trio I had grew out of the octet. We couldn't really work with the octet. So I took the rhythm section, Ron Crotty or Jack Weeks on bass, and Cal Tjader on drums, and the trio became very successful. It won as new combo of the year in *Down Beat* and *Metronome* and got a great review from

John Hammond. We were doing very well. Paul was always trying to sit in. People would ask me, Please don't let Paul sit in. We had already recorded, and they wanted it to sound like the record.

"The trio's first record was made for a label called Coronet. Jack Sheedy of Coronet wouldn't pay me so I could pay Cal Tjader and Ron Crotty. Sol and Max Weiss who ran the Circle Record Company told me, 'Go tell Jack Sheedy that you'll buy back the masters for what they cost him. Because we press them and we know they're selling.' They were originally a pressing company. So I bought back the masters for $350, four sides, 78s, *Back Home Again in Indiana, Laura, Tea for Two*, and *Blue Moon*. The Weisses started Fantasy Records to put them out. At first the Weisses just wanted to do our re-releases." Fantasy today, with its subsidiary labels such as Pablo, Milestone, and Riverside, is probably the biggest jazz record company in the world. It is also an important movie production house. And it all started with the Brubeck records.

Dave said, "Paul also made his first record for Coronet—as a clarinetist in a Dixieland group. Joe Dodge was the drummer.

"I was going along. I went into the Haig in Los Angeles. Gerry Mulligan and his quartet moved up from the Haig into the Blackhawk in San Francisco where we'd been playing. We just exchanged. Paul came along to sit in with us. We went into Zardi's in L.A.

"We wanted to buy a house. We'd been living in a flat in San Francisco. We were living in a little two-room on the sands, right here in Santa Monica, near the pier. You can see the area from here." He pointed out the window. The two-room houses are gone now. The sand is clean and yellow.

"We put the down payment on a house in San Francisco. I remember packing Iola and the two kids in the car and having her slap me all night to keep me awake driving. We got to San Francisco and the deal had completely collapsed, which it shouldn't have. The money was in escrow. But we had no place to live.

"A job came through in Honolulu, at the Zebra Lounge. I said, 'We have no place to live, everything we own is in storage, let's take this job.' We were so broke I bought a few cases of burned baby food. I always had to buy stuff at the dented-can food market, or stuff that had been in a fire. And the kids wouldn't eat it. So I had to eat it all in Honolulu.

"I got into a swimming accident about the first week. I was running and diving and a wave disappeared and there was a sand bar. Instead of hitting it head on as I should have, I turned. And there almost went my piano playing. Nerve damage, damaged vertebrae. It still bothers me down into my finger. I was in traction for twenty-one days, with a weight over me. I remember writing to Paul, overhead, he got this scribbled note. He saved it all his life. I told Paul, 'Maybe now we can start the quartet.' This time it just worked. This time around, we were ready for a horn.

"I went back to San Francisco. I couldn't work for quite a while, but finally we put the quartet together.

"The trio was really successful, and I had to build up again with the quartet on Fantasy. We did that *Jazz at Oberlin* album. Paul is so fantastic on that album.

"Eventually Fantasy Records and I made some kind of decision that we were going to split up. George Avakian came to hear me at the Blackhawk, with the idea of signing me for Columbia Records.

"At this point I was sick of the road. I told my attorney that I wanted to quit. I just wanted to stay around San Francisco and work gigs. He said, 'Dave, your big years are coming up. Do you want to educate your children? Go on the road for one year.'

"I said, 'I can't take it any more.'

"He said, 'Well what if you take your family with you and rent your house in Oakland to somebody for a year? You don't have any money.' And I didn't. I was penniless. At this point we were about ten thousand in the hole to the government for taxes. So I did need the money. I worked it out with Irving Townsend at Columbia Records. He was coming to California to become head of jazz for Columbia on the west coast. Irving said, 'You can rent my house in Wilton, Connecticut. The landlady likes to have artists around.'

"She was Alice Delamar. She owned about twelve houses there. Leonard Feather spent some time there. John Hammond lived there. Balanchine lived in one of the houses. Artists all over the joint.'"

"Gene," Iola said, "that's the house you visited." I remembered it, a lovely spacious house in the woods, and Dave had a piano in every room, including the kitchen.

Dave said, "We liked it so much, and life became so much easier, and I was with the family so much more, instead of traveling from the west coast to the east coast, that we stayed. At that time there wasn't that much work on the west coast. Now it's different, but at that time there was very little work for a jazz group. So we stayed on. We loved Wilton and we built our present house.

"Paul was on a percentage. He got 20 percent of everything. The attorney I mentioned, James R. Bancroft, set it up. He was also Paul's attorney. Paul and I never had an argument about money. He never looked at the books.

He never asked the attorney to see anything. He said, 'Whatever you say is right.' And Paul never would sign a contract with me. He made *me* sign one!"

"You mean, you were contracted to him, but he wasn't contracted to you?"

"Yeah," Dave said.

"Boy, he was slick."

"Yeah." Dave laughed. "He never would leave, but he never looked at anything and he would never sign anything."

Iola said, "That 20 percent goes to Paul's estate, and he left his estate to the Red Cross."

"Like," Dave said, "*Take Five*, everything he wrote, all his royalties go to the Red Cross."

"You know, Dave," I said, "Paul always said you were his favorite accompanist. He loved playing with you, and he loved the Modern Jazz Quartet."

The MJQ and the Dave Brubeck Quartet were dominant sounds in the jazz of the 1950s and '60s. There were areas of similarity, as well as difference. Both were led by pianists; both pianists had a taste for counterpoint, and both were (and are) composers of distinction with strong interests in European concert music. As soloists, they are different, John Lewis usually understated almost to the point of diffidence, Dave assertive and plunging, as eager and innocently enthusiastic as a player as he is as a man. But both men are generous and sympathetic compers, feeding the soloist with sensitivity, understanding, and restraint.

The Brubeck Quartet is generally thought to have reached its classic period after Joe Morello joined it on drums in 1956 and Eugene Wright on bass in 1958. This personnel remained stable until 1967, when it disbanded. Dave and Paul were an odd couple, the former devoted to his family, the latter to his own hedonism and a succession of gorgeous and sometimes quite kinky girls, and he seemed to live his true love life in gentle, distant, conversational affection for the wives of his friends. "Hi there!" he'd say on the phone in a bright cheery way I picked up from him. Gerry Mulligan says it too; maybe he also got it from Paul: Gerry was another of his close friends, and it fell to Gerry to give me the melancholy reports on Paul's declining condition. "This is your friend Paul Breitenfeld," his real name, he'd announce. Or sometimes it was, "Hi, it's me, Desmond."

Paul was family to the Brubecks. Darius told me that he was about twelve years old before he realized Paul wasn't actually his uncle.

Darius said, "Paul looked a lot like Dave when they were both younger and we always referred to him as Uncle Paul. His visits were not like those infrequent occasions known as 'having company,' which meant we had to make ourselves scarce. Paul always chatted with us, asked our opinions on things, laughed at our childish jokes, gave us Christmas presents, and even played chess with me. Our other uncles—our real uncles—were like that with us, but most adults were not, so I suppose it was only when I could grasp what 'uncle' literally meant that Paul Desmond was removed from my imaginary kinship system. Uncle Paul and Dave were so connected in our lives and theirs that the word 'uncle' became attached to Dave as well, and to this day, Chris and Dan, my brothers, and I often refer to Uncle Dave or UD for short. I've read that Native American cultures make little distinction between blood relations and kinship by choice.

"In South Africa, by the way, jazz musicians are addressed as Bra (for brother) within the fraternity. Therefore I am Uncle Darius to bass player Bra Victor Ntoni's offspring. Do the children know the codes of our in-group or will they, at some point, start wondering why their father's brother is white and doesn't speak Xhosa?"

Dave had a trick to annoy Paul on stage. Left to his own devices, Paul would play ballads or medium tempos all evening. Dave would kick off very fast tempos early in a concert, having discovered that Paul played his best when he was angry. Joe Morello angered him too. Joe is a deliciously busy drummer, and a witty one—Don DeMicheal, who was a drummer as well as a writer, said Joe could have written a joke book for drummers. Joe had a great rapport with bassist Eugene Wright. They would set up a loud, churning kind of rhythm, swinging like mad, as in their recording of *Let's Get Away from It All*, pushing Paul to some of his most inspired solos.

There was a tendency among critics to patronize Desmond during his life as too "white." He was considered derivative of Lee Konitz. I reject that out of hand. I know he admired Pete Brown. But I think I know where Desmond came from. If Lester Young, as he said, developed his tone and approach from trying to emulate on tenor the C-melody sound of Frank Trumbauer, Desmond, in my opinion, got his tone from trying to emulate on the alto the clarinet sound of Lester Young. You hear this if you listen to the Lester Young Commodore recordings in the Mosaic reissue package. What he did with his sound—high, lyrical, piercing yet soft, witty, allusive, sly, peerlessly melodic and inexhaustibly inventive—was his own. History has not taken his measure. He was a wondrous player, which I see more clearly now that I no longer have to question my bias toward him on grounds of friendship. Now he is gone into time, and I know just how good he was.

Dave Brubeck is a deeply religious man. His mother was a Methodist interested in Christian Science and Far Eastern philosophy. Ten years or so ago Dave wrote a Mass. After its premiere, a priest upbraided him for not including an Our Father in it. Dave took the family on vacation in the Caribbean and while there he dreamed the Our Father section in detail and in its entirety, and later added it to the Mass. He chuckled: "I thought that the church must be saying something to me." He became a Catholic.

Dave is enormously decent, sensitive, and moral and absolutely faithful to Iola. Paul Desmond, who was no more able to commit himself to a permanent relationship with a woman than he was to sign a contract with Dave, used to jest, "I spent seventeen years trying to get Dave Brubeck laid."

Dave is devoid of animosity. He seems almost naïve. But he has one deep anger: a lifelong hatred of racism. I reminded him of a tour he once cancelled. "Oh yeah," he said. "I cancelled 23 of 25 concerts in the South because of Eugene Wright. They said I could work them if I'd bring Norman Bates. And I wouldn't do it. We lost half a year's work. I was working at the Blackhawk, but you made your money going on a tour. I also lost out to Duke Ellington on the Bell Telephone Hour because they wanted me to put Eugene Wright where they couldn't put the camera on him. I wouldn't do it, and they hired Duke. I never did tell Duke. Because Duke was innocent; they just hired Duke instead."

The situation at Bell Telephone was peculiar: it was not that the company would not book black artists on their show; they would not let black and white performers appear together. Norman Granz got into a crunch with Bell over their effort to conceal from the camera that the guitarist in Ella Fitzgerald's trio, Herb Ellis, was white.

Dave has an abiding interest in the welfare and culture of the American Indians. He said, "I wrote a piece called *They All Sang Yankee Doodle*. It opens with an Indian song that Al Walloupe had taught me.

"The conductor at the concert at Yale University, Erik Kunzel, said, 'Dave starts this piece with an Indian song because he wants us all to remember they were here first.' There was a ruckus in the audience, and this man got up from his seat and made his wife and son, probably, follow him and leave the auditorium. The piece uses national anthems or songs from the melting pot, as we used to call it, all with *Yankee Doodle* going against *O Tannen-*

baum and *Meadowland* and the Portuguese *Holy Ghost March*. And then it ends with the Indian song, which is important."

The hatred of racism has been passed to his six children, all of whom have been trained in music, and four of whom are professionals. Darius, also a pianist, has for many years now been teaching jazz to young black South Africans. He is director of the New Center for Jazz and Popular Music at the University of Natal in Durban.

Iola told me, "Darius's wife, Cathy, was an assistant to Alan Paton. She was born in England and went to South Africa as a very young girl. Her history of working with the African National Congress and anti-apartheid groups is extensive. Her whole life has to do with the struggle in South Africa. When the ANC was no longer outlawed, she was in Lusaca where the ANC had headquarters. She got the first news that the ANC was no longer outlawed when it came across on a fax or something. She ran through the streets of the town, having to use the password to get through, getting to ANC to say, 'You're no longer outlawed!'"

Darius was at that point about to become an associate professor at the university. "They're even putting up a building for jazz in the music department," Dave said. I thought there was something interesting, even inspiring, about a one-eighth Modoc Indian devoting his life to teaching jazz in Africa.

No matter how misty the family history, the visual evidence is there. For years I've kidded Dave that he looks like the man on the buffalo nickel. "And I'll tell you something else, Dave. Darius looks a bit Indian. But do you know who really looks Indian? Danny." Danny is the drummer of the family. Paul's second favorite drummer, according to Dave.

Dave laughed. "Danny always *did*!" he said.

Iola said, "There is a photo of a young Modoc that looks almost identical to Dave at the same age."

On June 1, 1991, the Hartford Symphony and Hartford Chorale premiered a composition by Dave titled *Joy in the Morning*, using Biblical texts. Dave said, "It's really about my heart. Only I used this for the music. Ten years ago I was going to have my first angiogram. It was the first time I was in the hospital in real trouble. I was sitting up and I was writing Psalm 30. My doctor came in. It was about 10:30 at night. He said, 'I've never come into a room with manuscript paper all over the bed when someone was going to have an operation in the morning.' I didn't know him well enough to tell him what I was doing. When you read Psalm 30, you see: 'What good am I to thee if you put me down in the pit? Can the dust praise thee?' It goes on: 'Let me live!'

"Nine years after that I had another angiogram." (He also had a triple-bypass operation.) "I finished the piece that I had written that night for baritone and piano. I finished it for chorus and added to it for orchestra, to be the opening piece for the Beethoven Ninth, which threw me into a terrible panic. When they hired me to write, they didn't tell me I'm opening for the Beethoven Ninth, which can destroy any composer. The way I found out they wrote to say be sure and use the same instrumentation as the Beethoven Ninth so we don't have to hire anybody. They allowed me to add a tuba and third trumpet. Otherwise it's the same instrumentation. I poured a lot into this piece."

The piece has little to do with jazz, though one movement draws on string voicings used by the better arrangers in popular music and film scoring. Otherwise it is pure symphonic and choral writing in the European tradition, and at a high level. The piece is glorious, and filled with the sense of the unexpected that has always been characteristic of Dave's piano solos.

In 1852, Franklin Pierce became President—and Frederick Douglass questioned whether Negroes should celebrate the Fourth of July. In 1854, a politician little known outside of Illinois named Abraham Lincoln called for the gradual emancipation of slaves. In 1855, American interests built a railroad across the Isthmus of Panama to shorten the trip to California by 19,000 miles, thereby accelerating the extermination of California Indian tribes. Longfellow published *Hiawatha*, mythologizing the life of an Ojibway. And President Pierce proposed to the Suquamish the purchase of their lands, which at least was an improvement on appropriating them by genocide. Seattle, their chief, made a speech in reply, a speech Dave Brubeck has put to music. If Dave is one-quarter Modoc, and Seattle was all Suquamish, what do we, in our mad ethnic system of classification, call the piece of music Dave has made out of the speech? Five-eighths Indian? Whatever it is, that speech is a haunting document. Among other things, Chief Seattle said:

"The President in Washington sends word that he wishes to buy our land. But how can you buy or sell the sky? The land? The idea is strange to us. If we do not own the freshness of the air and the sparkle of the water, how can you buy them?

"Every part of this earth is sacred to my people. Every shining pine needle, every sandy shore, every mist in the dark woods, every meadow, every humming insect. All are holy in the memory of my people.

"We know the sap which courses through the trees as we know the blood that courses through our veins. We are part of the earth and it is part of us.

The perfumed flowers are our sisters. The bear, the deer, the great eagle, these are our brothers. The rocky crests, the juices in the meadow, the body heat of the pony, and man, all belong to the same family.

"The shining water that moves in the streams and rivers is not just water, but the blood of our ancestors. If we sell you our land, you must remember that it is sacred. Each ghostly reflection in the clear water of the lakes tells of events and memories in the life of my people. The water's murmur is the voice of my father's father.

"The rivers are our brothers. They quench our thirst. They carry our canoes and feed our children. So you must give to the rivers the kindness you would give any brother.

"If we sell you our land, remember that the air is precious to us, that the air shares its spirit with all the life it supports. The wind that gave our grandfather his first breath also receives his last sigh. The wind also gives our children the spirit of life. So if we sell you our land, you must keep it apart and sacred, as a place where man can go to taste the wind that is sweetened by the meadow flowers.

"Will you teach your children what we have taught our children? That the earth is our mother? What befalls the earth befalls all the sons of the earth.

"This we know. The earth does not belong to man, man belongs to the earth. All things are connected like the blood which unites us all. Man did not weave the web of life, he is merely a strand in it. Whatever he does to the web, he does to himself."

Dave was attacked by several critics when he made the *Time Out* album in 1959. He was being cute, he was being effete. That album was revolutionary, the first recording to break with the four-four time that was the uncontested norm in jazz and make compound time signatures not only acceptable but even popular. He has to this day not been given general credit for that departure. Before *Time Out*, jazz musicians were not all that comfortable even in three. Now they are.

At the end of 1992, the Sony corporation issued a four-CD Columbia Masterworks package titled *Dave Brubeck: Time Signatures: A Career Retrospective* that is revelatory.

I expected to love the Desmond solos. Paul too was an underestimated player. But time is lending perspective, and in the years since we lost him I have come more and more to admire his brilliance. He plays a solo on *Tangerine* that is no less than astonishing. His powers of melodic invention seem infinite, his lyricism as always lightened by his wit.

The surprise to me is Dave.

Back in those *Down Beat* days, I wrote an extensive article from an interview I did with Dave. The interview was not taped—the cassette recorder hadn't been invented—and I made notes as we talked. I edited the quotations rather carefully, knowing from experience that people seldom remember exactly what they said. After the article came out, Dave said something I've never forgotten: "You didn't quote what I said. You quoted what I meant." I was slightly shocked at the accuracy of his memory, and at the same time complimented by his recognition that I conceived my duty to be helping the subject make his point.

During that interview, I asked Dave who his favorite pianist was. I think I can quote his answer verbatim, and if I can't, I can certainly give you its essence. He said, "I like counter-rhythm, and I always try for it in my solos. I don't always bring it off, but when I do, it gets very exciting. That's what I look for, and since I'm the only pianist trying for what I want to hear, I'd have to say that I'm my favorite pianist." I think I may have left that out of the article, knowing how easily the last clause could be quoted out of context by anyone eager to make a case against him.

But the fact is that Dave's own evaluation was apt. Listening to this four-CD set, I am repeatedly astonished at the rhythmic complexity of his playing. Far from being effete, his playing is powerful, driving, complicated, and extraordinarily inventive. Dave said back at the time of that interview that he was anything but a classical player. Indeed, he said his playing was technically wrong. He was inclined to plunge at the piano, rather than sitting there in exquisite control, although he could play with great lyrical delicacy as well. I now realize that if there is one pianist with whom he has a certain something in common, it's Thelonious Monk.

I must have had a suspicion even then about the value of Dave's playing. Though the critics were chewing Brubeck up at every opportunity, I remember saying somewhat timidly to my friend Oscar Peterson, "You know, O.P., I have a lot of respect for Dave Brubeck's playing," thinking he would take issue with me. He said firmly, "So you should."

Yet still I was intimidated by those I thought must know more than I, keeping an uncourageous silence about Dave's playing, though I always recognized his gifts as a composer.

Listening to the Sony reissue, I made the rediscovery of one of the most interesting and individual players jazz piano has produced. The public was right; the critics were wrong. Dave Brubeck, part Modoc Indian, is one of the great jazz musicians.

December 1992

Growing Up
in Los Angeles:
Ernie Andrews

"How close did it come, Ernie?" I asked, a few days after the 1992 riot in south-central Los Angeles.

"Come on outside," Ernie Andrews said. We walked out his front door. The house was a sort of dark Wedgwood blue. It had wrought-iron grilles on its windows and all its doors. It was a modest house among other modest houses, but the neighborhood was slipping slowly downward with the neglect that city governments have traditionally gifted to black neighborhoods. Not many white people ever get into black neighborhoods. They don't know anybody there.

Ernie pointed. His house was almost at the crest of a sloping street, and from the little fenced garden in front of it, he indicated a business neighborhood about three blocks away. "All that," he said. "It was all on fire. The sky was orange. And the smoke! Everywhere."

Ernie has four sons and a daughter, ten grandchildren, and four great-grandchildren. His eight-year-old grandson Mark Andrews Jr., who lived across the street, came and went as Ernie and I talked. He was one of the children who had to watch the horror. One can only wonder what it did to him.

We went back into the house.

The New Orleans-to-Chicago legend of jazz genesis to the contrary, there was jazz in Los Angeles before 1920, played by Jelly Roll Morton, Kid Ory, and others. They and various local musicians made Central Avenue a greenhouse of the new music before the Jazz Age was born—and before Louis Armstrong set its direction in Chicago.

Black music history was being written in a small area centered on Central

Avenue, a street immortalized in Lionel Hampton's *Central Avenue Breakdown*. By 1920, as the scholar and pianist Ted Gioia tells us in his book *West Coast Jazz*, 40 percent of the black population of Los Angeles lived within a few blocks on either side of this vital thoroughfare between 11th and 42nd streets. The black population of L.A. had been doubling every twenty years since 1900, so that by the World War II years this area was a city within a city, a culture unto itself.

"Entertainment was just one small part of what Central Avenue was all about," Gioia writes, "and jazz was just one small piece of the entertainment picture, co-existing over the years with R&B, song-and-dance, comedy, blues, revues, shake dancing, vaudeville, and the like. The Club Alabam, the best known of the night spots that dotted the landscape, is sometimes spoken of by jazz writers as a West Coast Birdland or Village Vanguard, but it was both more and less. The Alabam featured lavish revues that covered the gamut of the entertainment spectrum, and though the jazz might be spectacular—with Charles Mingus, Dexter Gordon, or Art Pepper playing in the house band, it no doubt was—jazz was still just a small part of the show."

Black celebrities, among them Jackie Robinson, Joe Louis, and Bill Robinson, were there, often staying at the Dunbar, an elegant hotel next door to the Alabam. Duke Ellington stayed there when he came to Hollywood to be in the 1930 film *Check and Double Check*. Later, so did Louis Armstrong, Jimmie Lunceford, Don Redman, Sy Oliver, and Cozy Cole.

Two doors beyond the Alabam was the Downbeat, where Howard McGhee's newly organized bebop band, the first modern jazz group on the coast, performed several months before Dizzy Gillespie and Charlie Parker arrived for their historic gig at Billy Berg's. Art Tatum played in the neighborhood. Across the street was the Last Word, where Hampton Hawes played on the night of his high school graduation. A little south of there was the Memo, and Ivie Anderson's Chicken Shack, a restaurant favored by musicians. There were more. And that is not counting the after-hours clubs.

No one thought anything of it when white people came to hear the music, among them Mae West, Lana Turner, Frank Sinatra, Ava Gardner, Orson Welles, John Steinbeck, and William Randolph Hearst. And the entertainment roared around the clock during the war, when defense plants worked three shifts and workers would drop in on their way home.

At first you couldn't get the new bebop records. They were carried to the coast by railway porters and sold like bootleg whisky, sometimes out of a shoeshine stand by a man named Emery Byrd, who also supplied Mexican green and heroin. His nickname was Moose the Mooche. Charlie Parker made it the title of one of his compositions.

Ted Gioia's account is augmented by a documentary film often seen on the Public Broadcasting television network. Centered on the life and times of Ernie Andrews, it is called *Blues for Central Avenue*.

Jimmy Witherspoon, himself one of the great blues singers, said once that he considers Ernie Andrews the greatest singer he's ever heard. This is considerable praise from a qualified commentator for a man whose career has been characterized by long stretches of obscurity, neglect, and frustration broken by sudden sunbursts of recognition. The late pianist and arranger Nat Pierce and drummer Frank Capp, with whose Juggernaut band Andrews performed, shared Witherspoon's esteem for the singer. Yet you can search the standard jazz dictionaries and encyclopedias in vain for Ernie's name. And one of the few that does take note of his existence dismisses him in six lines.

"I was born in Philadelphia on Christmas day, 1927," Ernie said back in the house. He brought me a cup of coffee, set it on a low table, and sat down on a sofa facing me. The living room was pleasantly cluttered, with a studio spinet piano against one wall and stereo and videotape equipment on another. "I left Philadelphia when I was nine, went to Louisiana, and lived with my mother's folks. A little place called Jeanerette, where I stayed four years, maybe five."

Ernie on a stage has enormous energy. He can shout "Well!" on the flat third with more conviction than anyone you ever heard. But his speech is quiet, spaced and paced, the voice rich but soft. The letter *r* is always softened to an *ah* sound, probably a vestige of his years in the South. Singers usually soften *r* after a vowel anyway; it is not one of the prettier sounds in the English language. Ernie is trim and has a mustache, coppery skin, and hair that is surprisingly free of gray.

"Bunk Johnson was teaching for the unified school system. I started out playing drums in school there with him. And then I left Louisiana and I came here to Los Angeles the last of 1944 with my mother. My mother and father were separated. My mother was a chef. She could cook. She could knit, she did a lot of things in her life, supporting me. My grandmother was a great cook too. She cooked for one family for fifty-three years.

"My mother was a wonderful singer. Her mother before her was a wonderful singer. Her brothers were great singers, church singers. My father came from Virginia, and he was a wonderful singer. His sisters were great singers.

"I went to school here. I went into Thomas Jefferson High School. Sam Browne had the band there. I took a drummer's class, but I never did get to play with that band.

"Drumming's a lot of work," Ernie said with a little laugh. "You've got four things going for you. Right foot, left foot, right hand, left hand. Oh man! Ambidextrous! Oh man, you've gotta get with it now! You've gotta tune 'em up, make 'em sing! So it wasn't hard for me to put it down for singing. It was easy.

"Starting out on drums made me a kind of time addict. I'm a stickler for time. If a drummer lays back too far, I have a problem with that. It labors me, because it keeps me pulling all the time, something I want and am not getting. But then if you get too far in front of me, then I'm in trouble again. Buddy Rich, God bless him, God rest his soul. Buddy would run over you. What a great player. But you had to get on your little pony to stay up with Buddy.

"I was six years with Buddy with Harry James.

"And then I had one of the most broken-time players but was always there on one. Sonny Payne. He'd stick some things in, you had to be thinking all the time. Frank Butler was one of the very fine players. I was quite a few years with Frank. He was one of my favorites, too. Larance Marable, he used to live next door to my wife and me on 23rd Street. He'd be next door with a number 12 tub as a bass drum, snare drum, cymbals, sock, sticks, and brushes. He'd wear me out all day long, playing the drums all day in the garage.

"For a while I worked in the Lincoln Theater as an usher. I worked all the amateur shows. That's where I was found by Joe Green, the songwriter. He opened a label with me, G and G, for Green and Green, his father. He wrote and I recorded *Wrap It Up and Put It Away Till Daddy Comes Home from the Army, Soothe Me, Green Gin, Dream a While,* and *Don't Let the Sun Catch You Crying.*

"Then I took off out of Jeff and went on the road. Started my first job in Oakland, California, in a place on Seventh Street called the Villa. I went from there to the Backstage in San Francisco, Say When, California Theater Restaurant on Post Street. Then I ended up at the Blackhawk. André Previn, Dave Brubeck, Miles Davis, Chet Baker, we all ended up over there. Then I played Jack's Tavern on Sutter Street. I traveled up and down the road.

"I made my debut in New York in 1954 with Jimmy Jones on piano, Earl May on bass, and Percy Bryce on drums, at Birdland. Opposite Dizzy

Gillespie and Charlie Parker! I was scared to death! Charlie Parker used to come up to me every night and sing 'When you open it to speak,' because he wanted me to do *My Funny Valentine*."

He paused a moment, then said, "You've never seen the TV show I did?"

"Nope," I said. I knew it turned up from time to time on public television, but for some reason I'd missed it, despite hearing it acclaimed by anyone who saw it.

"Let me show it to you." Ernie turned on the VCR.

"When I was seventeen," Ernie says, voice over a sequence of him in a nightclub, singing *Round Midnight*, "I had three or four hit records. I made that great mistake. I thought it would never end . . . ."

Curtis Peagler is playing an alto obbligato.

"The bottom fell out, for some reason. It's been a scuffle ever since. The cars and the clothes and the moneys—like it would never run out . . . .

"The record shows: I stood the blows."

A black-and-white photo sequence. A total-immersion baptism in a river or maybe bayou in Louisiana. A white frame church. "I would sing in church . . . The flo' would rock when the church gets t' goin'. . . ." He has slipped back into a deep Southern sound. "Somebody would have a half pint of whisky in their hip pocket, and they was singin' church songs, and swingin' out the door!"

He says that he moved with his mother to Los Angeles when he was fifteen. Black-and-white shots of Los Angeles streets in that long-ago time, mid-1940s, the famous big old Red Cars, the interurban trolleys that were bought up by automotive, tire, and highway interests and deliberately dismantled to force people into automobiles, leaving the working poor without transportation, no way to get to jobs, and now you see them, weary men and women, waiting interminably on the clumsy bus system to get home from underpaid jobs all across L.A.'s vast summer-dusty smog-brown palm-scattered sprawl.

Shots of movie posters. *Stormy Weather* with Lena Horne and Bill Robinson. Benny Carter wrote her charts. Such was the segregation that he was allowed to write only for black performers. He told me that himself. Astounding. A movie called *Sepia Cinderella*. Another called *Jiving in Bebop*, starring one Dizzy Gillespie. Herb Jeffries talking on-camera, about the four black westerns he made, including one called *The Bronze Buckaroo*. Stupefying. The real West was full of black cowboys. The movies weren't. Jeffries talking about how he always stayed at the Dunbar. He wasn't allowed into the hotels along Sunset and Wilshire.

A headline on the *California Eagle*, a black newspaper.

> **Protest Police Brutality**

You couldn't live north of Wilshire Boulevard if you were black in the 1940s. Ernie says, "King Cole, Lena Horne—they had a lot of problems."

> **Court Reviews Right of Negroes to Live in Their Own Homes**

A story saying the California Supreme Court was reviewing lower court cases on whether blacks could occupy homes in Los Angeles that they actually owned. Surrealistic.

> **Police Beat Family of Shooting Suspect**

"There was a fantasy," Ernie says in the film, "in the black world that there was going to be a way out in the movies, that they were going to be the first blacks to really break through. . . ."

Shots of Frank Sinatra, Ava Gardner, and others in the nightclubs of the black community, "hanging out in Central Avenue with all of us. . . . You see, blacks were trying to get into Hollywood, and the whites were trying to get into Central Avenue."

A black-and-white shot of Central Avenue at night, all aglow, the street crowded with cars. Ernie's then-young voice singing *Soothe Me*. He was a little Eckstinish in those days. He even looked a little like Eckstine.

A contemporary color shot of the façade of a school, a gray stuccoed structure in what we might call 1930s Hollywood *moderne*, the name Thomas Jefferson High School spelled on its face in dated sans-serif letters. Ernie talks about the kids who went there, Chico Hamilton, Hampton Hawes, the Farmer brothers (Art and Addison), the Royal brothers (Marshall and Ernie), Dexter Gordon. He forgets Don Cherry, Sonny Criss, Edmund Thigpen, Frank Morgan, Big Jay McNeely, choreographer Alvin Ailey, and actor Woody Strode.

A club owner says in the film that two-thirds of the patronage of some of those Central Avenue nightclubs was white. A black-and-white still shot of

Ernie singing at the Club Alabam with Andy Kirk's band. Then some shots of latter-day Ernie, guiding us along Central Avenue. Empty lots where those great clubs used to be.

Sweets Edison talks on camera, describing how the cops hassled the club owners.

> ## White Policemen Jail Man Walking with White Friend

I believe that. Long after that, in the 1970s, when Daryl Gates had assumed command of the Los Angeles Police Department, it was going on. My son Phil, then nineteen, was close friends with London McDaniel, son of the singer and songwriter Gene McDaniel.

Whenever they would go somewhere in Los Angeles, cops would stop the car. A white kid and a black kid together. It didn't happen some times. It happened every time. Flashlight up the nose. Hand frisking. Batons exploring the crotch. Draw your own conclusion. I began to worry about them hanging out together.

I didn't want them killed. LAPD cops don't require much excuse.

I can use his name now, because he's dead.

He was chief paramedic for the San Fernando Valley and, if I recall, West Los Angeles, a man so expert in his work that he sometimes lectured on cardio-pulmonary resuscitation in university medical schools.

His name was Arlen Nine, nicknamed Shorty, because he was—short, stocky, sturdy. Like all truly tough men, men secure in their manhood, Shorty Nine had no need to give demonstrations of machismo. Genuinely tough men are often quite kind, and Shorty was like that. He was from Cleveland. He had served as a paratrooper in Korea, and he was a weapons expert. Shorty was the paramedic who attended Robert Kennedy when he was assassinated. All reports on that shooting said Kennedy was shot with a .22. Shorty wrote on his report, a copy of which he showed me once, that Kennedy was shot with a .38 from close range.

Shorty hated the L.A. cops. And so did many of the paramedics under his command.

"I live in fear," he said to me, "that one day one of my guys is going to kill a cop because of what they see when they get to these police shootings."

Shorty told me of a case involving a black boy of thirteen or fourteen who lived in a good neighborhood of the San Fernando Valley. The boy had been attempting to slip his own father's car out of the driveway to go for a joy ride. Two cops on a stakeout of a nearby house saw him do it. When he realized they had seen him, the boy panicked and tried to climb a fence. A cop put a bullet in his brain.

When Shorty's boys arrived, they found the kid face down on the ground, his hands cuffed behind his back.

"Get those things off him," one of them said.

"That's procedure," the cop said.

"I don't care," the paramedic said. "He's not going anywhere with a hole in his head like that. Get 'em off."

Shorty arrived on the scene. Ever afterward he was haunted by what he saw. The boy lying there in his nice clean bluejeans and tee-shirt, weighing all of ninety pounds, blood pouring from his head. He died.

The cop was cleared. Surprised? The cops who beat Rodney King were cleared, despite irrefutable evidence on videotape. A Ventura County jury was persuaded that they should not believe their own eyes.

After the riots, you saw LAPD officers whimpering on television about their safety (more L.A. cops were killed in the 1920s than the 1980s), moaning that they were not appreciated, some of them saying they were going to quit. "I'm outta here," one of them said.

Good. Gooooood. Write if you get work.

In the film, Buddy Collette sits at a piano, his tenor across his lap. He says the police didn't like white women coming to Central Avenue "and mingling in the clubs."

Sweets Edison comes on camera, saying, "The police department mostly closed up Central Avenue . . . (They) would mostly hire their policemen from down south. They were pretty rough, most of them. They were pretty prejudiced. They burned up a lot of the places all along Central Avenue. Central Avenue became just another street."

A black-and-white shot of a burning nightclub.

The newspapers, whose owners, editors, and reporters were through most of this century so cozy with corrupt cops, politicians, and judges that they simply did not report crime in the city. "Law is where you buy it in this town," Raymond Chandler wrote in *Farewell, My Lovely*, and "this town" was the sleazy world of his fictional private eye Philip Marlowe. In 1938, a captain who headed the LAPD's Special Intelligence Section blew up the automobile of a reform investigator who was making the police brass and the politicians nervous. Do you think that he or his colleagues would have any compunction about burning down black nightclubs? And that the white press would cover it? Stephen Reinhardt, former president of the Los Angeles Police Commission and now a judge on the U.S. Ninth Circuit Court of Appeals, recently said, "Historically, the press has not done an adequate job of investigating law enforcement in this city. Generally, the press here has been a patsy—a press agent—for the police."

Why were the clubs burned? Only because of "mingling"? Or were there more practical business reasons? "For most of the first half of this century," the *Los Angeles Times* reported recently, "Los Angeles was a corrupt, vice-ridden town. A member of the 1937 grand jury said there were 1800 bookmakers, 600 whorehouses, and 200 gambling dens in the city and—as in other cities—the criminal elements who ran these illicit enterprises regularly paid off police and politicians to keep their enterprises open."

And maybe to burn out competitors along Central Avenue?

Thoughts like these pass through my mind as I watch those sequences in the film.

Ernie's wife, Delores, is on camera, telling how she met Ernie when she was a cashier in a nightclub, going to school to study nursing. She talks about an aunt who was very wise, telling her she mustn't go sneaking around spying on Ernie, reminding her that she knew he was an entertainer when she married him. She says that Ernie has been ripped off by a lot of the business people.

"These people will *hurt* you," Ernie says, possibly establishing the show-business understatement of the decade.

Buddy Collette says, "It got very quiet for [Ernie] for a long time. He had to be amazing to handle it as well as he did." Collette remembers Charlie Parker getting one gig a week for $25. Bird came over to Buddy's house for dinner at a time when Buddy was doing studio work, playing the Groucho Marx show a half-hour a week for good money. Bird said he wished he could be like him. Buddy was shaken by it.

Rock-and-roll and rhythm-and-blues came in. "I really did try to change," Ernie says. "Just to give it a shot. It just didn't feel right with me."

Shot in a dressing room of Ernie and Sweets and others. Sweets says, "The one thing you give me, we have: friendship."

"Well," Ernie says, "that's all you're gonna get." And they laugh.

"Well that's all I require."

Then they start doing the dozens, trading insults.

One of the happy periods of Ernie's life was the ten years, starting in 1959, that he spent with the Harry James band. Ernie had in past spoken warmly of James, yet there was little about him in the film. So I asked him about the experience.

"Working with Harry James was wonderful," he said. "It was a great experience, an honest experience. I didn't make a lot of money, but I sure got a lot of experience. I got the feeling he loved me like a son. We worked around the country. We had good times. And a few tough times in some places."

He was talking about the problems of being a black performer with a white band. Artie Shaw has described how Roy Eldridge, when he traveled with his band with star billing, would sometimes check into a hotel by announcing himself as Mr. Eldridge's valet, thereby getting the room key. J. J. Johnson told me that the main reason he and Kai Winding broke up their very successful group was the unceasing hassle of trying to get hotel accommodations together.

Ernie said, "I'd look around and Harry would look at me and say, 'What is the problem?' I said, 'I don't know. They called my name for my key.' You never go on the road without a confirmation from the hotels. When the bus pulled up, they'd start passing the rooms out. So when they called my name, they told me to wait. Harry said, 'What's the problem?' I said, 'I don't know, they called my name but I haven't got a key.'

"So Harry got up and said, 'Mr. Monty . . .' Pee Wee Monty, his road manager. Harry said, 'Do we have a manifest?' Harry looked at it and saw my name on it and he said to the room clerk, 'Now what is the problem?'

"He said something like, 'Well we don't have a room for him here but we could put him two blocks down the street and he'd be close to the band.' So Harry would say, 'Pee Wee, go down the street and see if they can accommodate 28 of us. Take the stuff out of this lobby, put it back in the bus, and let's go.' And they would say, 'Well wait a minute,' and Harry would say, 'What are we waiting for?' And the clerk would say, 'Well we might find something here,' and Harry would say, 'Well find a corner room.' And they'd say, 'Why a corner room?' And he'd say, 'Because that's the biggest room. It gets plenty of air from both sides, and right now he needs it.'"

Ernie laughed. "I never opened my mouth. It didn't happen often. But it happened.

"We'd be in the South somewhere. A guy would ask me to sing *The Yellow Rose of Texas* or something. I'd tell him I don't know it and he'd tell me to sing it anyway. When it was time for me to sing, he'd say, 'I thought I told you to sing *Yellow Rose of Texas*.' Naturally he'd call me 'boy.'

"Harry would stop the band and say, 'Just a minute. I don't know how big boys come where you come from, but this is a grown man here. We don't have *Yellow Rose of Texas* and if we *had* it, we wouldn't play it. And furthermore, we're going to pack this band up if they don't put you out of here *because we're leaving now*.' And the guy would get tossed out.

"Harry was born in Georgia and raised in Beaumont, Texas. He was a truly wonderful fellow. He used to tell me sometimes, 'I know how you are, and I know you're strong, and you're a wonderful person. Sometimes it ain't gonna work. We're gonna have a problem.' He would let me know where we would have our biggest problems. I realized I wasn't the only one with problems. He wanted something one way, and they'd say, 'Do you wanna go home or do you wanna play?'

"We did a television show in New York. They didn't want a singer. Harry fought, fought, fought for me to be on that show. They got really hacked at him. I just looked at him and said, 'Hey, do the show and let's get outta here.' Then they made up their mind they'd let me on. By the time the show was aired, you didn't see me at all. They'd cut me out.

"Same thing in Philadelphia. They said to Harry, 'Where'd you find him? Wonderful singer.' He said, 'He's from right here, Philadelphia.' We were doing *That's Life*. You wouldn't see the show for a couple of weeks then. When it came out, we were in Las Vegas. Wasn't on it. There was cooking in the spot where I was."

The movie nears its end. Ernie says, "Jazz is a wonderful thing. You have to *apply* to play jazz. . . . It isn't over yet. I don't ever want to stop or slow down. I don't ever want to get that tired. That's the only thing that keeps me going. Because if I stop to think about the things that happened with me, the ache and the pain that I have, if I gave in to that, I'd be in big trouble. . . .

"I know that the lights are coming up, I know that the mikes are going to be on, and I'm going to forget about the aches and pains for a minute."

Then the movie's over, but Ernie isn't. A new generation, a much younger generation, seems to be discovering him. Among his admirers are the Harper Brothers, Winard and Philip, whose album *You Can Hide Inside the Music* featured the work of some of the heroes of these two brilliant young players: Sweets Edison, Jimmy McGriff, Jimmy Heath, and Ernie Andrews. Ernie had been touring with the group led by the Harpers.

"They came and got us," Ernie said. "They invited us to perform on the album. We were delighted that the young men wanted to keep us all going. It was kind of a thrill.

"I think no one can critique me, because they don't know anything about me. They say what they think they know about me, or what they think that I may feel, but basically they can't critique me. 'Cause one day I'm one way and another day I'm another way. It depends where my feelings are for the day. My metabolism goes this way, that way. One day I'm singing something up, and the next I'm singing it down. It's knowing how to do it either way. That's art. A lot of people want to hear you do it the same way all the time." The words are strong; but there are suppressed sobs in the voice.

"You're making a record," he said. "You've got all these people watching the clock. 'Cause it's money. The engineer might say, 'Would you stand closer in to the mike.' No. You've got the dials in your hand. Pick it up. Let me perform, let me do it the way I feel it. They don't like you to do that. It's the managers, the agents. They don't like you to like yourself. They don't like you to have confidence in yourself, and it takes every bit of that. They want you to run scared all the time because of what they think or how they want you to be. And if you don't comply, then something happens.

"They want to make you what they want to make you—*if* they want to make you. In the meantime you're dying inside, because you're not doing what you want to. I know no one's going to get in the box for me when the time comes. I'm just going to enjoy myself doing what I like to do the way I like to do. I like to sing songs. Predominantly I live. It makes it honest, because I'm telling the truth when I'm singing, and it comes off much better than to just sing a pretty song because someone had a hit record on it and I've got to follow them. Sometimes it isn't fruitful for you to do that, because certain songs fit certain people. Johnny Mathis sings songs that I could sing, but they fit his style so great. Billy Eckstine used to sing songs, and hey! you couldn't get past it. Dan Grissom. Billy Daniels. King Pleasure. All special people. A lot of wonderful people who did things that fit them. I take funny songs. I took *Tie a Yellow Ribbon*. I haven't recorded it yet, but I took it and swung it to death. I've had jazz people say, 'You know, I never did care about that song until I heard you do it.' It swung right on out the window.

"So the ups and downs of life can be tough. If you let it. If you really realize what it is, or how it is, and you're by yourself, you can't fight city hall. If you like living, you can continue on going. If you balk upon it, something happens to you. I don't mean like getting killed or anything like that. I'm talking about one'll tell two, and two'll tell ten, and they'll tell twenty people. And then you find obstacles in your way of trying to be who you really are.

"I don't have what I want, but I've got what I need.

"And that's common sense to deal with life, because I love life. It can have a little hassle every now and then, but I love it. Since I'm here, I just wanna be around and not worry myself to death or run into obstacles too tough. I'm like all my brothers and sisters, but I know that I have to do the best that I can with life. And I speak for my people all over the place."

Delores came home from work. She looked a little older than she was when the film was made but still a pretty woman with a warm smile. She and Ernie had been married forty-four years. She is a private nurse with as many as eight patients a day. Ernie's son Mark Sr., a handsome man of thirty-five, came in, greeting me warmly. We had talked on the phone. One of these conversations took place immediately after the riot, when I called to find out if the Andrews family were all right. They were. But it was close, Mark said.

I left, driving over cement streets bleached white by time and sun and patterned with meandering cracks. The streets and modest bungalows are from the Raymond Chandler era. It was late afternoon. I drove the business streets in the vicinity of Venice and LaBrea. Lebanon West. Tangles of blackened metal. Stores burned out. Boarded up with plywood. Even those whose walls were still standing, Ernie had said, were gutted. An auto supply store at LaBrea, bearing a sign saying, "We will soon be back to serve you."

I was thinking about Shorty Nine and Eulah Love as I looked at this devastation. In early May the *Los Angeles Times* ran a soul-searching five-part series on the cozy past relationship of press to police. It was critical of its own past behavior as well as that of other papers. One of the stories in this *mea culpa* orgy began:

"Before Rodney G. King, there was Eulah Love.

"Love was a 39-year-old black woman who was shot to death by two Los Angeles police officers early in 1979 as she was about to throw a kitchen knife at them."

That's bad journalism in the second sentence. The reporter does not know that she was about to throw a kitchen knife at them, only that the cops said she was.

The incident occurred January 3, 1979. A man from the gas company had come earlier in the day to cut off her service. He told police that she had assaulted him with a shovel.

The two cops arrived. They claimed later that they drilled her when she was about to throw this 11-inch kitchen knife at them. First, have you ever attempted to throw a knife so that it lands point first? It's all very nifty in the movies, but try it some time. It's a developed skill. Second, will anybody stand there and tell me that you can't jump out of the way when you are braced and ready to do so? If I can duck a snowball, I can duck a knife. And two strong male cops couldn't take a knife away from a lone woman? Or talk her into putting it down? I forget how many times they shot her, but it was a lot. They ventilated Eulah Love very thoroughly.

I was fascinated by the later statement of Daryl Gates who said, in that quaint jargon, that the shooting was "in policy." He did add, "Any way you viewed it, it was a bad shooting."

So. There were good shootings and bad shootings.

In 1964, the year before the Watts riot, only five of forty-two L.A. cops accused of brutality were disciplined. A masked police officer told a television reporter named Wayne Satz in 1977 that "most officers are extremely eager to be in a shooting." As for racism, he said that "a majority are definitely prejudiced."

The police department was predictably outraged and sued the station, KABC. The case was thrown out of court. But this is a measure of L.A. cop mentality: they put photos of Wayne Satz on the figures of bad guys on their shooting ranges and pumped them full of holes. The worst that can be said is that each man who did this was a would-be killer. The best you could say is that they were infantile fantasists with no sense whatever of being accountable to the civilian community. This contempt for the public is manifest in a remark common on the LAPD: "If you want to be liked, join the Fire Department."

Shorty Nine told me, within weeks, possibly days, a detail of the Eulah Love killing that did not make the papers. One of his paramedics arrived in time to hear a cop say over her corpse, "Well, there's another nigger who won't threaten any more police officers."

My conversation with Ernie still running in my mind, I stopped a few blocks from his house to get gasoline. A black man of perhaps forty, his right leg missing below the knee and the stump covered in a white tube sock, moved his wheelchair among the gas pumps, begging money. Another black man, handsome, youthful, and apparently prosperous, about to get into his Mercedes, gave the man money. The man then wheeled his way toward me. "I got burned out in the riot," he said plaintively.

I too gave him a few dollars, got into my car, and went home to my safe world in the mountains north of Los Angeles.

June 1992

Father and Son: Horace Silver

"My father used to tell people that when Horace was coming up, there were only two things a black guy could be successful in and make money and be something: sports or music. He said, 'Horace wasn't interested in sports, so I really pushed him with the music.'"

"I gather your father was very, very important in your life," I said to Horace Silver. We were sitting in his living room, whose wide window overlooked the bright afternoon slab of the Pacific Ocean. The traveler zips up the coast through Malibu on Highway 1, aware only of the crushed-together and vaguely shabby houses on postage-stamp seaside properties costing millions, in which movie people and coke dealers live in symbiosis. But above the bluffs, unseen as you go by, is a large middle-class and modest colony of homes. It is in one of these that Horace lives with his son, who was then eighteen.

I was thinking of that 1964 Blue Note album, *Song for My Father*, whose cover showed a man sitting on a rock or log or something in front of an autumnal wooded pond, hands clasped around his knees, a straw hat with a wide band on his head, a stub of cigar in his mouth, a smile on his face, and some sort of unfathomable happiness in his heart.

What brilliant groups Horace led, with the classic trumpet-and-tenor front line, groups through which passed Bob Berg, Donald Byrd, the Brecker Brothers, Roy Brooks, Billy Cobham, Junior Cook, Bob Cranshaw, Art Farmer, Blue Mitchell, Tom Harrell, Joe Henderson, Roger Humphries, Carmell Jones, Benny Maupin, Larry Ridley, Woody Shaw, Clifford Jordan, Gene Taylor, Louis Hayes, Teddy Smith, and John Williams, among others—extraordinary alumni, comparable with those of the big bands of Woody Herman and Count Basie. Many of them were discovered by Silver. Although Dave Brubeck and John Lewis have written extensively and beautifully for their quartets, probably no other leader of a small jazz group ever has written so much material for his. Horace has recorded little that he didn't write, and many of his tunes have become jazz standards, among them *Doodlin', Strollin', The Preacher, Sister Sadie,* and *Nica's Dream*. In 1959, three years before the samba made its incursion into jazz, he recorded *Swingin' the Samba*. Others of his tunes hint further of his heritage: *Senor Blues* and *The Cape Verdean Blues*, for example.

Horace Ward Martin Tavares Silver was born September 2, 1928, in Norwalk, Connecticut. The name originally was Silva.

Horace and I used to be friends, back in the early 1960s. I say "used to be" because I hadn't seen him in years. I have always remembered him with affection, and a soft series of images of an evening we spent floating around clubs in San Francisco, visiting friends, lingers pleasantly in my mind. It was one of those nights of your youth when you are exploring, learning, and you talk until dawn. He had an enthusiasm for life and one sensed a certain spirituality. His speech had a plunging, energetic quality, like his piano work, and it was outgoing and devoid of evasion. That was probably the autumn of 1959, after the Monterey Festival. I trusted Horace Silver.

The years do slip by. Yet from the moment I walked in his door, we were talking as easily as if the intervening years never had occurred.

The first subject that came up was his father. "Both my parents were important to me, but my mother died when I was nine years old," Horace said. "So I didn't have much time to spend with her. But I love her dearly, and I think about her a lot.

"My father raised me, with a little help from my mother's aunt, my great-aunt, my Aunt Maude. I went to Catholic grammar school, and I used to get my lunches at my Aunt Maude's. Her house was about two blocks from the school.

"She was kind of a stout lady, and she was sickly, and she couldn't get around too much. So I used to do a lot of her shopping for her. She'd give me her grocery list and she would cook all the nice things that I liked. She was a great cook. She used to be a chef in restaurants when she was younger. She kind of helped my father bring me up.

"Me and Dad lived together in our own apartment, and she lived with my uncle. I spent a lot of time visiting her, and she spent a lot of time telling me about my family history, and who my relatives were on my mother's side. My mother was born in New Canaan. Almost all those people were born in that area. Later on some of them lived in Bridgeport."

Horace's father was born in the Cape Verde Islands; "verde" is green in Portuguese. They lie just off the bulge of western Africa. They are dry and hot. When they were discovered by Europeans in the mid-fifteenth century, they were uninhabited, but the Portuguese, who took them over, established plantations and imported African labor to work them, and after the discovery of America, made the islands a staging area for the export of slaves.

The Portuguese settlers on these islands mixed with the African population, and Horace's father was one of the consequences. The islands have a song and dance called the *morna*. With the decline and eventual abolition— as late as 1876—of slavery, with deepening drought and administrative corruption, the economy of the islands deteriorated rapidly. By the start of the twentieth century, a flow of emigrants to the United States was under way, and it continued until the U.S. government imposed a quota. Those who got in before the cutoff sent money home to help their families.

"Your father spoke Portuguese, then," I said.

"Oh yeah."

"Do you?"

"No, just a few phrases."

"So the mixture, then," I said, "occurred both there and here."

"Both. Dad was a brown-skinned man. My mother was very fair, very light. You'd think she was a Caucasian woman. Her father was Caucasian. My grandmother was black. My family's very mixed on my mother's side. I never knew my mother's father.

"And there was some American Indian. My Aunt Maude would sit me down and tell me that background. Her mother was American Indian. My mother's family was intermingled with the Blade clan, which had a lot of Indian blood in them. I come out of those two clans, plus my father's people, Silva, from Cape Verde.

"At home, in Norwalk, my Dad and his brothers would have kitchen parties, and they'd play the Cape Verde folk music. Violin, Spanish guitar, sometimes mandolin. I was a little boy. The women would make fried chicken and potato salad, and they'd have drinks. People would come on a Friday or Saturday night, and they'd pull the furniture back, and they'd dance in the kitchen. Some were family, some were neighbors.

"I had a brother and a sister, but I never knew them. My sister was a miscarriage. My brother was born, but he caught pneumonia and died when he was about six months old. I think about what it would be like if they had lived. Growing up as an only child, I always thought how nice it would be to have a brother, an older brother especially, to hang with and protect you when the kids come around to pick on you.

"I know I've got a brother. He isn't in this world. He's in another world. I've got him, and he's there, and I think about him, and I say a little prayer for him now and then, or talk to him in my head. And my sister too. When I pass over into that other dimension, I'll meet him."

I asked how hard his father had pressed him to pursue music.

"After I started taking lessons, he had to force me to practice, because I thought I was going to play in two weeks. When I found out I had to do all these boring scales and exercises, I wanted to quit. But he wouldn't let me quit. He stayed on my back and made me practice. He said, 'You're gonna thank me for this some day.' And I do thank him for it today.

"But what really made me decide that I wanted to become a musician was Jimmie Lunceford and his band. First band I ever saw live."

I shared some of that memory with Horace: the Lunceford band was one of the first I ever saw. A crisp and crackling band, it was noted for its discipline, swing, and showmanship. It featured arrangements by Sy Oliver and the band's pianist Edwin Wilcox. Wilcox later led that band, at first with tenor saxophonist Joe Thomas and then on his own. He had a degree in music from Fisk University. Lunceford too had a bachelor's from Fisk. Indeed, when he formed his first professional orchestra, in 1929, its members included Wilcox, alto saxophonist Willie Smith, and trombonist Henry Wells, all of whom he had known at Fisk.

"I must have been around ten when I saw that band," Horace said. "There was an amusement park. After my mother died, me and my Dad used to go down there every Sunday and we'd ride the roller coaster or the merry-go-round or throw darts at the balloons and eat cotton candy and hot dogs and just have a nice Sunday afternoon, me and Dad.

"They had a dance pavilion down there, and they had dances every Sunday night. Some of the big bands would come in. It was getting toward sundown. We were on our way to the parking lot to get into the car. And I saw this Greyhound bus come in with all these black guys on it, and I saw 'Jimmie Lunceford Band' on the side of the bus. And I said, 'Hey, Dad, can we stay to hear just one song? Please? Just one song?' He said, 'You have to go to school tomorrow. All right, just one song.'

"We had to wait maybe an hour or so for them to get set up. Blacks weren't allowed into the pavilion. It was an open-air pavilion. It overlooked the ocean. It had slats on it. Blacks and whites who didn't want to pay to go in were on the outside, peeping through the slats and listening to the music. I edged my way up to where I could peek right in through the slats. And they started. And oh man! That was it!" Horace laughed aloud at the memory.

"First of all, they were dressed nice," he said. "Immaculate. I think they had white suits, and ties, and shiny shoes. They played out of this world. The band was so well rehearsed, so tight, and they had their little choreography, y'know, the trumpets doing this and that. They had Dan Grissom singing, and a trio singing, a glee club. Some numbers the whole band would sing, like Johnny Long used to.

"I was *fascinated* by that band. And that was when I said to myself, 'I know what I want to be! I'm gonna be *a musician*.'

"I used to pester the record-store man to death for the next Jimmie Lunceford release. I'd go in and say, 'Anything new coming out by Jimmie Lunceford?' 'Well let me look in the catalogue. Oh yeah, he's got a new one.' 'Do you have it?' 'No.' 'Well order it, I wanna get it!' And I'd go in every two or three days. 'Has it come in yet?'

"Then I'd take the record home, and put it on my Victrola in the living room. I had me a big stick, like the baton Lunceford used to have. He didn't hold the baton the usual way. 'Member how he used to hold it? Paul Whiteman used to hold it the regular way, but Lunceford held it backwards. I used to get me a big stick and stand in front of the mirror and put his records on and make believe I was him!"

The laughter trailed off. "I had a big thing with Jimmie Lunceford," Horace said. "I remember one time his band was playing a dance at a ballroom over in Bridgeport, Connecticut, long since gone. I was in high school at the time, sixteen or seventeen. And I dressed up in my zoot suit and everything. I tried to look older. And I got in. I stood near the band all night. I stood right in back of the pianist, Edwin Wilcox.

"During the intermission, I got a chance to talk to Wilcox. He was telling me Art Tatum stories. I told him I was a piano student. It was a thrill to stand there and listen to that band and talk to the piano player. The next day, I think it was, Jimmie Lunceford was due to do an interview on the local Bridgeport radio station. I read about in the newspaper, so I took the bus from Norwalk over to Bridgeport and stood outside till he got there to get his autograph.

"I was ga-ga on Jimmie Lunceford.

"A few years back I was in Hawaii, and I ran into a Chinese lady who was a disc jockey. I did an interview on her show. After the show, I said, 'Doesn't Trummy Young live here in Hawaii?' She said, 'Yes. I know him very well. Incidentally, today is his birthday. Let's call him up.'

"I got on the phone with him and wished him a happy birthday and told him what a big Lunceford fan I was.

"He said, 'Yes, I can dig that. I'm familiar with your music, and I can tell by listening that you dig Lunceford.'

"I didn't get a chance to meet Trummy in person, but on the phone we had a long conversation. I asked him about Lunceford. And he said that when they got to New York, Lunceford would take three weeks off, and the band would rehearse every day. They'd rehearse in sections. The saxophone section would be in one studio, the trumpets over here, the trombones over there, the rhythm somewhere else. They'd rehearse separately and then he'd put them together. So when I was a kid, I was a big Lunceford fan.

"I studied with Professor William Scofield, the organist at one of the leading white churches. He was a nice guy, and a hell of a piano player, classical. He was very strict. He scared me to death sometimes. He'd get on me and take the ruler and crack my knuckles, or curse at me, 'God damn it, you didn't practice this week!' I'd jump." Again he laughed. "But he was a great guy. He really saw some potential in me, I think.

"I'm a firm believer in the legit foundation. I'm sorry, really, that I didn't go further with it. I took classical for a couple of years with Professor Scofield, and then I quit. I was so into the jazz thing. I was playing boogie-woogie at that time.

"I liked classical music then, I still love classical music. What turned me off as to playing it was that I used to get all these tunes for lessons, *Clair de Lune, Fantasie Impromptu,* Gershwin's *Rhapsody in Blue.* When I'd get through the piece, he'd say, 'Now I want you to memorize it. Memorize the first two pages for next week's lesson.' But, you know, I knew nothing about harmony, I knew nothing about the chord structure of the piece, and I would be playing the tune by rote. If I made a mistake, I'd have to stop and start from the beginning. I couldn't fake it and keep going.

"But if I was playing my boogie-woogie—I had a certain arranged boogie-woogie that I had rehearsed—and I made a mistake, I could cover it up and keep going. But if I made a mistake in *Fantasie Impromptu*, I couldn't carry on.

"That bugged me. I got into learning some basic harmony. I got a fake book. The very first tune I learned the harmony on, and learned to improvise a little on the chord structure, was *What Is This Thing Called Love?* With the first chord C-seventh. I would play it in root position, C E G B-flat. Finally I got I could play some tenths, you know. I kind of copied Teddy Wilson. Tatum and Teddy Wilson were my idols before Bud Powell and Monk.

"When I first started my band, I played the Newport Jazz Festival for George Wein. We were playing *Filthy McNasty.* George was backstage. I'm playing my solo. I'm playing some octaves 'way up on the high part of the piano, maybe rolling some octaves. And I hear him yell out, 'Earl Fatha

Hines, Earl Fatha Hines.' And I'm saying to myself while I'm playing, 'What the hell is he talking about? I don't know nothin' about no Earl Fatha Hines, I ain't trying to copy him, I'm not aware of what his style is like.'

"After that I began to realize that I used to copy Nat King Cole, and Nat King Cole copied Earl Fatha Hines, so I got it secondhand through Nat. I didn't realize it was Earl. I was invited to his home for Thanksgiving dinner one time when I in San Francisco. He asked me to play something, and he played something, and he was fantastic.

"One time in Italy, I had a day off, and there was a festival going. He was on as a solo pianist. Now he came out on that stage by himself, and just took over, played forty-five minutes or an hour by himself. It sounded fantastic, and he had the audience spellbound. It really made me stand in awe of him."

"After you quit formal study," I asked, "what were the influences?"

"Well, the first was the boogie-woogie and the blues. I just knew the boogie-woogie and blues changes. But then when I started to learn harmony, I started to get into records of Coleman Hawkins and Prez, and the swing era guys, Buck Clayton and Tatum and Teddy Wilson and Ben Webster. And then I heard my first bebop record, which was *Groovin' High*, with Dizzy and Bird, and I said, 'Wow! What is *that*?' That floored me. I started copying a lot of bebop records."

"Where were you getting the harmony?"

"I learnt my harmony from Frank Skinner's *Modern Arranging*. I went over to Bridgeport to take a harmony course. I took it for several weeks, and I didn't learn a damn thing, it was so complex. I learnt my harmony by myself, from the fake book and the Frank Skinner book, which showed you the intervals, a third, a perfect fifth, a major seventh, a minor seventh, and the minor third, and the diminished. Just the very basics, but it was what I needed to start. I got into thirteenths and all that later on. Once I got that basic stuff, the rest of it came from stealing stuff off the records. I'd take it down into my basement and put it on the old-fashioned wind-up machine. My piano was in the basement. I'd slow the turntable down. It would change the key, of course. You'd hear the notes in the chord and go to the piano and try to figure them out. I was playing a lot of chords that I couldn't name.

"I'd go to an older pianist I knew and say, 'What do you call this chord?' He would look at it and tell me."

In 1950, Stan Getz played a gig in Hartford and heard about Horace from a local bass player. Getz took a trio led by Horace on the road with him. In 1951, Horace settled in New York City, and soon had a freelance recording career. Word of the strong, bluesy pianist spread quickly, and he worked with Coleman Hawkins, Lester Young, and, most significantly, Art Blakey. In 1953, he, Blakey, Kenny Dorham, Hank Mobley, and Doug Watkins formed a group they called the Jazz Messengers.

"It was a co-operative group in the beginning," Horace said. "We didn't go to a lawyer and have papers drawn up. It was a gentlemen's agreement that the group was to be a co-operative. So nobody was the leader. We got the idea from the Modern Jazz Quartet. They did it, and they did it successfully. We did it, and we didn't do it successfully. People in the group weren't taking care of the business, and so it fell apart on a business level.

"Several times I was very dissatisfied with the business aspect of it, because the guys were goofing off. Sometimes the guys would show up late for the gig and we'd get docked money. Several times, I told myself I'm gonna quit. But I *couldn't* quit! Every time we'd hit a gig, the band would be cookin' so tough, I said, 'I can't go nowhere. Where'm I gonna find guys like this to play with?'

"The thing that made me leave was the drug problem. Art and myself and Nica's daughter, we got arrested in Philadelphia." He referred to the Baroness Nica de Koenigswater, the famous patroness of jazz for whom he named the tune *Nica's Dream*.

"We were on our way back to New York in Art's car, Art and myself and this guy who used to hang out with Art, setting up his drums, and the baroness's daughter. I didn't use drugs. I didn't even drink. But on the way out of town, I guess the cop saw a white girl in the car. Automatically, to him that's a pimp and a whore. He stopped the car. He made us get out and he searched the car. He found a gun in the glove compartment and some shells, and in the baroness's daughter's bag a box of benzedrine tablets. So bam! We're down to the station. They book us.

"I had to stay in the precinct station over the weekend until my father came and got me out. I had to go to a hearing. They released me, because I didn't have any drugs. The only thing I had on me was an ordinary pocket knife.

"I wouldn't want to go through that experience again. First they had us in the little precinct jail. That was overnight. Then they took us to the local penitentiary, the tier thing like you see in the movies. And I was in there for two and a half or three days, until my father could get down. That was a nightmare. I'd seen this in movies, but to experience it! I was in a cell with two other black guys, and all they did was talk about all the different jails they'd spent the early part of their lives in, and where they're going to send them next. At three or four o'clock in the morning, there are guys flippin' out down on the lower tier, hollerin' and screamin'—they had to run in and put a straitjacket on this guy.

"The FBI questioned us. At three o'clock in the morning they'd wake you up and bring you down to the office, and question you, and try to scare you."

"And no doubt succeed."

"Well *yeah*! But I couldn't tell them nothing but the same story. They couldn't trap me in a lie, because I was telling the truth. I was just working with these guys. The rest of them had gone back to New York."

Once more, his irrepressible chuckle: "I was so glad to get out of there, man!

"Some of the guys in the group were into drugs. I said to myself, 'I love these guys, they're all beautiful guys, and they're great musicians, and where else can I go to play with guys of this caliber? Long as I'm clean, if they bust them, they're gonna let me go. I got no track marks on my arms, I'm not in possession, they'll let me go.

"But when I got busted, and I had to spend three days in the jail, and had to go to a hearing, and hire a lawyer to defend me to make sure they didn't send me up for nothing! My father had to pay this money, and then I had to pay him back. It cost several hundred dollars. I said, 'I gotta leave these guys now, because as much as I love them, they're just too hot.'

"Doug Watkins is dead, Kenny Dorham is dead, Hank Mobley's dead. They're all gone except Art and myself." (Not long after this conversation, Art Blakey was dead, leaving Horace the last member of that quintet alive.)

"I left," he continued, "with the idea of cooling it for a month or two and trying to get a job with another group. I did a couple of record dates with other groups. It wasn't my intention to start a band, be a bandleader, that was the farthest thing from my mind. I guess it was fate that had it to be so.

"I had recorded *Senor Blues*. That record came out shortly after that period when I left the Messengers, and it was successful. Jack Whittemore had booked me for years."

Jack Whittemore was a small, stocky, feisty Irishman who at one time was head of the Shaw booking agency, then went on his own. He was probably the best, the most decent, and certainly the most respected booking agent jazz has ever known, with on outstanding client list of artists. His death of a heart attack a few years ago was a major loss.

"Jack called me one day," Horace said. "He was booking the Messengers, too. He said, 'Horace, they're playing the hell out of your record in Philadelphia, and the guy who owns the Show Boat wants you to go down with your band.'

"I said, 'I don't have a band. That was just a put-together session. We rehearsed and made a record.'

"Jack said, 'Well why don't you put some guys together and go down and play a week? He wants you.'

"I said, 'Well, okay.' So I got together Arthur Taylor on drums, Doug Watkins on bass, Hank Mobley on tenor, and Art Farmer on trumpet. We went on down there and we played and we did good—we packed the joint. The guy said, 'Look, I want you back. I can't bring you back too soon, but I want you in a couple of months.'

"We had a week off, and after that Jack got us another week someplace else. And that's how it started. Jack gave me a push. I hadn't thought about being a bandleader.

"Oh, he was a good agent. I liked him."

"So. You were never a side man from that day on."

"No."

"Have you ever recorded standards?"

"A few in the beginning, in the formative years. The few standards I did on Blue Note were things that I liked. One thing I can happily say is that Alfred Lion or Frank Wolff never came to me and said, 'Look, we want you to record standards.'

"When I left the Jazz Messengers, I wanted to be with Alfred. But we were signed to Columbia. I went to George Avakian and he said, 'We'll let you go to Blue Note, but we want you to do one album for us first.' So I did *Silver's Blue* for Epic, which has been released many times. I wanted to do an album of originals, but they wanted three standards, so I picked standards I liked and did arrangements on them. They came out quite nice.

"But Alfred never once said to me, 'We want a few standards.' There was only one exception. When we rehearsed *The Preacher* with the Messengers, he said, 'What is that tune?' I said, 'It's just a little tune I wrote on the chord changes of *Show Me the Way to Go Home*.' He said, 'Oh no, that's Dixieland. No, we don't want that. Why don't you just jam a blues, and we'll take that one out?' I was kind of crushed. I'm grateful to Art Blakey. He pulled me over in a corner and said, 'Man, ain't nothin' wrong with that tune. Tell him you want to do it. They'll do it if you insist.' I went to Alfred and said, 'Look, Alfred, if you don't want to do that tune, why don't we cancel the session until I can write another tune? Because I don't want to jam no blues.' He said, 'Okay, go ahead and do it.' And it became a big hit."

I mentioned to Horace—not that he needed to be reminded—that the roster of players in his group constituted an astonishing alumni association. At one point he had Donald Byrd alternating with Art Farmer on trumpet.

Horace said, "Donald worked with us on and off. Art Farmer was our regular trumpet player. He was working with Gerry Mulligan too. He'd come to me from time to time and say, 'Look, Horace, I've got a chance to go out for a couple of weeks on the road with Gerry, and it's paying some good money, man. Can you get somebody to take my place?' So then I'd say, 'Let me call Byrd.' Donald was going to Manhattan School of Music. Farmer would go off with Mulligan for a few weeks and Byrd would take his place."

"You've never had a color line in your band," I said, and mentioned a mutual friend who had been criticized for hiring white players.

"Nobody has said anything to my face," Horace said. "But I have heard from my fans that some cats say, 'Why does Horace hire white guys?' I just want the best musicians I can get, I don't give a damn if they're pink. Polka dot.

"If I could get the caliber of musicians I want all black, I would hire them. How can I put this? I want to give the black guys an opportunity—if they're capable musicians. But if I hear a white guy that plays better and suits my band, I'm going to hire him. I want the best musicians. And I know Miles does and a lot of other guys feel that way.

"Even before the Brecker brothers, I hired Teddy Kotick on bass. He was the first white musician I hired. And he's a hell of a fine bassist, he can swing his butt off. So I'm just looking for the best musicianship, to make my music sound right. That's what I'm about. If I can find that from black guys, I'll hire them first, because I want to give them an opportunity. There aren't many opportunities out here for black people, or black musicians, so if I can find a black guy who can play my music to my satisfaction, I'll probably hire him first. But if a white guy comes along and he plays better than that guy, I'll get him. I'm not going to hire somebody just 'cause they're black. Or 'cause they're my uncle or my cousin. Or my mother. I'm going to hire somebody because they're doing the job musically.

"I was invited a couple of years ago down to Orange County, along with Gerald Wilson and Shorty Rogers, to be a judge at a big band competition, high school and college bands. I'll tell you, man, the bands were fantastic. One thing bothered the hell out of me. They played the section work, they were in tune, they had the phrasing, they sounded like old pros. They'd get up to take a solo, there was nothing happening. They didn't know their changes. I went back and had a talk with some of them. I said, 'Get yourself some Jamey Aebersold play-along records, get to the piano, learn your harmonies, and apply them to your horn.'"

Horace had not recorded for a major jazz label in several years. This has tended to lower his visibility. Indeed, for a while I had the impression that he had more or less dropped from sight. The reason is that he started his own record label, which is always a hard way to go. But he had his reasons, and the idea of doing so has crossed the minds of many musicians.

Horace traveled now only in the summer. One reason, he said, was that his son—Horace had been divorced for a number of years—was still in high school. Horace was devoting his time at home in California to composition and running his record company, which now had two labels, Silveto and Emerald.

He said, "I'm trying to operate my record company here in my house. We do mail order. We try to get into the stores, but our distribution is not what I'd like it to be. I had no intention of having two labels. I had no intention of even having a record company.

"In 1969, '70, '72, I did a series of records called *The United States of Mind*. Andy Bey and his sister Salome sang on them. They had a spiritual connotation to them, kind of a metaphysical connotation. Some of my fans maybe were not into them. Jazz fans are kind of narrow-minded, and some of them are die-hard instrumentalists. If you're recording with Sarah Vaughan or Ella Fitzgerald, they'll accept it. But if you record with some of the lesser-name singers—some very fine singers, like Andy Bey—some of my fans didn't dig it because they figured I should be playing only instrumental music.

"I was very proud of the records, and lot of people dug them, but they didn't do as well as my other records. I'm a student of metaphysics and have been for years. Naturally, when something becomes a part of your life, it becomes a part of every part of your life, so it crept into my music too.

"When I did the first of those *United States of Mind* albums on Blue Note, they called me into the office. Alfred had sold the company by then. Frank Wolff was still there. Frank didn't want to call me in. Maybe he felt a little embarrassed to talk to me, because we were kind of friendly. But another guy, an English guy who worked for United Artists, who bought Blue Note, he said, 'Horace, this *United States of Mind* project that you're involved in, I understand you've got two more albums you want to do on it. It's not selling like your usual stuff. Why don't you go back and do your regular thing and then finish this?'

"I said, 'My contract says I have free rein here. It's like a three-act play. You can't tell what it's going to do until you finish the third act. This is only the first act. I want to finish it. If it's not successful, you can me.' So they let me finish it. The albums weren't that successful, but they didn't can me. I went back to making regular, straight-ahead instrumental records. But every now and then I'd try to throw in some of my metaphysical thing. I tried not to throw in too much of it, because I didn't want to alienate my fans or the company.

"I could see the handwriting on the wall. They were phasing out jazz at Blue Note. When the contracts expired, they never picked up the options. I was the last one there. I had two years to go on my contract. I knew they weren't going to pick up the option, and I thought I might as well be looking someplace else.

"I was playing the Keystone Korner in San Francisco, and got the newspaper to read a review on our performance. On the other side of the page there was a review on this book *How to Make and Sell Your Own Record*. I sent for the book and that's what turned me on to saying maybe I should put my money where my mouth is.

"I had a couple of offers from labels. I said to myself, 'If I'm gonna do straight-ahead, it's okay, but if I want to do this metaphysical thing, they're gonna fight me on it, knock me down, I won't be able to do it. So why don't I just go ahead and start my own label, so I can do my spiritual thing?'

"That's why I started the Silveto label. About eight years ago. I wasn't thinking about another label. I was just thinking about doing what I wanted to do without fighting anybody. After I had made at least three albums for the Silveto label, I thought, 'Why not start another label, the Emerald label, for straight-ahead?' Instead of losing the fans who didn't want to go this way. With what I'm doing they can have both.

"What I'm trying to do now is catch up on my Emerald label. The Silveto label is slow-moving. The Emerald label is selling better. The straight-ahead thing. I came into possession of a tape that was done at the Cork and Bib back in 1964, with Joe Henderson, Carmell Jones, Teddy Smith, Roger Humphries, and myself. It had *Filthy McNasty* on it, and *Senor Blues* and *Tokyo Blues* and all those tunes. I made arrangements to bring it out on an album. It's on the Emerald label. It's called *Horace Silver Live 1964*. So far that's my best seller."

Meanwhile, all those marvelous Blue Note albums have been reissued on CD, causing a sudden rise of awareness of how much Horace has contributed to jazz.

"I don't want to be on the road fifty-two weeks a year," he said. "I do a lot of writing while I'm home. In recent years, I've been getting into extended pieces. A couple of years back I was commissioned to write a piece of music for a concert in New York honoring Duke. I wrote a three-part piece for string orchestra, flutes, piano, bass, and drums, and a mini-chorus of singers. It was called *Message from the Maestro*.

"I came home and wrote another piece for string orchestra. I have written three or four more extended pieces. I hope someday to do something with full symphony. I have things involving choreography, things I want to put on eventually."

When the day was over, it seemed to me that Horace had changed little with the years, except that he has a mustache and his hair is a little long. He still is a gentle man, and I have always thought him to be eminently sane. And I still trusted him.

April 1990

The Nine Lives
of Red Rodney

By all accounts, Red Rodney ought to have been dead.

Instead he was flying all over the earth in glowing good health, leading a quintet whose members were often a third his sixty-seven years, playing better than he had ever played, and enjoying what one critic called "one of the most celebrated comebacks in jazz history."

"In fact," Red said, "the odds were against my coming back and doing anything."

They certainly were. Heroin was the elixir of bebop, but few of those who succumbed to its blandishments in the 1940s and '50s are using it today: they have either quit, like Red, or they're dead. A few, like Art Blakey, maintained their habits with such aplomb that they managed to reach a good age before dropping of other causes. By and large, dirty needles, self-neglect, improper nourishment, sojourns in the slammer, and all the other concomitants of heroin addiction took a devastating toll. Red Rodney is almost able to say, with Job, "And I only am escaped to tell thee."

Red is briefly portrayed in the Clint Eastwood film *Bird*, which attracted both high praise and a bored condemnation in the jazz community. They've never made a good movie about jazz, you'll hear it said by those who have not bothered to notice that they've almost never made a good movie about music—period. Red is listed in the credits as being an adviser on the film, but his advice, he says, was limited largely to telling the young man who plays himself how to hold the horn and stand. There is a scene in which the Charlie Parker character upbraids him for having taken up heroin. Something like that happened in life: Bird, according to accounts I've heard from several musicians, urged his proselytes not to follow him into drug use. Few of them paid attention to his admonition; they paid attention to his example.

The question of drug use among artists is a complex one. You cannot say you have examined a question until you have entertained all sides of it. I believe we have reached the limits of what the mind now can do and are trying to exceed them. Asked what it took to be a writer, William Faulkner said, "A pencil, some paper, and a little good whisky." A doctor wrote a book two or three years ago to consider why writers are such drinkers— Faulkner, Steinbeck, Jack London, and many more. The loneliness of the work, he said, is one of the causes. Nonsense. It's the sheer hunger for ideas. The writer sits there *in a loneliness he or she actually likes*, glass in hand, slipping into reconciliation and a resigned revery until something comes that is worth putting on paper. I have said repeatedly that you can write drunk, but you have to edit sober. Susan Sontag has written of her use of speed as an aid to writing. She suspects that Sartre wrote on speed, because of the sheer uncontrolled verbosity of his work. The problem is that all drugs suspend judgment. But isn't that, in an improvisatory art, just what you want them to do? Free you of that incessant, cruel, unsleeping, inner monitor that judges your every action even before it is completed?

I have a recurring suspicion that the next major leap in human intelligence will be chemically achieved. We seem to have no objection to the use of a drugs such as dopamine for those with Parkinson's disease or Dilantin for epileptics, both neurological disorders; not to mention all the tranquilizers in virtually unrestricted use in our society.

Loren Eiseley in *The Immense Journey* compared the human mind to a telephone switchboard that you encounter in a small motel. The motel has only a dozen or so rooms, but the circuitry is sufficient for thousands of rooms. The expansion of the brain and the brain case occurred comparatively quickly in evolutionary time, Eiseley reminds us. What is all that extra circuitry for? Will we some day learn to use it? Some day, I suspect, and perhaps soon, we are going to find a drug that will so expand our capacities that the man of the future will look back on us the way we do Neanderthal man. The odds are rather better that, given the ravages of nationalism, ethnocentricity, class distinctions, avarice, overbreeding, and all the other manifestations of our madness, we won't make it. But if we do, future man will see us as the last of the savages.

I suspect that it is this yearning for the balanced function of intellect and feeling, what Blake called the marriage of heaven and hell, the recurring suspicion that it can be achieved and that there is something *more* somehow, a something we glimpse occasionally and fleetingly through mist, a subliminal flash of a divine future, that has drawn men such as Charlie Parker and Bill Evans into heroin.

I asked Red Rodney what he thought, but his answer must be heard in context and so I will withhold it for the moment. Certainly no one can speak of drug addiction with a greater depth of experience than Red.

On the other hand, we should not dwell only on that aspect of his life. This is, let us keep constantly in mind, a brilliant musician, a gifted man. One of the protégés of Charlie Parker, for three years a member of Bird's quintet, standing night after night beside Bird's horn and hearing its outpourings, Rodney was one of the first white bebop trumpet players. Red is uninhibited about discussing his past, and he is frank about it when young musicians ask him about it in music clinics.

It is an astonishing story. Red was in and out of narcotics hospitals, various jails, and other institutions of restraint and spent long periods of time when he didn't even pick up his horn. He was hunted by the FBI, insurance detectives, and other investigators. He survived by cons and scams and fraud. This was, he will tell you bluntly, a time of his life when his improvisatory skills were devoted to criminal schemes. Some of his activities, in retrospect, are funny: they have all the elements of a caper movie, except for those secondary characters script writers insert into the scheme to make dialogue. Red was a loner.

"I wasn't," he said, "the type of guy to go steal your horn and pawn it. If I were going to do illegal activities, I was going to beat the banks, the government, and the insurance companies. Those were the biggest thieves anyway in American life, and they were legal thieves."

He was born Robert Rodney Chudnick in Philadelphia, Pennsylvania, on September 27, 1927, the oldest of three children.

"My father was born in Kiev," Red said. "My mother was born in Minnesota. For a while she was one of those traffic crossing guards. We were a very close family. Most Jewish families are very close."

Red's father ran his own little sheet-metal business, working as a subcontractor in construction. One of his clients was the firm headed by John B. Kelly, Grace Kelly's father. No one in Red's family was musical, and he is not sure himself where his interest in music came from, although it began early.

"I joined a bugle-and-drum corps when I was ten years old," he said. "It was a Jewish War Veterans post. My father was a member. I wanted to be a drummer, and they gave me the little snare drum to march with. They took it away because I was too small to carry it and gave me a bugle. I was heartbroken. It's funny. Within six months I was the best bugle player of that whole organization. There were kids in there fifteen, sixteen, even a little older. I was eleven by then. I took to it very quickly.

"The first of January, Philadelphia has a big Mummers Parade. All kinds of bands and acts and floats are in that parade. It's like Macy's Thanksgiving Day parade in New York. I remember marching in it. I played in other parades, Veteran's Day affairs, with my bugle. I won a competition: best bugler in Pennsylvania. And my reward was a piston bugle, the old one with a valve on the side that you play with your thumb. The piston bugle was the progenitor of the trumpet.

"As a bar mitzvah present when I was thirteen, I got a trumpet. I already had chops, because I played the bugle. When I got the trumpet, wow! Now I had three buttons to push, that would give me all the songs that I heard. I still couldn't read.

"The trumpet my parents bought me was the same trumpet I play now, a Blessing. The company had a deal with Gimbel Brothers. If you bought a trumpet there, you got fifteen free lessons. Then of course you continued. That was their pitch. So my father bought me the trumpet at Gimbels' and I got fifteen free lessons. But I had already had chops. The teacher didn't know what to do with *that*. I could play all the songs.

"And then of course I had to go home and learn how to read. I had all the textbooks that come with learning how to play the trumpet. I took to it very well. I was very good. That was my main interest. Most kids were out on the street playing ball. I liked that also, but I made sure to play, I always loved to play.

"It came very naturally. I guess that's the reason I learned how to improvise. I could play before I could read and play the text book material. I could hear it and play it. Then I did learn how to read. I've known some very great players who didn't know how to read, like my dear friend who's long gone, Bill Harris. He had to learn how to read with Benny Goodman and with Bob Chester's orchestra. Charlie Ventura had the same problem.

"If you're in a band and reading, doing it all the time, it's like reading the newspaper. But I find now that if I'm put in an all-star band, my God! Like a few friends of mine, now that we don't do it all the time. Old guys who can't even *see* the music, let alone read it! You end up fighting for the fourth trumpet chair.

"I went to school in Philadelphia with Joe Wilder. It was the Jules E. Mastbaum Vocational School. We had a great music course. Joe Wilder and Johnny Coles and I were in the school band. Buddy De Franco was there.

"My next adventure—and it was a big jump—came when the war broke out. All the good trumpet players were drafted. Here I am now, fifteen, sixteen, and working for all the top bands in Philadelphia and for Alex Bartha, the house band at the Steel Pier in Atlantic City on weekends. Ziggy

Elman had been in that band. We'd play the first hour, then the name bands would come. And so I played with a lot of name bands because they'd come to Atlantic City minus musicians. They were getting drafted left and right. I played with Benny Goodman, I played with Jimmy Dorsey, whom I went with later, I played with Tony Pastor. It was very good experience. When I was about sixteen years old, Jerry Wald heard me at the Steel Pier, and asked me to go on the road with him. And I did. That was really my first road job. I stayed two or three months—I really wasn't ready. I came back and went back into the Steel Pier house band.

"My hero at that time was Harry James. I liked Charlie Spivak. I didn't know *anything* about jazz. Not the slightest thing. James was a great player. He was a Louis Armstrong type jazz player. To the day he died, I loved him. He was tremendous. And he was a decent man.

"I went out with Jimmy Dorsey for about five months. I really wasn't ready to play that chair. He was going to replace me. He let me stay until we got to Philadelphia.

"I was married when I was eighteen. She's dead. We separated, and she got killed in an automobile accident in 1960 or '61. We had two boys, who stayed with my aunt in Las Vegas. One lives in Los Angeles now. He's working as a disc jockey on a couple of radio stations. The older one is in Las Vegas. He's superintendent of an apartment building. He's got two children."

Settling back into life in Philadelphia, Red joined a CBS radio band led by Elliot Lawrence. It is hard for people born after that era to grasp the range and creativity of radio's role in American musical life. Today it is a force for decay and debasement, but it wasn't in those days. In addition to all the remote radio broadcasts of the big bands and the various commercial network broadcasts that featured Woody Herman, Benny Goodman, John Kirby, and many more, and even full symphony orchestras maintained on staff by NBC and CBS in New York, various local stations had studio bands of their own, some of which were heard nationally through network hookups. The Elliot Lawrence band was one of these. Though it is little mentioned in big-band histories, the Lawrence band—Lawrence in recent years has been a conductor of Broadway musicals—was notable for intelligent, advanced arrangements. One of its writers was a young Gerry Mulligan.

"I got Gerry in that band," Red said. "We stayed a year. That was the first I heard jazz.

"The studio band was a day gig. I would go around to the Down Beat club at night. It was the modern jazz club in that town. Bebop was starting to be played there. Dizzy had worked there two years before as the house trumpet player. His mother lived in Philly, and Dizzy lived in Philadelphia for quite some time. I didn't know who Dizzy Gillespie was, though. I went up there and tried to play. The piano player was a guy named Red Garland. I knew *Exactly Like You* and *Body and Soul* and that's it. And Red Garland said to me, 'Young man, if you want to play with us, you're gonna have to learn some new tunes. So if you come in early tomorrow, I'll go over some with you.' How sweet.

"Next day I came in early and he taught me how to play the blues and he taught me *I Got Rhythm*. I didn't know what the changes were. I had no idea. All by ear. And I played in that band, a quintet, with a tenor saxophone player named Jimmy Oliver, who's still living in Philly.

"There was a streetcar conductor who used to stop the streetcar and run upstairs and sit in on drums. His name was Philly Joe Jones. He had the 11th Street run, and that's where the Down Beat was. The cars would be blowing their horns, people would be yelling, 'Get that damn streetcar moving!' They finally fired him, so he wound up working at the Down Beat.

"Red Garland left, to go to New York. The piano player who replaced him was Jimmy Golden, a wonderful player. He's dead now. He influenced more young jazz players from Philadelphia than anybody. He was a big influence on me. He was very prominent. He was the first of all the young bebop players. He was a little older than we were. He was really our mentor. He was between swing and bop. He taught me how to play all the standards. He was very good to us, especially all the white kids that would come around. Everybody at the Down Beat was black except me.

"There was a big night coming up. Gene Krupa's band came to town with Roy Eldridge. I'd already heard Roy on a big hit record, *Let Me Off Uptown*. I thought, 'Wow! That's sensational!' But it didn't have any attraction to me yet. That wasn't the Harry James tone. It was different. I thought it was sensational, but it didn't mean anything to me. Then I realized. Oh yeah. Roy Eldridge came to the Down Beat. Dizzy Gillespie was coming. And they were going to have a jam session.

"That was the night that Dizzy made me think, 'Oh my God.' I heard that Roy was great, but Dizzy was new. It was apples and oranges. You couldn't compare them. That night Dizzy showed us—we were very young; I was eighteen years old—the way to go. I even thought in my head, 'You know, if this guy didn't play such weird notes, he'd be great.' Roy played the notes that I could understand. Dizzy was playing harmonically things that I'd never heard.

"Three weeks later, I realized they weren't weird notes.

"There was my influence.

"Then I started listening heavily. I tried to play like Dizzy, which of course I couldn't do. The notes that he made were sensational. The fire, the time that Dizzy had! He's truly one of the greats of the instrument. We have to say Louis Armstrong, Dizzy, Clifford Brown, Miles of course. Miles is one of the greatest innovators. The only one I've ever heard play like Dizzy is Jon Faddis. Who does it very well.

"I was pretty lucky. Even back then I had my own sound. Like it or not, it was me. You could always say, 'Well, that's Rodney.' But Dizzy's influence was already set.

"Now I became quite friendly with Dizzy. Such a nice man. And he always was. He took such an interest in little young players, and he still does. He's a great teacher.

"I was still with Elliot Lawrence. We were becoming the heroes of Philadelphia, broadcasting every day in two sustaining coast-to-coast programs. It was a good band. And I played at the Down Beat club at night. I was earning about fifty bucks a week at the Down Beat, another sixty from Elliot. My God, I was rich! Living home with my parents.

"Dizzy was coming to visit his mother all the time. He'd always stop in at the Down Beat after his mother went to bed. His mother lived on 13th Street, two or three blocks away. He'd walk over. I was always so happy to see him. He was my hero, he was my idol.

"He said to me one night, 'It's time for you to come to New York and hear my quintet. We're opening at the Three Deuces. And you'll hear Charlie Parker.' I'd already heard *of* Charlie Parker. Dizzy said, 'This weekend, you have to come to New York. You're ready.'

"So I go to New York. I go to 52nd Street. Dizzy puts me right in the front row. And I hear that quintet with Max Roach and Al Haig and Charlie Parker. And I . . . freak . . . out. It was like a religious experience. I sat there like I was listening to one of those evangelistic gospel preachers. Oh my God. It left me talking to myself. I stayed until four o'clock in the morning, when they closed. And then I started walking around 52nd Street.

"I knew right then that that was what I wanted to do. That was going to be my life's work. Charlie Parker came over to me. Dizzy had introduced us. He said, 'So you work in Philadelphia. Where you going now?' I said, 'Nowhere.' He said, 'Come on with me. By the way, can you loan me ten bucks?'"

Red laughed at the memory. "I would have loaned him a hundred. Anything I had. So I went uptown with him. Then we came back downtown. We became friendly. I don't know why. It certainly wasn't the ten bucks. He befriended me.

"I asked him if he'd come to Philly to play with us. He said, 'Yeah.' And he came just a couple of weekends later to play with our group.

"He was wonderful.

"And I played with him. It was fantastic.

"And that was it. I was on my way to learning how to play the kind of music I had chosen. Of course, had I known I was going to take the same kind of twists and turns he took, I might have pulled up and thought a little differently.

"In those days, a lot of the older jazz players were putting the music down. I remember when bebop started how people put us down, including Louis Armstrong. I was very hurt when Pops put us down, because I loved him so much. So was Dizzy and so was Bird. In later years, he did admit he was wrong.

"Another hero of mine was Jack Teagarden. I remember how he looked at me, and I felt 'Why you little bebopper,' although he didn't say it. And that hurt me too. But he was so great. I loved him.

"As we get older, change is harder for us to assimilate. We must never let ourselves get that way."

For all the complexity of the music, Red was playing it by ear. Bebop had expanded the vocabulary of jazz, not only harmonically but rhythmically. The rhythmic displacements were disconcerting to some listeners, and musicians too. And the way Parker and Gillespie built melodies out of the harmonic extensions, the upper partials, produced disorientation in some listeners, and indeed still does. One of the things of particular interest in Red Rodney's remembrances is that he takes polite issue with those who think of Parker's work as the product of a complex intellectual process rather than the fluid intuitive process that is the wellspring of any unpremeditated art.

"At this point," Red said of his early days with Bird, "I was doing it strictly by ear. Some of our leading players still do. Look at Stan Getz. Anything Chick Corea threw at him, Stan played right off. Anything.

"I to this day feel that Charlie Parker didn't know where he was either. He seems to have proven it to me. Many times I asked him, 'Bird; where's the bridge go?' And he'd say, 'B-flat.' And it would be F-sharp minor or B, one of those kind of things. And I'd look at him and I'd see Al Haig laughing. And I'd ask him again, for another tune, similar type, difficult bridge. And

I'd say, 'Where's the bridge?' 'B-flat.' And he'd give me that sheepish little smile and say, 'Well that's what I play.' So I often thought that maybe *he* didn't know. Now I know that he's written tunes. I know that."

"Well," I said, "I know from Dizzy that Dizzy often wrote them out. Bird would come over to Dizzy's apartment and play the tune."

"And," Red said, "Dizzy would write it down."

"So you're suggesting then," I said, "that this was entirely the invention of an astonishing ear."

"Yes," Red said. "I have no way of proving that except my own experience with him. A lot of people say, 'No no, he knew, he was very knowledgeable.' I don't think so. Dizzy, yes. Not Bird.

"At that time, I was harmonically very unaware of how things went. I was using my ears to hear everything. And, you know, that will take you a long way. In fact, I go to colleges today and listen to all of the materials they have to deal with and especially Jamey Aebersold, who is awesome. He puts his things on the screen. He's so good, and so long, that he gets me sleepy, let alone the kids.

"Twice I've followed him, and I got up there, and said, 'I agree with everything he said, but he didn't speak about these two little things God gave us on the side of our heads. Two ears. They can give us the added salt and pepper and the catchup, the condiments, the color tones and the beauty. You must be able to hear to make beautiful music.'

"A lot of times I'll emphasize that. But of course I know the importance of harmonic training. When I was in the Public Health Service hospital at Fort Worth, Texas, which is like Lexington for the west coast, I took the Berklee correspondence course.

"When I got to the chapters on chord progressions, I'd sit there and play them and laugh, because these were things I'd been playing all my life. And now they were telling me what I'm doing. I remember writing my first arrangement for the band at Fort Worth. They were young musicians. It was thrilling. I never really became a good arranger, but I learned a little harmonically. This with all my experience helped me a great deal. Knowledge is important. A little bit of knowledge is what I have, and sometimes that can be dangerous. The reason for the way I'm playing today, though, is that I have such young people with me. They're very young and modern. For the last twelve years I've had that. And so with the little bit of knowledge I have and a great deal of knowledge they have obtained—they're all college graduates from great music schools—I've come a long way. I didn't turn my ears off, the way a lot of people my age have done. They say, 'Whoa, wait a minute.' They're in their comfort zone, which is great. What they've done is enough. But it isn't my comfort zone. I have to go all the way, until I can't play any more.

"I stayed with Elliot a little while longer and at the Down Beat. Gerry Mulligan went with Gene Krupa's orchestra as arranger in January of 1946. Gerry was the first arranger, back then, to write contrapuntally. He was young—he was eighteen like I was. He embraced the new music. He was a tremendously talented man. A whole generation of new young musicians do not know what a great musician he is.

"Don Fagerquist was leaving the Krupa band. Gerry recommended me, and they called me, and I was interested, partly because Dizzy and Bird were going to be at Billy Berg's on the west coast. The Krupa band was going to make a movie and play at the Palladium, and be on the coast for three or four months. I was offered $250 a week, the biggest salary I had ever dreamed of making. And Bird and Dizzy were going to be at Billy Berg's.

"And I liked the way Gene spoke to me on the phone. So I joined the band. I didn't know then how great a man he really was. Oh! The greatest! He was the greatest leader of men I ever met. He was sensational. He was a beautiful man. He was a real intellectual. Artie Shaw was supposed to be the intellectual, and maybe he was. But I know Gene was. Gene was well versed on any subject you wanted to speak about. He was a teacher. He would come back in the bus and speak with us. He was a mensch.

"Gene embraced anything new. Nothing frightened him. And he had what was really the first white name bebop band. He tried, he did it, he let it happen. He let the young guys do what they had to do. I remember he billed me as the surrealist of the trumpet. I didn't know what the hell it meant. I had to go to him ask, 'What does this mean?'

"Bird and Diz were not successful at Billy Berg's and the engagement did not last very long. Diz came back and Bird stayed there and got into Camarillo. He went berserk, he was so sick. Whenever he couldn't get drugs, he drank too much. It was like a nervous breakdown.

"I stayed with Gene's band a year. We worked all over.

"But 52nd Street was beckoning. I wanted to come to New York and really become a full-fledged jazz player. I left the band at the Capitol Theater in New York. It was a difficult thing, because of Gene. I loved him. To the young ones he was like a father. He was never an employer or a boss. Never. He was so good. I've never met one like him. I loved Woody equally as much. But they were different.

"I said, 'Bobby Scott always claimed that Gene was never a pot smoker.'"

"Never," Red replied unequivocally.

"Gene claimed those charges against him were a frame and Bobby believed it."

"It *was* a frame. It was definitely a frame. The band boy got busted in 1942. He set Gene up. He had the marijuana in his pocket. The charge was contributing to the delinquency of a minor. That case was a disgrace. Pat Brown, who was the prosecuting attorney who put Gene in prison, became the governor of California."

"When did you leave that band?"

"The beginning of 1947. I was nineteen. I was playing Monday nights at the Three Deuces or the Onyx or whatever club. I was doing the jam sessions that Monty Kay ran. And of course it still wasn't enough to live on.

"I went to join Local 802, and saw Sammy Musiker in the dues line. He had been a clarinet player with Gene's band. He's long dead. He asked what I was doing. I said I was trying to work out my union card, which took six months. He said, 'Well, you know you can play single engagements. I'll hire you.' Sammy was married to a woman whose father was a big, big leader in Jewish weddings and bar mitzvahs. Sammy took me with him, taught me how to do it, gave me the gigs. I'd work a lot of weekends. There was enough to make a living. In fact, they made me a third leader. They'd get three gigs in a night, they'd make me a leader.

"The bands were terrible, but Sammy himself was great. It taught me the standard tunes, and it gave me a way I could always make a living. I know how to do that. The bands of that kind today are much better than they were in those days. These kids can play jazz.

"It was an enjoyable year. I was learning, I was playing, I was hanging out with guys like Miles Davis and Fats Navarro on 52nd Street. We were all friends. Fats was far ahead of us.

"There was something Bird saw in Miles before anybody. And then I started seeing it. I didn't know what it was, but I knew I liked what he was doing. I liked his musical mind. I didn't think he could play the trumpet. He didn't do that until years later. But there was something about Miles that was fascinating. And, you know, he was a charming young man. Unlike his projected image. He was always pretty well-spoken when he wanted to be. You could see the breeding he had. That was obvious, even though he played it down. Miles was a gentleman, when he wanted to be, despite the terrible things you hear.

"I always knew that he had something. What it was I didn't know yet. It didn't take long. I was the third one of the triumvirate. We got all the gigs. We were sort of friendly rivals.

"For the whole of 1947, I did those weddings and bar mitzvahs. For about six months I was with Claude Thornhill. It was a lovely band. This was the end of '47, beginning of '48. Lee Konitz was in the band. Gerry Mulligan was writing for the band. Sometimes he played. Gil Evans was of course the chief arranger. Gerry learned a great deal from Gil, and I think vice versa. Gerry was twenty years old. The music was well written and well played. It was nice. But I wanted to be a bebopper.

"I came back to New York in '48 and did the same kind of work, the weddings and bar mitzvahs. Now we had the Royal Roost open, and I used to do a few gigs in there. A few jazz clubs would open and I'd get my share. There were about four trumpet players who were the journeymen. It was Fats, it was Miles, it was Kenny Dorham, who was wonderful, and it was me. We would compete for work. Fats was still the best of the four. He was still 'way ahead of all of us. Clifford Brown came directly from Fats. Directly. But then of course he died so young.

"Then I went with Woody Herman, the Four Brothers band. Marky Markowitz decided to stay in New York and go into the studios, and they offered me the gig. I pondered it. It was the fifth chair. Bernie Glow and Stan Fishelson were the two lead players. Ernie Royal played the high-note lead, plus the high-note jazz. Shorty Rogers was the fourth chair, and the jazz chair, and my chair was the fifth chair and the jazz chair.

"But Shorty was such a sweetheart. He'd write the solo on my chair—like *Lemon Drop*. I said, 'Shorty, now that's not fair. Your wrote the arrangement.' He said, 'I want you to play it. It'll be good for your career.' He put all the good solos on my chair. And it was very good for my career.

"One of the incidents I remember is the time Dizzy led Woody's band. We were on our way back from California to play at the Four Hundred Club, I think it was, in New York. There was a gigantic blizzard, and we were stranded on the train right outside Salt Lake City. The picture of that train snowed in made the cover of *Life* magazine.

"Dizzy had a one-nighter there that night, and because of the blizzard couldn't get his band there. So Woody and all of us got off the train, and we went to the place and Dizzy led our band with Woody. We played all of Woody's things, and some of Dizzy's. He didn't even have his music. But it was great.

"I loved the Woody Herman band. But I was getting to the point where I needed to play in small jazz groups. I was looking for a way out. Zoot had left. Stan Getz had left. People were starting to leave.

"A lot of them were addicted to drugs. And I was accused of it then. I was not. I had never used drugs. I knew who was doing it and who wasn't. Most of the sax section was addicted, excepting Sam Marowitz. The Swope brothers. Bernie Glow. That band was crumbling. And all of a sudden I got a call from Charlie Parker. Wow. That was a call from God.

"I went to Woody and told him where I was going, with his blessing, of course. I joined Charlie Parker in 1949. The first gig I played was the Three Deuces in, I think, September. I'd been in a big band for a year. And here I was with Bird, and those fast tempos! That first night! Oh man." He laughed.

"Fats Navarro and Miles were there. Those two were in the audience. I was petrified. Petrified. It worked out all right. I rose to it. After I finished the set, they both came over and hugged me. They said, 'Man, you were great!' And it was so nice, feeling accepted by your peers.

"That was the turning point of my career and my life. Now I was going in a different direction. It was as if I had graduated high school and now I was going to college. This was my college entrance. It was college and graduate school together, my time with Bird.

"Bird was a very kind, considerate, thoughtful, humble, modest human being. He was genuinely concerned with everyone, and with all issues. He was a very brilliant man, though he had a limited formal education. I guess his natural ear enabled him to speak perfectly when he wanted to. He spoke like a college graduate, and more. He was a nice man.

"He knew that he was that great. He knew the adoration other musicians had for him. He handled it very humbly and modestly. A lesser person wouldn't have been able to handle it as easily. I've seen guys who were great but not that great and got similar adoration, and it completely turned them around. It brought out the negative in them, rather than the positive. It didn't do that with Bird. He was a lovely man, a charming man.

"The first one who really told me about Bird and the heroin was Miles Davis. That's when I realized Bird was a junky. This was in 1946. Miles lived on the second floor and Bird lived on the third floor of an apartment building up around 145th Street. I went up to see Bird. He said he was busy and sent me down to see Miles. Miles was laughing. He said, 'Don't you know what they're doing?' And he told me.

"When you're very young and immature and you have a hero like Charlie Parker was to me, an idol who proves himself every time, who proves greatness and genius . . . that's a hard word to throw around. But you can't say less. When I listened to that genius night after night, being young and immature and not an educated person, I must have thought, 'If I crossed over that line, with drugs, could I play like that?'

"Drugs were heavily involved in that part of jazz music. It wasn't the swing players who were using junk. It was the new bebop generation that did that. And I was one of the last. I saw all these people doing that. I watched Bird, and I knew what he did.

"You want a sense of belonging. You want to be like the others. And so I tried it. And, you know, the euphoria can be compared to having an orgasm. It's so tremendous. I started snorting heroin. And then when my nose was too burned out, I started to use a syringe.

"It didn't take me long to get hooked. If you did it once or twice a week, it would take months. If you continue to do it every day, it can happen very fast.

"When Bird found out that I was strung out, he was *furious*. His attitude was: Don't do as I do, do as I say. He was disappointed in me. He was very sad, very angry. But he was smart enough to know that once you're involved, there wasn't anything he could say. So we shared. Now we were on the road together and we shared all the time. He was great even that way. He was a genuinely nice man. He was disappointed that I had gone out and messed up, but once it was done, it was done.

"I was with Charlie Parker for most of the next three years. Some of that time, I was with Charlie Ventura. He had a big band. There were times when Bird would go out as a single, and I was with Charlie Ventura's big band only, not the small band. We did three weeks in Chicago at a place called the Silhouette. That's where I first met Ira Sullivan. His father brought him to see the band, and he came up and said, 'Well I play trumpet too.' He was playing saxophone across the street in a little club. I invited him to sit down next to me and read the music with me. I didn't know he didn't read music at all.

"At the end of that three years, the strings came in—Bird with strings—and there wasn't enough money to keep a trumpet player with the strings. Bird hated it, but he'd a had a bit of a jazz hit with it. It was very restrictive for him. The agents and managers did it. Bird never knew how to say, 'No.' He'd say yes to everything, then just wouldn't show up.

"And the rest of the time he was getting a lot of single work."

I said, "You can clarify an issue. The myth of bebop is that the music had a negative genesis—an act of hostility to keep the white boys off the bandstand. If Dizzy and Bird didn't want them on the bandstand, why did they hire and teach them? Look what you tell me about the way Dizzy treated you in Philadelphia. Why did they hire people like Al Haig and Stan Levey? Why did Bird hire you, if that were the music's purpose? You cannot create out of hatred. And no one who has ever known Dizzy could believe it."

"I don't think that was a problem then," Red said. "I was treated like anyone else. Of course, there was a lot of Jim Crow in those days. A lot of it.

And yet a young white boy came around, and man, I never felt any, any animosity. I never felt anything but love.

"I don't know whether it's the same today, with the younger ones. I know if I were black, I would feel the same way. I would feel very antagonistic. I would probably rebel without good cause, instead of rebelling with sensitivity, but you don't know that when you're so young. And I can understand. I don't have to like it, but I can understand.

"But a man like Clark Terry and like Dizzy, and so many others I can think of, no matter what they've been through, I think they do differentiate between those of us who feel for and believe in their cause and other people who may not. Still, they handle themselves beautifully. I have never once been made to feel anything but a friendly equal to Dizzy. I don't consider myself his equal, but he treats me that way. Clark's another one, a dear man. Clark goes out of his way to recommend me on things. I do a lot of college clinics now because of Clark. He never told me he recommended me. But I know who got me there.

"But the younger ones, I can see how they feel. I've felt uncomfortable on certain tours with certain young, excellent players. Years later, those very same people were much nicer. I got a very different feeling."

It came time to ask the loaded question: "Do you think it's possible that dope did help your playing?" Red's answer, when it came, was in accord with that of every other former addict to whom I have posed it.

"No," Red said, immediately and emphatically. "First of all, you have to be healthy to play well. And you're not very healthy using drugs. Nothing is working. Your cells are deadened. It's the greatest cure for the common cold there is." He chuckled. "I didn't have a cold for twenty years. That's about all I can say for it. Now I know why there are codeine-based cough syrups. If you take some of that, you stop coughing.

"With heroin your cells are dead. All of them. You know, when a woman addict gets pregnant, she doesn't know it, because she doesn't menstruate anyway on heroin. It suspends menstruation. And addicted women don't show as quickly. They may be in the fourth or fifth month before they start having cramps and have to find out why.

"It puts all of your cells to sleep. That's why you have such terrible withdrawal when you awaken them. Your nervous system goes spattering around and around and around and up and down and it's completely berserk. And that's why you have such terrible discomfort. Your hair hurts, your toes hurt, your feet hurt, you're sweating profusely. You're shaking. You can't sleep. You can't eat. Your nervous system is upside down."

I said, "Philly Joe Jones told me he never had withdrawal symptoms when he quit. Philly said he never even got sick."

"I can't believe it," Red said. "I've seen him where he's had to go out and do crazy things in order to get enough money for drugs." Red laughed. "He took my car one time. We were on a record date. A Red Rodney–Ira Sullivan date with Tommy Flanagan and Oscar Pettiford. Philly Joe took the car and sent in Elvin Jones to finish the date. I said, 'Where's my car?' Elvin said, 'He's got it.'

"I loved Philly Joe. He was one of the most brilliant men I ever met. He was well versed in any subject you could speak about. I gave a twenty-fifth wedding anniversary party for my parents. Philly Joe was playing drums at the gig. He immediately went behind the bar and started talking Yiddish to all of them. I freaked out. He spoke better Yiddish than I did. I loved him dearly.

"He came back with my car two days later."

"Did you try to quit?" I asked.

"Oh! Many times! And, you know, a lot of people who stayed involved either died or got very sick or disappeared. Some of them left music, went into other fields to straighten their lives out. Stan Levey did. He became a photographer.

"I stayed. I stayed in music, and I stayed a junky."

After those three years with Charlie Parker, Red was badly strung out.

When I first encountered the term "strung out," it struck me as grimly vivid. It suggested an image of an expiring soldier, arms outstretched in a tangle of barbed wire, the posture of crucifixion. But language is diluted by use. "Turn on" originally denoted to get high on dope. Now it has all manner of bland meanings, even in television commercials. A breakfast cereal can turn you on. "Strung out" has been so weakened in its absorption into the general vernacular that you might be strung out on your credit-card payments.

But it originally meant to be addicted to heroin—no other drug—and it was a mercilessly evocative term. Red went home to Philadelphia strung out. His parents were devastated, his cousins and other relatives bewildered.

He floundered through 1955 and '56, working occasional local jobs, impeded by vice and narcotics cops, who would accost him and shove up his shirt sleeves to look for fresh tracks. There's another vivid term: the scars that follow the lines of violated veins look like the symbol for railway tracks on maps. Red said, "If you had recent marks, you were dirty. And that was a conviction in Philadelphia, as it was in L.A. at one time. They could put you in jail for it. So I didn't do it there."

There was a direct quality about Red Rodney. For all the ingenuity of the scams he designed, he had a disposition toward forthright confrontation. Furthermore, I think Red could charm his way out of hell. I never heard him derogate his tormentors, never heard him speak ill of the police, and indeed, over the course of his improbable life, he seems to have encountered a remarkable number of sympathetic authority figures. Red went straight to the cop in charge, and thereby hangs a tale: how Red Rodney, archetypical bebopper, became the Lester Lanin of Philadelphia, playing businessman's bounce, the antithesis of jazz, the music jazzmen all cordially loathe, although more than a few of them have turned to it *in extremis* to put a little bread on the table.

"The captain of the vice and narcotics squad was a man named Clarence Ferguson, whose name struck fear in all the vice and narcotics offenders of Philadelphia," Red said. "And I went to his office one day, and I said, 'Cap, every time I get a job, your men come around, and shake me down looking for marks, and I lose the job.'

"He says, 'All right, you're right, and I'm going to help you.' And he takes me to a kosher catering house called Davis Caterers. Harry Davis was the owner and proprietor. But Clarence Ferguson owned the building and had a lot of money in the catering business. And he made me the bandleader.

"There was a false door there. I never knew why. It was a door with a glass to it that led to a brick wall. Maybe they built another building after that one had been built. And they printed 'Red Rodney Orchestras' on it. I didn't do it, they did it. It sounds like something I would have done, but I didn't. They did.

"When someone would come in to book a party or a wedding or a bar mitzvah, Harry Davis or somebody would ask, 'Who's doing your music?' And they'd say sometimes, 'We don't know yet.' Harry would say, 'You should get Red Rodney there, but he's not in right now. We'll call him and book him for you.'

"So the caterer booked me. He packaged me. And I hired all the good jazz guys in town. Billy Root lived in town then. There were a lot of good players. I hired Bernard Peiffer, the pianist. I was the first bandleader that had black musicians playing weddings and bar mitzvahs in Philadelphia. I had Butch Ballard playing drums, Specs Wright on drums, Nelson Boyd the bass player. I hired everybody that could play jazz, especially when I had some big-band work. But of course the music was crap.

"I even played Captain Ferguson's niece's wedding. I offered to do it free, but he paid me full price. Captain Ferguson never took a nickel. Everybody else said Captain Ferguson was this, he was that. But he was good for me.

"I had an office. I was making money hand over fist. Plus the guys in

Captain Ferguson's squad would not mess with me when they saw me on the street. And I was strung out again. The music was so horrible. Of course, a junky doesn't need an excuse, but this was as good as any: the music is terrible! Look what I'm playing!"

This phase of Red's career lasted about two years. Eventually he sold all his bookings and band business to a club-date agency and left town, settling in San Francisco. "You're always running away," he said of the junky's life. "You figure, if you leave this you'll straighten up. But you can't run away from yourself."

He was insolvent again, back at the bottom, and with an expensive habit to support. It was in San Francisco that he embarked—with what seems an oddly detached logic—on the first of a number of elaborate schemes to get money.

"When I started getting into criminal activity," he said, "it was well thought out. I became Garfield Levy the lawyer. I'd already spent a few little bits of time in Lexington and Fort Worth as a volunteer, trying to get off heroin. You could volunteer then. I'd been with prisoners, and heard things. I met printers, I met this, I met that.

"I had a friend, a young lawyer named Tom Cochran, who was also a drummer. He worked in Melvin Belli's office in San Francisco. The firm in those days was Belli, Asch, and Geary. Tom worked for Lou Asch. I saw on the walls checks for awards from insurance companies for personal injury suits—big-time awards. These were photostatic copies. They didn't have Xerox in those days. And I stole them one at a time and took them over to my printer. He'd duplicate the checks, saying, 'Manhattan Marine Fire Insurance Company' and things like that. I'd cop one and put it back, cop another one and put it back on the wall of Melvin Belli's office. All checks he'd won in damage suits.

"Each one had the signature of the officer responsible and the co-signature. My printer used magnetic ink at the bottom of the check, so that when it went through the banking system, the ink was kosher. It wouldn't kick it out.

"There was a bandleader-booking agent friend of mine named Howard Frederick, who's dead now. I rented a little space from him and put up a sign saying, Garfield Levy, Esq.

"I went to the Bank of America and said I was a brand new young lawyer, just starting in practice. I opened an account with a thousand-dollar deposit in the name of Garfield Levy, Esquire. I came in ten days later or something like that with my first award, a $30,000 check made out to Gussie

Goldstein—that was my grandmother's name—and her lawyer, Garfield Levy, Esquire. That's how it's done, the lawyer deposits his check and then he makes one out to the client. I got some old junky lady to go in and cash the second check for me.

"That was the first one. I probably got away with about $75,000 in that six months.

"When the auditors figured out what had been going on, they started looking for Garfield Levy, Esquire. But he had disappeared. He was gone. I became Dr. Ronald Berger. I had a little doctor's office to write prescriptions for myself. I had my printer make the prescriptions. I'd send somebody to the drugstore for Dilaudid. It's a derivative of morphine, used for cancer patients."

I asked a friend, a pharmacist, about Dilaudid. Dilaudid, he said, is more powerful than morphine, almost as strong as heroin. "It is used for deep pain," he said. He buys it wholesale for 40 cents a capsule. These capsules, sold illegally on the street, go for $40 each—one hundred times their wholesale value.

Red said, "I'd send a girl to the drugstore. My phone would ring, and I'd say, 'Dr. Berger's office,' and okay the Dilaudid prescription.

"I went back to Vegas, and one night I broke into the Bureau of Vital Statistics office. There was no money in there. I went in and got death certificates. And while I was there, I stole the imprint seal.

"But I couldn't really figure out all of the things to do right. I'd read in the paper that so-and-so was killed in a hit and run or whatever. So I'd send away for their death certificates. They cost three dollars. When I got them, I'd erase the name, as clean as possible, with an electric eraser. And then I'd type over the name. You had the cause of death, the medical examiner's written statement, the doctor's statement if there was one. You had everything you didn't have to touch. I just had to change the name and the date.

"When I had a clean copy, I would Xerox it. Xerox had been invented. I'd Xerox over and over and over until finally it was perfect.

"All the insurance companies want is a copy of the death certificate. And my copies always included the seal of the State of Nevada, which made it look very official. I insured all kinds of people. This took some time. While I was putting this claim in, I was buying another insurance policy, then making out the death certificates and then cashing the policy.

"I was wanted for a phony narcotics sale. A kid came to me from Philadelphia, a horn player, who wanted help. It was one of the times I was trying to straighten up. The kid was so sick. I went upstairs to the connection, bought five dollars worth of heroin, and gave it to him. He gave me $50. I tried to refuse, but he insisted. It was marked money. I got out of the car and got busted by federal narcs. The kid had set me up. I made bail and ran. My hair would be gray, my hair would be brown. I couldn't play in any of the Las Vegas clubs or hotels.

"Life was very hard, and I would think up these outlandish ideas.

"But checks were a forte. Checks were very good.

"I always had the greatest ideas from this printer I had. I had a couple of printers, but this one was special. I had the American Express card. I had credit cards in teak wood. If I opened the flaps of the wallet, they looked real. You couldn't use them, you couldn't put them in a machine, but they looked good. I had all kinds of ID. I had ten different licenses in ten different names.

"I got along like that. It was a horror. I'd look at myself and say, What am I doing?

"The first time the insurance company came after me, they arrived with a state investigator. The insurance investigator started screaming at me. I noticed that the state guy wasn't saying anything. He's got a little twinkle in his eyes.

"The insurance investigator is screaming at me: 'Don't you realize what we can do to you?' And I'm saying to myself, 'Lord have mercy, they don't wanna bust me! They don't want the publicity!' Now the state detective, *he* can bust me. But he's just there for show.

"So I say, 'Yes sir, I'll never do it again!'

"So when they left, I thought, 'Wow! I've got a license.' And I had more certificates made out. I didn't even remember the names, who was dead, who wasn't.

"You know, I recently got my file through the Freedom of Information Act, and they've got more things crossed out. It's this thick. You wonder how they catch people, as badly as they did this. I know damn well that if I were arrested today for something, any detective or FBI agent would have my full record at his disposal. But I couldn't get it even through the Freedom of Information Act. They goofed. They said, 'You're still subject to punishment for impersonation.'"

"That's nonsense," I said. "There are only two crimes that have no statute of limitations."

"Right," Red said. "Murder and treason. They said I was still subject for impersonation. But they didn't even charge me with that. They turned me over to the narcotics agents for that phony sale. I was on the run from that. Hiding out. I was hiding out in the home of an old lady. She knew the whole story, and I was paying her. What am I going to do? I'm wanted, I can't play anywhere, I can't work."

It was then that Red came up with his most bizarre caper. Red passed himself off as a general in the United States Air Force and almost succeeded in stealing a payroll. This is how it happened:

"I was reading a newspaper and saw a headline: *Shortest General in U.S. History*. The story says Air Force General Russell T. McIntyre is five foot five. I'm five six. He's the auditor and comptroller of the United States Air Force. I was looking at a picture of me with gray hair and a gray mustache. He looked very much like me.

"I'm not thinking anything, just reading the story. And then it says that this guy makes spot audits. They never tell where he's going. They never tell what air base he's going to visit. He just shows up. And immediately the books are opened to him, and the safes.

"There's an atomic energy test site there in Nevada. It's big now, but at that time it was just a little hole in the wall, on Nellis Air Force Base. It was maybe five miles away from Nellis. It was a separate division. Once when we played the Flamingo Show Room, we went out there to play a show with the Mills Brothers. The guys who were stationed there could not get out. They were there for their tour of duty, eighteen months or whatever it was. So shows would come to them. I'd been in there three or four times.

"I read that there was a payroll there like $300,000 every other Friday. I started forming a plan to get it. I thought, 'If I'm going to go, I'm going to go righteously.' What could they give me for sale of drugs? Five to fifteen? What are they going to give me for stealing on an air base? Five to ten? I'm already going to get something. I'm already wanted.

"I went to a costume store. I told the guy in the store I was playing a part in a movie. I got a general's uniform. The story didn't say whether Russell T. McIntyre was a brigadier or a lieutenant general. It just said 'general.' So I made him a brigadier. And I got the salad for the chest.

"I went to a beauty salon that I knew in that area, and they grayed my hair. I grew a mustache and touched it up gray.

"I had to sneak into San Francisco and get my printer to make all the applicable ID. I didn't know what kind of ID I was looking for, but *he* knew. Department of Defense. He made me up perfect ID. And all the teak credit cards and right driver's license and all that. And people like ID. You go to banks, stores, to cash something, you show this ID and you're all right. I even had a Masonic card.

"So I drive up in my car. Man, I'm loaded. On heroin and methedrine. Wired. If I'm going to go, I'm going to go swingin'. 'Cause I expected to be busted any minute. I never thought I'd get away with that.

"But from the very beginning, salutes! They take me back to the colonel who was in charge of the base. It was a little teeny base. I had all this ID ready. He didn't even want to see it! It was: Yes sir! No sir! People believe whatever they see. If I put on a pilot's uniform, they'd think I was a pilot.

"I'm pretending to look over the books. I couldn't tell one thing from another. But the pretense was good. Now I'm thinking, How am I going to get him to open that safe? I didn't even have to. He opened it without my asking and walked away.

"There was 30 grand in there. There was no 300 grand. I found out later I'd missed the payroll by a week. But I took the 30 grand and I took some other papers, parchment papers and what I thought were securities. They saved my life.

"I see that's all I'm going to get. This colonel wants me out of there. They might have been doing something too. I don't know. Later on, when I was busted, this guy came in with the FBI and said, 'That's him! That's him! I'll never forget him! His hair was gray, but that's him!' He'd have killed me if he could have got through the bars.

"So I leave. Now I'm so wired. There were a lot of whorehouses in Nevada. They're legal. I stopped at the nearest one. I picked this one girl. We go in the room. I see she's got tracks. I said, 'Hey, have I got a present for you!' And like an idiot I whip out the works and some good shit, and I turn her on, and I turn on. And she says, 'What the hell kind of general are you?' A dope-fiend general!

"That was a big mistake. The FBI traced me to that place and figured out who the general was. Rodney!

"I was going east. I stopped at Provost, Utah. I put on the uniform again. Walked into a bank. Got a check. Fixed it up with a check machine. I asked for the bank manager. I got one who said, 'Oh yes sir!' and wanted to take me to lunch. Cashed a check for $1800. I did that almost cross country. Every time I had to go into a bank, I'd put the uniform on.

"I was running and running, and more strung out. You always need money when you're not working and you're shooting drugs and running from place to place and hiding. It's very expensive.

"That life is a horror, a 24-karat horror. By then I was strung out on the depressant, which was heroin, or morphine or Dilaudid, and I was always shooting methedrine. It came in little vials. You go up and down and in and out, and you're very paranoid. I was very forlorn. You think, 'When is this going to end?' You almost ask to be caught.

"There was nothing east for me. I couldn't work. This was 1965, and the whole jazz scene had changed. I drove back west. I was in bad shape. I had gone through a lot of the money and I was thinking of new avenues. And I got busted in San Francisco copping. I went to somebody's place to cop and crash! the door came in. They were there to bust the connection. They took me in and of course they found out who I was and that I was wanted by the feds.

"They put me in the San Francisco County jail. They sent a guy from Washington. They freaked out. This guy asked me about the securities and other pieces of parchment papers I'd taken. It was gobbledygook. He said, 'Have you got 'em?' I said, 'Yeah, Bank of America, in a safety deposit box.'

"He said, 'If you'll give them back, we won't charge you with the imper-sonation or the theft. We'll just turn you over to the narcotics bureau, and you'll get tried for the narcotics charge.'

"I had to sign something to let them get into the box. It was not very far from where I was. I had all kinds of things in there. They got them all out and they gave me back what didn't have anything to do with them—like, for example, a check writer, which I had no use for in jail.

"The papers they wanted were classified information. I had no idea. They made the deal with me. They wanted to make a deal anyway. They didn't want the publicity either. Penetrating a secured area. They wanted to keep it out of the papers.

"But one of the detectives there was a friend of mine named Jim Hurley, a trumpet player. He's retired now. He was telling the reporters, 'This guy's a great trumpet player.' And they gave me a horn, and that picture was on the front page of the *San Francisco Chronicle*. There was another story in the *Examiner*. It was ridiculous, a side show. When I went back to the county jail the next day, I was a hero, everybody calling me 'General'.

"One of the papers had a story about the general; the other one had a story that Garfield Levy, Ronald Berger, and Robert Lehman, the stock broker, all were Red Rodney.

"I took the name Robert Lehman because there was a Robert Lehman, who was Governor Lehman's brother. And there was Lehman Brothers, investment bankers. The name sounded very good, in case I ever wanted to come up with a brokerage or stock scam, but I was never good enough to figure one out."

There is a great irony about this, which I pointed out. Maybe he couldn't figure it out, but Ivan Boesky and a few more got away with millions of dollars. Even that is as nothing to the collective handiwork of the manipulators who plundered an entire nation through the savings-and-loan institutions, comparatively few of whom have been charged with crimes, much less punished, and whose depredations ultimately will cost the American taxpayer upward of half a trillion dollars. Since they got away with it, and you and I will have to make up losses, they stole our money on a carom shot. Seen from this perspective, Red's thefts seem almost innocent by comparison.

"You were a callow amateur," I said.

Red laughed and said, "You're right. They're the real thieves."

All the names Red took, one will note, were Jewish, a fact not lost on some of the authorities who questioned him: "The FBI guy said, 'Well, you're very loyal to the Jews.' I said, 'Of course! Who thinks of them as committing crimes?'

"If I'd gone to trial, I'd have lost anyway and got a big sentence. So I made a deal. I pled guilty to the narcotics charge and I got five years. And the five years wound up being twenty-three months. They sent to me the Fort Worth Public Health Service hospital. It was not a prison then. I had a beautiful room. Now it's a prison. Lexington and Fort Worth have become correctional institutions. Ever since the methadone programs came out, they didn't need any more government treatment centers, as they were called.

"After I finished that sentence, I was back in Las Vegas. I had no teeth, I was in bad shape. I was able to play fourth trumpet in a show band there. It was horrible. It was a tough period, and I was strung out again. And I went back to the insurance fraud, figuring they're not going to bust me anyway. This time they did.

"I was living in my aunt's house in Las Vegas. I had a nephew—he was really my cousin, but because of the age difference, I thought of him as my nephew. He was going to college and found a little apartment and moved out. He had some insurance. It was a college policy, a lot of money for a little bit of premium money, and it was double indemnity in case he got killed. My aunt, his mother, was the beneficiary.

"She was very sick at the time. We had a joint bank account, she and I. I took care of everything, her Social Security money and her pension money. And it all went together. So it was very easy for me to do this. My nephew had the same name as his father, who had been killed. I took his father's death certificate and I copied it. The copy I made was better than the original. And I had that official state stamp. When I declared my nephew dead and got all the documented evidence that he was dead, and killed in an accident at that, the check came to her. I just deposited it. Forty thousand dollars.

"The fraud was great, the scam was great. They couldn't get me. But they came around and said, 'We're going to get her. Now you cop to it or we're taking her.' So what was I going to do? And I was ready then. This time I knew if they put me away, I'd never mess up again. I wasn't going to let them take my aunt, even though she probably would have got a probation. She's still alive, by the way; she's ninety. She didn't even know what the hell happened. I had to tell her. I copped to it. Pled guilty. They gave me three years."

But he wouldn't serve even that much time. Furthermore, he went not to a prison but back in Lexington, where he encountered a sympathetic warden, as he had so often encountered sympathetic cops and FBI men.

Red recounted: "Now I'd been there three times as a volunteer, long before I ever started any criminal activities. And now I was ready. This was 1976–77. The warden at Lexington was a nice guy. Warden Rauch. He had come from a tough penitentiary, McNeil Island. And he's suddenly at a place like Lexington, that was co-ed! He sees girls sitting there with practically nothing on, sunning themselves, walking up and down the yard with their boyfriends—no physical contact. That was a no-no.

"Once the word got around that I was there, one of the disc jockeys at the University of Kentucky called and asked for me. And then the school asked for me. The warden finally called me in and said, 'What is this about?'

"I told him, and he said, 'I think it's good community relations for you to go out. And this is a community-custody institution anyway, so we'll have to get you your proper classification, and you can go.'

"So then I was going to the University of Kentucky, giving a little jazz theory class. One of the professors—who was also the head of the dental school—played saxophone. He got me out to play with the University of Kentucky pep bands for the basketball games.

"A great trumpet player named Vince Di Martino was a professor of trumpet there. He got me to do classes, to speak. I would get out a lot. The warden would laugh and say, 'Hey, you think you could spend the weekend with us this week, Rodney?' And I'd say, 'Well, I'll have to see my schedule, Warden Rauch.' He loved that.

"By now I was forty-eight or forty-nine. I _knew_ that once I got out of there, I'd never mess up.

"The parole board came, and they weren't going to let me go. You know, those guys who work on the parole board are former employees of the prisons. They're Bureau of Prisons people. They may have been unit managers or hacks or guards or whatever. My unit manager went with me to the parole board. It was, 'Hey, Jim, Harry, how are you?' They all knew each other. They said, 'What are you doing here?' He said, 'I'm here for this man. I want him out.'

"I made parole. It was cut and dried: you've got a year more to do. Which was great: it gave me twenty-three months, and three months before that I went to a half-way house in New York.

"Remember the Bryant Hotel at 54th and Seventh? It was like a flophouse. Musicians used to stay there. Years ago it was nice. That became the half-way house. And that's where I was. From there I looked out and I said, 'This is going to be tough.' Here I am thrown into New York with very little money. In the back of my mind, I still thought I would go back to Las Vegas. I still had some leaders who would put me in their bands. But I said, 'No, man, I don't want that. If I'm going to play, I want to play jazz.'

"I was downright scared. I had no teeth. I needed implants, which were very expensive. This was 1979.

"I didn't know what I could do when I got out of the half-way house. I knew only that I wanted to get back into jazz and do the best I could. I had no idea that anything good was going to happen. I just knew that there would be no more nefarious activities."

And at this point Red's life changed completely. The woman's name was Helene Strober. She was then a buyer of women's wear for the 2000-store Woolco chain, which meant she had a great deal of power in the garment district of New York, that crowded and shabby area, not far south of Times Square, of narrow streets and double-parked trucks where workmen push carts full of dresses hanging from horizontal poles along the sidewalks from one establishment to another. It is incredibly busy in the daytime, bleakly deserted at night.

Red said, "I knew two garment manufacturers and a Mafia guy, trucking guys from the garment center, who were in the half-way house for income tax when I was there. They befriended me. One time they said, 'We want you to go to dinner with us. There's a lady we want you to meet. Be nice to her, she's very important to us. She's a buyer with a big pencil.' I didn't know what a buyer was.

"That's how I met Helene. That was the first date. I'm sure at first she thought, 'Who is this so-called musician who was in jail for something?'

And then we talked and I told her why. Another date, and I took her to a jazz club. And they introduced me. She didn't know anything about it, but I guess she thought, 'Somebody must know him.'

"After the half-way house, I planned to get my own apartment. But I moved in with Helene. Out of a flophouse to a gorgeous apartment.

"My first gig was in a restaurant called Crawdaddy's at the Roosevelt Hotel. It was only a trio gig: piano, bass, and me. An old publicist named Milton Karle, long dead, who had Stan Kenton and Nat King Cole, got me the gig. And on piano I hired Garry Dial, who was then twenty-three. That was the beginning of a long association. We worked there five or six weeks. We did good business, because Helene had the place packed with garment center people. The job was 6 to 11; they'd finish work and come over. The manager wanted us back quickly.

"She had her natural mother instinct. Here I was in trouble, just getting out of it. She saw that I was really trying. She watched it very carefully at first. By the time we were ready to get married, she knew everything was fine.

"I was very lucky, because now I didn't need to take any other kind of work. I got my teeth taken care of. I needed endodontic implants. I still had some teeth on the bottom. They could do root canal and put steel pins in. A dentist in New York did them for me. He said, 'If you're lucky, they'll last five years.' They lasted five years. By that time, I needed new implants, a kind they developed in Sweden, which I've got now. They're great.

"My chops were good. I started working. I went to a gig in Florida and we bought an apartment in Boynton Beach. Ira Sullivan had the house band in the place, Bubba's, in Fort Lauderdale. I spoke to Ira. I said, 'I'm supposed to go into the Village Vanguard. Why don't you come in with me?' I talked him into it. He never traveled. So we had a band together for almost five years, Rodney-Sullivan. Garry Dial on piano. We had Joey Baron on drums for a while. My favorite kid, man, he was sensational. I started recording quite a bit, some for Muse, some for Elektra Musician, for Bruce Lundvall."

The association of Sullivan and Rodney was to produce a series of memorable albums.

"I was finding much more success than I did in my early life," Red said. "And of course I was now a much more mature person, a healthier person, one who knew what the pitfalls were, and one who knew the advantages of a clean, healthy, good home life. It took many years for me to straighten my life out. But once I did, my career went along with it. Today, I guess I would say it's a human triumph. That's the term I would use.

"Because I really hit rock bottom. I neglected all of the talent I had. When I did play, it was in show-room orchestras and funny bands in Las Vegas. The crimes I committed were outrageous, outlandish. They may seem funny. And they are funny, when you look back and say, 'Wow. This guy had the balls to do all of this?'

"It wasn't balls so much. The improvisational quality was there, of course. But I realized, 'Hey, I got nothing to *lose*. I'm in bad trouble anyway.' And when I did get caught, it wasn't that bad. I *needed* that rest."

Red was sitting on a low sofa in the basement of his home on the bank of a stream in New Milford, New Jersey. With his stocky body and almost full head of wavy red hair, he looked like a bank manager or the owner of an automobile dealership. It was late February, and to his right, beyond a picture window, a premature spring was coming up in the garden. Clear water flowed full in the creek, and a dusting of green tinted the faded winter lawn. Red said:

"I think going through that kind of ordeal makes a kinder person. You're more sensitive to other people and human frailty and to other people's feelings and thoughts and ambitions and desires. And you're also more alert to people's needs. You know, you'll find someone in the audience who can't wait for you to finish and to come over and talk to you. Well, years ago, I'd just say 'Thank you' and walk away. Now I realize this man perhaps needs to talk to me, so I'll give him a little time. I find that most of the time I'm right, that they need it.

"You know, adversity stinks. Adversity usually knocks a person down forever. But if someone can overcome and bounce back from adversity— and not many do—then it makes you a better person, a much more understanding person. Believe me, adversity is a horror. And I'm not going to say I was an exceptional person, or exceptionally strong, because I don't think I was, or am. I think I was very lucky.

"Now my ability, of course, is not luck. That had to be nurtured. And when I stopped playing, I didn't play well. When I started playing again, all of those years of pent-up frustration of not playing came out. And that is one reason I am playing better now in these last twelve years than I've ever played."

"How much do you practice?" I asked.

"Ummm, not as much as I should," Red said, which is an answer to that question you'll hear frequently from musicians. "When I'm off, I should practice more. I'm not a practicer. Many guys are. Like, a Buddy De Franco. All the time, he's practicing. It's not good. The first night I go to a gig, I suffer! Is the sunlight in your eyes?"

"Not really," I said.

"Yes it is," he said, and got up to draw a curtain against the afternoon sun. He sat down again.

"By now, I've been back in the music scene for twelve years and what I hope is the next thirty or forty years. My sights are squarely set on making the best music I can make, embracing all of the newer forms of jazz that specifically fit my style. I'm not going to take anything that sounds like snake-charmin' music and fit that in, because it doesn't fit in.

"So that's what's happening to me now. I'm enjoying a nice run of success. The music I'm involved in, I'd like to say it's bebop of the '90s, but it's even a little more. I think I'm leaping into the twenty-first century, using the new electronic instruments, but being me. We're playing jazz and using those instruments as colorations. I don't want to do what other experimenters have done, even though they've been very successful, like Weather Report. And they're very good. I just don't want it that way.

"And even what Wayne Shorter is doing—I don't think that's jazz. It's very good, very neatly done and marketed and packaged. But I don't hear the Wayne Shorter I love. I may not be right. But certainly I want to try it this way and keep growing. And I'm taking the younger players, because I think they've got so much more to offer me. I offer them the roots and tradition, but what they can offer, I can take. One thing I've learned. Whatever they bring in, I usually am in charge of arranging it, without writing down a note. So I do rearrange everything.

"Having been with Charlie Parker did me a world of good. But what I did before is not what I'm working on and how I'm getting my work today. Life isn't lived yesterday. If I had to live through yesterday, I think I'd commit suicide. I look back at all these things and say, 'Oh my God! How could I have done that? It's not me, it's a different person.'

"Yet, when I look at it realistically, all I can say is, 'Well it was me.' I'm very proud that I could overcome this. I didn't expect anything.

"I've seen so many very fine players never come back: lose their health, lose their ability to play, lose their careers, then lose their lives.

"This in a sense was not planned. It was hoped-for. I didn't expect to accomplish this much."

I asked Red about his wife, who was away at work, in Manhattan.

"My wife," he said, "is a very nice lady, six years younger than I, a business woman. She's very sensible. She didn't know anything about jazz until she met me. She's given me a whole new life, and she's also made it possible for me to stay in jazz without having to embrace club dates or weddings and bar mitzvahs and whatever else you had to play to make a living. She could afford me not to work until things came along.

"We've both developed in this marriage. She didn't know anything about me. She gradually learned. She's no longer a buyer. She works for a big manufacturer. She now sells to the buyers who were her friends.

"In colleges," Red said, "all of the kids ask me about the drug years. I'm up front about drugs. I always let them know that it was very heavy in jazz during the late '40s, through the '50s, and into the '60s.

"I love it today. There are no drugs in jazz today. It's all in rock-and-roll. These kids have learned from us what not to do as well as what to do. Today, smoking is unsociable, which is great.

"The young musicians are very serious. They're involved. One good thing about music in the schools: Learning music teaches you how to learn. I would say 75 percent of the kids in the music programs will never embrace music as a profession. But it will help them in learning whatever they choose as a profession.

"Art Blakey said, 'If you pass through this life without hearing this music, you've missed a great deal.' And this is very true.

"Our fans listen to our music with their ears and not their feet. Sure, a taste has to be acquired for our music, just as it does for classical music. You have to listen for a while before you see the value and the beauty of this music. That's why it'll probably never have mass popularity, like rock-and-roll.

"But at this stage of my life, I'm glad it doesn't. I would rather play for the select, special few than for a mass. You know, rock gets worse every year. It doesn't get better. The old rock-and-roll bands—and they were never good either—were better than the new ones. Whereas the new young jazz players coming up are very proficient, they're educated, they play their instruments beautifully.

"Clark Terry, Nat Adderley, Snooky Young, and I just judged the Thelonious Monk Foundation's Louis Armstrong trumpet competition. The winner was a seventeen-year-old kid from Sioux City, Iowa, named Ryan Kisor. He was magnificent. But the others, all nineteen of them, were magnificent. I told the *Washington Post*, 'I would not want to have been a contestant in this contest.' And the others agreed. The one who won was top of the line, but he wasn't that far ahead of the last of these trumpeters. They were so great. We sat there and laughed, saying, 'Look what the hell we're confronted with. Look what's happening to the trumpet.' These kids, no one ever told them, 'You can't do this,' so they go right ahead and do it. They're more proficient, they're technically better. They do everything better than those in my generation. Now of course they've got to learn how to play with experience, how to play with ensembles, which they will. But I can see from that contest what the trumpet players are going to be playing like ten years from now.

"And this is not only happening with the trumpet. The music is just going to perpetuate itself. The players are going to get better and better and better. The writers are going to get better. It's going to be great.

"I want to embrace it. I want to continue with it as long as I can stand up and hold the horn. We're not supposed to be moldy figs. We're supposed to keep two ears open."

In the early evening of Friday, June 18, 1993, Red performed in a two-fluegelhorn duet with Clark Terry in a huge tent on the lawn of the White House, during a concert presented by President Bill Clinton. He played magnificently. That was the last time I saw him.

A few months later, he told me on the telephone that he had an inoperable lung cancer for which he was receiving chemotherapy. He was so short-winded that he could not play. "My job right now is trying to save my life," he said during one of several talks; he was remarkably cheerful. "But if I go down, I'm going down fighting." And so he did.

Red died on a morning in May, 1994. Mort Fega, the disc jockey, told me, "My biggest fear was that he'd suffer. Thank God he was properly medicated at the end.

"There was a memorial service in Delray Beach. It was a lovely observance, and the chapel was standing room only. Red's son, Jeff, spoke about his father with great respect and love.

"A few months before, Red asked me to deliver his eulogy. I feel especially honored to have been chosen by him, and I spoke my thoughts with truth, affection, and the hurt that comes with losing a longtime, valued friend.

"It will comfort all of Red's friends to know that his departure, so painful to all of us who loved him, was free of pain for him. He was such a gentle man."

March 1991

The Philadelphia
Connection:
Benny Golson

The role of cities in the development of jazz seems not to have been examined in the history books. In the early days, New Orleans was the primary incubator of jazz musicians, but in the 1920s Chicago, after a kind of mass migration of jazz players to that turbulent Mecca in the north, took over that role. It has consistently turned out major jazz players, and a glance through any of the standard biographical dictionaries suggests that only New York produces more of them. Part of this is a function of demographics. New York has the largest population of any American city, and Chicago long was in this regard its second, although that increasingly dubious honor has devolved on Los Angeles, which lies there in a basin of subtropical smog slowly strangling in its own effluents.

Often you can trace the genesis of a body of jazz musicians to a particular school, such as Cass Tech in Detroit, which has turned out fine players, from Donald Byrd and Frank Rosolino to Geri Allen, for decades. And there are subtle regional styles of playing. Chicago, many of whose jazz musicians have owed their careers to the inspiration of a single teacher, Captain Walter Dyett at Wendell Phillips High School, since the early days has produced jazz players of a particular feeling: strong, tough, and individual, like the city itself, players of a nature that reminds one of what Carl Sandberg called it, the city of the big shoulders.

Davenport, on the eastern border of Iowa, abutting Illinois and due west of Chicago, produced only one important jazzman, although that one was of a stature to give the city forever a place of honor in jazz history, namely Bix Beiderbecke. Council Bluffs is at the western side of Iowa, right on the Nebraska border, and it produced two jazz musicians: the twins Art and Addison Farmer. They did not develop there, however; they spent their childhood in Phoenix, Arizona, and then moved to Los Angeles, attending another of those incubator schools, Jefferson High, where they came under the influence of Samuel Browne.

Pittsburgh, in the extreme west of Pennsylvania, the birthplace of Art Blakey, Billy Eckstine, and Billy May, and home in a formative period for Billy Strayhorn (who went to high school and got much of his training there), produced a lot of jazz musicians. American states are bigger than most European countries, and Philadelphia, a long drive to the eastern side of Pennsylvania, has little in common with Pittsburgh, except that it too contributed a large number of players to the roster of jazz musicians:

Donald Bailey, Kenny Barron, Joe Beck, Mike and Randy Brecker, Ray Bryant, Stanley Clarke, Warren Covington, Ted Curson, Spanky De Brest, Bill Doggett, Ziggy Elman, Stan Getz, Bill Harris, Tootie and Jimmy Heath, Gregory Herbert, Billy Kyle, Eddie Lang, John LaPorta, Jimmy McGriff, Lee Morgan, Paul Motian, Tommy Potter, Luckey Roberts, Red Rodney, Jimmy Rowser, Rex Stewart, Lew Tabackin, McCoy Tyner, Charlie Ventura, Jimmy Woode, Reggie Workman.

And Benny Golson.

In addition, the city was the home during formative years of a number of important players, including Joe Venuti, Johnny Coles, Gerry Mulligan, and Joe Wilder. In part this fecundity can be traced to the work of a particular institution, the Granoff Studios, where a number of Philadelphians got the solid classical training so widely assumed not to be part of the making of jazz musicians.

Jazzmen often reveal a preference for the professional company of natives of their hometowns. This is not to be ascribed to regional chauvinism or racism. It probably has to do with compatibility or even mere familiarity. Everyone knows you cannot just throw three persons together and get a rhythm section; there must be a consensus about time and dynamics and other things, and sometimes one more readily achieves it with those who grew up in your own cultural ambiance. Witness the devoted association of the late Pepper Adams with Donald Byrd, the latter still angry that Pepper didn't get the recognition Donald thinks he deserves.

Whether he is consciously aware of it, Benny Golson has often revealed in his professional associations a taste for the company of hometown boys, although his most celebrated association over the years has been with the aforementioned Arthur Farmer. It was Art with whom Benny founded and co-led the Jazztet in 1959 and then revived it in the 1980s. It was a group that featured outstanding writing by Golson, and some striking soloists, including Curtis Fuller and Benny's fellow Philadelphians McCoy Tyner and

Tootie Heath. Curtis Fuller gets just about the biggest sound ever heard from a trombone, and he was integral to the original Jazztet. When he left the group, he proved irreplaceable.

Golson was a highly lyrical tenor player whose sound, since his return to the jazz world after a long absence, has become rougher, deeper, and bigger. He is an outstanding soloist. Yet from the beginning his playing was over-shadowed by his writing, and he has contributed a substantial body of compositions to the jazz catalogue. His tunes include *Stablemates*, which Miles Davis established in the repertoire, the lovely *Whisper Not*, *Along Came Betty*, *Blues March*, and *Are You Real?* His tunes are characterized by a simplicity that will fool you. It is their harmonic elegance that makes them popular with jazz players. His *I Remember Clifford*, an *homage* to his friend Clifford Brown, is one of the loveliest of all jazz ballads, and it has been widely recorded.

Benny's writing remains a forte and is the primary source of his income. He gets not only the royalties of his jazz standards but also those from the performances of all the television shows for which he wrote scores during his many years in the Hollywood film industry.

Benny went to the west coast during that period when jazz had become fashionable in film scoring. He was far from being the first black musician to penetrate that profession. Benny Carter wasn't even the first; that distinc-tion belongs to Will Vodery, who had got into film scoring by the 1930s. But when Benny Carter did it, such was the nature of the bias in the industry that he was assigned largely to writing arrangements for black singers when they appeared in film.

By the time Benny Golson got into film, Oliver Nelson had already done so, along with a number of white jazz composers such as Johnny Mandel. Then J. J. Johnson began scoring films and television. Jazz had arrived in Hollywood.

Its day appears to be over. The synthesizer has ruined film scoring, not to mention what it has done to employment in the west-coast music industry. A great many jazz musicians, composers and players alike, have gone back to playing jazz, J. J. Johnson, Roger Kellaway, Herb Ellis, and Bud Shank among them. Along with Benny Golson, who now lives most of the time back in New York, although he still maintains his home in the Hancock Park district of Los Angeles. His four children are in their thirties and forties.

I met Benny, another of the Art Blakey alumni, when I met Arthur Farmer, that is to say when they formed the Jazztet in 1959. Their manager, Kay Norton, called me when I was editor of *Down Beat* to solicit publicity for the group. The mating of two such talents with that of Curtis Fuller seemed eminently noteworthy to me, even if the name McCoy Tyner didn't yet mean much. Norton, a tall and handsome blonde who lived on New York City's fashionable Upper East Side, was well-liked in the business, worked hard for the Jazztet, and died some years ago after a protracted bout with cancer. I arranged a photo by the imaginative photographer Ted Williams—he shot them in elegant suits, holding their instruments, in the rubble of a south side Chicago apartment building that was being razed—and I put it on the cover. Arthur and I became fast friends and have remained so.

In February, 1991, I dropped by to spend a pleasant afternoon with Benny at his apartment in the West 90s of New York City. It was tastefully and simply appointed with mostly modern furniture. Its windows commanded views of the towers of Manhattan, receding in planes of aerial perspective to the south, and the glinting Hudson River and New Jersey on the west. I asked Benny questions I had never had occasion to raise, and he answered joyously, warmly, and with humor. The dynamics of his speech are broad, ranging from conspiratorial secretive whispers to bursts of laughter. His face is round and animated, and he is fairly shiny on top.

He was born January 25, 1929. "My parents were non-musical," he said. "And non-academic. Intuitive. My mother and father separated early on. I never remember living with him. Years later we got together. My mother's gone now and I sort of watch out for him.

"My mother was my champion. If I'd said I wanted to go to the moon, she'd have tried to figure out a way to get me there. She was very supportive. We didn't have much money. Piano lessons were 75 cents. That was quite an outlay at that time. She was getting six dollars a week in tips as a waitress. We'd just come off of welfare, and 75 cents a week was something. One week the piano teacher came and my mother asked him to come out to the kitchen. She didn't want me to hear. I found out about this years later. She told him she didn't have the 75 cents. He said, 'Mrs. Golson, don't worry about the 75 cents. I think Benny really has talent. Don't ever do anything to stop him. Let him go ahead to reach his full potential.'

"And he gave me my lesson. After that he would let me come out to his house. I'd go spend the weekend there. He'd have this music together. His godson came. We went to elementary school together. His godson would be out playing stick ball, and I'd be inside having an adventure going through all this music he had on the piano. Going through it and trying to play it, all day long. He had all kinds of stuff. You name it.

"That was my pleasure. It was an adventure to me. He told my mother.

"I got to be a good reader. I can still read pretty well on the piano.

"And then I heard Lionel Hampton. He featured a guy named Arnett Cobb. I took a day off from school when I wasn't supposed to. I went down to the Earl Theater in Philadelphia. And when that curtain opened up, my life changed—dramatically. The bandstand rolled forward. The lights made the horns sparkle, playing a flag-waver. I was in awe. And when Arnett Cobb stepped out there to play that solo on *Flying Home*, all the kids were screaming. I was screaming emotionally, inside. That did it. Earl Bostic was in the band, too, playing snakes. The snakes didn't get me, but Arnett Cobb did!

"I told him about eight years ago that he was the one responsible for me playing saxophone. And tears came into his eyes and he said, 'I never knew that.'"

"Time and again you'll hear something like that from musicians," I said. "Horace Silver said it was hearing the Jimmie Lunceford band at an amusement park in Connecticut. Lou Levy said it was hearing the Glenn Miller band at a dance in Chicago."

"Speaking of Glenn Miller," Benny said, "I was the only person in the whole black neighborhood listening to that band. And that was my favorite band. Nobody could understand."

"Billy Mitchell told me the same thing," I said.

"Tex Beneke was my hero!" Benny said. "I wrote a letter to him about two months ago."

"Henry Mancini told me Tex Beneke was one of the finest tenor players technically he ever worked with."

"I knew it well," Benny said. "The arrangements! Some of them were pearls. Really. *Chattanooga Choo Choo, In the Mood*! I liked Count Basie. Duke Ellington at that time I didn't understand. A little arty for me, a little artistic. Basie was more straight-ahead. Jimmie Lunceford. Trummy Young was with him. *Cheatin' on Me, Blues in the Night Parts 1 and 2*. Then I started to really get into it and broaden out.

"My mother didn't have the money to buy me a tenor saxophone."

I asked what a good tenor would cost today.

"Don't even mention it!" Benny said "Three thousand dollars, maybe more. We were talking even then five or six hundred bucks. I couldn't get a saxophone. So what I did was, at night, I'd do my homework and turn the radio on and listen to the jockeys play the music and listen for all the tenor solos. I became a fan of Eddie Miller, Bud Freeman, Chu Berry, Coleman Hawkins, Ben Webster with Duke on *Raincheck*. *What Am I Here For?*— things like that. *Cotton Tail*.

"One day my mother came home from work. And she had this thing in her hand. And I was looking. And I said, It can't be. And my heart was beating. And she got closer and she said, 'Guess what I got for you, baby. A saxophone.' It was a brand new one that she bought at Wurlitzer. And it happened to be a good one, a Martin saxophone.

"I was beside myself. I was ecstatic instantly. Then I realized when I opened it up that I didn't even know how to put it together."

If there is a common condition in the lives of major musicians, it is the support of parents, one or both of them. Sometimes a gifted teacher plays an important role too, but for the most part it will be found the one thing major musicians tend to share is an early start supported and encouraged by a parent.

"There was another friend of mine who lived near my aunt," Benny continued, "a fellow named Tony Mitchell. He showed me how to put the saxophone together, how to put in the reed and the strap and everything. I said, 'Play something!' I wanted to hear my horn, I wanted to hear my horn speak! He played the Ben Webster solo on *Raincheck*. I couldn't believe it. He said, 'Try it.'

"I put it on. It sounded like an insane mule. Nothing.

"My mother arranged for me to take lessons at Wurlitzer. And it turned out that this guy, Raymond Ziegler, used to play with Charlie Barnet. He'd decided to just settle down in Philadelphia. He was a good teacher, and I got a lot out of him. Right away we got into what the saxophone was all about. I spent so much time on what the instrument was all about, reading and transposing and stuff like that, that I couldn't play solos.

"After about four months, I joined a little band. We were playing stocks, of course. Another guy was the soloist. This started to concern me as the months rolled by. They said, 'Black people got rhythm, and they can *play*.'

"I said, 'I can't do a thing!'

"Then there was another band I started to play with. The bandleader said, 'Go see so-and-so, he'll show you.' But I didn't realize: nobody can show you how to play solos. Unless you copy what they're playing. But eventually I learned. By trial and error. Syllogistic reasoning. I arrived at it. I became very eclectic, like all beginners."

"But of course," I said. "That's how we assimilate techniques. Imitation is a vitally important phase of training."

"Yeah, absolutely! I was sounding like everybody. First time I heard Bill Evans, he sounded like Milt Buckner. Next time I heard him he sounded like Bill Evans. I said, 'Bill, what happened?' He said, 'Well, it was time for a change.' We used to laugh about that. He was playing with Herbie Fields when I knew him. He was patting his feet. He locked both legs together, and he lifted his heels up. And that's the way he played, he bounced on the seat like Milt Buckner. When I saw him again, he was so smooth, and he had this other thing going.

"You go through it."

It was during his early years of playing that Benny met one of the important figures in his life, one who was to influence his career.

He said, "When I was in high school, a friend of mine who lived in the Projects, where Bill Cosby is from, said, 'There's a fellow in the Projects who plays alto just like Johnny Hodges.' I said, 'Bring him by.'

"Sure enough, next day he knocked on the door, and he came with this fellow. He was standing there, and I said, 'Play something for me.' Me! As though I'm an authority." Benny mocked himself with laughter. "So he whipped out his horn, put it together. Johnny Hodges was his idol. So you know what he played? *On the Sunny Side of the Street*. My mother heard it. She said, 'Who is that?' I said, 'Oh, it's a new fellow I just met. His name is John Coltrane.'

"My mother heard John play and said, 'He sounds great!'

"John Coltrane and I became fast friends. John was like a country bumpkin at that time. Very quiet. He was from North Carolina. Any time I wanted to have a session, John would come, Ray Bryant would come. And my mother would holler downstairs and say, 'Is John there?' And he would say, 'Yes, Mis' Golson.' And he knew he would have to play *On the Sunny Side of the Street*. And then the session could start.

"We were together every day, just the two of us. He would come by. There was a big old stuffed chair by the window. He'd sit there and put the alto together. I would try to play some kind of chords for him on the piano. Terrible. And then he would try to play chords for me, which was even worse. He was eighteen and I was sixteen.

"We wound up playing in a lot of local bands together. Jimmy Johnson's big band. And we would live for those gigs, just playing out in the public. Even though we were playing stock arrangements. By Spud Murphy and Val Alexander. I remember one day we were looking forward to playing a gig. And the bandleader told us it had been canceled. We thought this was kind of strange. And the night of the gig, we were sitting down in my living room, looking at each other. My mother said, 'Why are you looking so dejected?' I said, 'We were supposed to play this job, and it's been canceled.' And she said, in her wisdom, 'It sounds to me like he didn't want you to play tonight. If I were you, I would walk down there and just see what's going on.' John looked at me and I looked at him. And we walked. We walked everywhere because we didn't have money for carfare. So we walked over there. It was only about six blocks. And as we approached, we heard the band playing!

"It was in the basement of this building. In order to see, you'd have to lay down on the ground and when they opened the door you could see down the steps. You have to imagine this. We lay down on the ground and looked, and it was them! He'd cut the band down from a big band to a sextet.

"We were really down in the dumps. After we walked back to my house, we sat down. My mother came down and John said, 'You were right, Mis' Golson.' She said, 'Look, don't worry, sweethearts. One day both of you are going to be so good that that band will not be able to afford you.'

Benny laughed. "We didn't see that in the near future. They were just words at that time.

"Years later, we were up playing the Newport Festival. John had his quartet by then, with Elvin Jones, McCoy Tyner, and Jimmy Garrison. John started laughing, and said, 'Remember when we had that gig and got canceled out? Remember what your mother said? Do you think they'd be able to afford us now? And do you remember that time you came in the Ridge Point and caught me on the bar, walking the bar?' I remember it well. He was walking on the bar, horn in hand, stepping over drinks. As I came in, he had his foot poised, stepping over a drink, and he saw me, and he took his horn out of his mouth and said, 'Oh no!' I just about died laughing.

"We had rhythm-and-blues gigs like that. He was with Daisy May and the Hep Cats, where they were singing. I had gigs doing the same thing, playing with Trudy Briscoe. She was playing the cocktail drums and singing *Rag Mop* and I was singing. But hey! Until we got a chance to do something else. He'd gotten into the tenor by then."

Coltrane, one of those who studied at the Granoff Studios, gained experience in bands led by Joe Webb, King Kolax, Earl Bostic, and Johnny Hodges, along with some obscure groups. Benny went off to Howard University in Washington, D.C.

"I was not an A student in high school, but I had good enough marks," he said. "A friend of mine who played alto was going there. He was telling me, 'Oh it's great!' Even though he was in liberal arts, he was telling me what he saw in the music school. I didn't want to be a music teacher, but that's what was set up for me. Music education. It's a cover-all.

"I went to take my entrance exam. I prepared this thing. I worked on it diligently on the saxophone. Something by Rudy Wiedoeft. He was a very legit, very technical saxophonist. Rudy Wiedoeft, Marcel Mule, Dick Stabile, Al Galladoro, these guys were technicians. Al Galladoro was probably the best I ever heard in my life, my entire life. He used to play for Paul Whiteman. This guy was unreal. He must have been from Mars. Double tonguing, triple tonguing. He used to play under Ormandy, he used to play jazz. He could improvise. He was on a weekly radio show, he played a *Flight of the Bumble Bee* on the clarinet that was breathtaking. He was amazing. I felt an effervescence inside when I heard this guy. This guy from the past turned me upside down. I've heard him within the last year, and I've talked to him on the phone. He put Rudy Wiedoeft to shame, but at that time I was listening to Rudy Wiedoeft.

"Anyway, I went down to Howard with my saxophone. They let me play the piece. And then they told me, very nicely, 'No saxophones here. Only clarinet. Legit.'

"So I had to lay the saxophone aside, and do *allll* the work, *allll* the practicing, all the things I wanted to do on the saxophone, on the clarinet. So at night, I would go down to the laundry room in the dormitory, shut the door, and transfer all the stuff to the saxophone. So it was double work for me, trying to learn how to get over the scales and things.

"I liked it down there because it was big, cement, had a nice echo—built-in echo. It made you sound better than you were. And that's what I did. They had practice rooms for the piano—no jazz.

"And then we got into the harmony. In the third year they were supposed to be doing some advanced stuff. And I'm really feeling like a rebel. So I go to the practice building early in the morning, around seven o'clock, before anybody was there. And the instructor for the violin had the office right across. And I kept playing this tune that I was trying to put together. I couldn't get the ending. And so I would start over again and get to the ending and stop. It didn't bother me. And all of a sudden I heard the door open across the hall and I said, 'Oh my God, he's here.' His name was Louis Vaughn, a classical violinist in charge of the violin department. And I was in trouble, because I wasn't supposed to be playing jazz there. He walked over to the piano and said, '*Resolve* it! Resolve it!' And he went out and slammed the door. And I knew I was all right with him."

I said, "From what you've told me in the past, and what I've heard from others, it seems that there was in the black academic community a deeper hostility to jazz than in the white community, reflecting a sort of aspiration to white middle-class respectability."

"Yes. Tell me about it!" Benny said. "That's what was going on. The director of the music school, Dean Lawson, his pride and joy was the choir. It was Mozart and whatever. All classical stuff. No jazz. And I had a job out in the city, off campus, playing jazz. They used to lock the dormitory door at night. The wall that prevented me from coming in was about eight feet high. And I had this gig. I went to play, and I had extra money. Instead of my mother sending me money, I was sending money home.

"There was a monitor at the door. I became very chummy with him. We worked it out so that he would let me in. And nobody would know about it, you see.

"One night, when I was up there playing, here comes Sterling Thomas, the one of the guys who taught theory. And he sat at the front table, right in front of the bandstand. It was terrible. I kept playing. But after the set was over, he said, 'That was really nice.'"

"So, then, the whole faculty wasn't opposed to jazz," I said. "It was just official policy. Somebody on top."

"Right," Benny said. "That's right. Fools in high places. Some of the teachers went along with it, but some didn't.

"At the end of my third year, I took *cantus firmus*." (The Latin term means "fixed melody." It refers to the practice of using an existing melody as the foundation of a polyphonic composition.) "I knew all the rules. I went home and my heart said, 'Why don't you do it like you feel it, like you hear it?' And I did. I broke the rules. It was then that I concluded that school teaches you the rules but experience tells you when to abandon them.

"I took the class the next day. There were only ten or twelve in the class. The teacher reviewed the work of each of us on the piano. She'd play and say, 'Oh, very nice, Mr. So-and-So.' And she started playing mine, and the red pencil went like the sword of Zorro! Swish. Swish. And she did it again. And again. Then she just *stopped*, and turned around, and said, 'Mr. Golson! What have you *done*?'

"And in my belligerent way, I stood up and said, 'That's the way I heard it.' And next day I packed up my car, and I was gone. I just left."

The incident reminded me of Debussy's encounter with Cesar Franck when the latter was his teacher at the Paris Conservatory. Franck was an extension of the German Romantic tradition, whose dominating influence on French music Debussy resented. Debussy objected to the methods of modulation by which the increasingly complex chromaticism was accommodated to common practice, and one day in class he rose to his feet, said indignantly, "Monsieur Franck, you are a modulating machine," and left.

Benny said, "I left Howard and Washington and went back to Philadelphia.

"I started working for a local band there. We were playing rhythm-and-blues type stuff. The leader would sing songs and we'd get up on the bar sometimes and walk the bar and put on funny hats.

"And then a guy named Bull Moose Jackson came through town. Some-body told him about me and he called and asked if I would be interested in joining the band. I said, 'Yeah!' This was an opportunity to get out of town.

"While I was with Bull Moose Jackson, I met Tadd Dameron. He was in the group. When I left Bull Moose Jackson, Tadd Dameron was putting together a band to play a show down in Atlantic City. He hired Philly Joe, Jymie Merritt, Johnny Coles, Clifford Brown, me, Gigi Gryce, Cecil Payne, and a couple of other people. When I left that situation, I joined Lionel Hampton. This was in 1953. With Lionel Hampton, I met Art Farmer, Quincy Jones, Monk Montgomery, Jimmy Cleveland. And of course Brownie and Gigi Gryce had been in the band in Atlantic City with us. We all left at the same time. Tadd had given the band up. I'm not going to tell you why. But the police were looking for him and he had to get out of town. . . ." The ellipsis, as it so often does in conversations with musicians who lived through that era, told the story. Tadd Dameron's problem was, alas and yet again, heroin. Dameron died in 1965 of cancer.

Benny continued, "I told the club owner, 'Okay, let him go, I'll stay here and make sure that the new guys have got the show down right.' When everybody had it down, then I split and went with Hamp.

"And the money was so *bad*! I think I stayed with him for all of two weeks. Later I wrote some music for Benny Goodman, and the way he negotiated the price, you'd have thought the man was poor." (Hampton and Goodman are often mentioned in the same paragraph by musicians who worked for both. Indeed, Hampton sometimes is referred to in black musical circles as "the black Benny Goodman.")

"I remember how Hamp used to jump on the tom-toms. I used to watch his heels digging into the heads. And one night we went daht-daht-daht daht-daht-daht-daaaah!" Benny sang the famous lick from *Flying Home*. "And boom! he went right through the big tom-tom. And it fell over and rolled, and he rolled. Right offstage. In front of the people." He laughed.

"Oh boy, the things we used to do with that band. During the summer-time, one of the guys used to wear these straw shoes, almost like women's shoes. And they used to kid him about the smell. And Lionel one night grabbed one of his shoes off and came by the reed section and waved it in front of our faces and said, 'Faint, Gates, faint!'

"This guy would go out and play a solo. He had like an act he got together. He would kick his foot up in the air and the shoe would fly off. Oh man. Sometimes we would go out off the stand and go marching around."

I said, "Al Grey told me they had a guy who specialized in walking on the backs of theater seats while playing."

"Oh yes," Benny said, laughing helplessly. "One night, one of the trumpet players, Emory Thompson, weighing 335 pounds. . . . They had a riser for the trumpet section, and he lost his balance, and when he tried to catch his balance, the whole trumpet section disappeared. Boom! They all went over backwards. Nobody but the trombones sitting back there.

"Regardless of the money, I'm glad I was with that band. It was really an experience. I wasn't on the Swedish trip."

That "Swedish trip" has assumed almost legendary proportions, largely because of a recording session that occurred in Stockholm. Art Farmer and Clifford Brown crept surreptitiously from their hotel and made an LP with Swedish musicians and the writing of Quincy Jones. The album enhanced the reputations of all those involved in it. Hampton was angry, apparently not because it had been made but because he had not been invited to be a part of it. But Farmer, Brown, and the others were all young, the new crowd, and Hampton was of an older school. For this exclusion, according to these witnesses, Hampton came close to firing the participants in Paris.

"I quit the band just before that trip. Me and my principles! I quit the band when it got to New York. I said to myself, 'Why are they going to Europe for that little bit of money?' Quincy sent me a letter from Stock-holm: 'We just did two record dates today, outside the band.' Then I got another card: 'We made an album last week. Sure wish you'd made it.' They made more money on the side than they did with the band.

"Philly Joe Jones had already left Philadelphia, but John Coltrane had not gone yet. Philly was older than us and played better than we did. He was quite a pro by then. Miles enjoyed Philly so much, he said, 'Do you know anybody?' Joe said, 'Yeah. His name is John Coltrane.' Miles said, 'Can he play?' Joe said—understatement of the world—'Yeah. He can play.' Later Miles came to love him.

"When John left, we all left vicariously with him. About two weeks after he joined Miles, I ran into John on Columbia Avenue, one of the main streets of North Philadelphia. I said, 'How's it going?' He said, 'Great. You know, Miles needs some tunes. Do you have any tunes?' Did I have any tunes! That's all I was doing, writing tunes. I gave him a tune that I had written for Herb Pomeroy, who was playing at the Stables up in Boston.

"After I'd been out on the road with Bull Moose Jackson, I went with Tiny Grimes, with Screamin' Jay Hawkins. Then I got into the Earl Bostic group. Blue Mitchell was in the band. Stan Turrentine had just left. John Coltrane had been in that band. Earl was a monster on that saxophone. John told me about it before I joined the band.

"While I was in Boston with Earl Bostic, I met Herb Pomeroy, who asked me to send him some tunes. I'd been writing a thing in bits and pieces. We would play an hour and a half and then take a half-hour intermission at these dances, one-nighters. I would stay on the bandstand and use that half hour. I finished this thing in Wilmington, Delaware, and sent it to Herb. Since he was playing at the Stables, I called the tune *Stablemates*.

"I gave this thing to John. Didn't think anything about it. And I ran into him about a month later. And he said, 'Remember that tune you gave me? Miles dug it. We recorded it.' I said, 'What?' I couldn't believe it. James Moody did my first recording, a thing called *Blue Walk*, but it didn't get any kind of acclaim. But wow! It was through John Coltrane and through Miles that I got put on the map as a composer. Because I'd been passing out music all across the country. Nothing ever happened. Now people went back and got those tunes, and they started recording my stuff like there was no tomorrow. And never stopped. And I kept writing. Of course, I have to tell you, I had a lot of dogs, too, that will never see the light of day. A lot of dogs in my piano bench.

"Eventually I moved to New York. I figured this was where all the action was. And it was. It was good for me. I did *Stablemates* in '55. And I moved to New York after I joined Dizzy. So that would make it '56. I'd been married, and now I was divorced. I started to gig, and worked with Dizzy in the big band. Quincy Jones, Lee Morgan, Wynton Kelly, Nelson Boyd, Billy Mitchell were in the band. Phil Woods. That's where I met Phil. I took Ernie Wilkins' place. Ernie had recommended me.

"I got a call from one of my idols, Art Blakey. He said, 'Look, I need a sub just for the night. Can you make it?' And he told me how much he'd pay. He didn't know it, but I'd have played for free. So we went down to the Cafe Bohemia and played. Bill Hardman was there and Spanky De Brest. And I really enjoyed it. And I thought that was it. Art said to me at the end of the night, 'Do you think you could make it tomorrow night?' I said, 'Oh yeah, I think I can make it.'

"And then the next night, he said, 'Look, do you think you can finish the week out?' I said, 'Yeah!'

"Now I was really into it. We finished the engagement. He said to me, 'Do you think you could make one week with us in Pittsburgh?'

"I thought, 'Well, one week is not so bad.' So I went to Pittsburgh with him. And just about the day before we closed, he said, 'We just got a call to go to Washington. Do you think you could make it one more week?' He suckered me little by little.

"So I went to Washington, and I'm glad I did, because I met my present wife, Bobbie. She was a ballet dancer. She was good, too. I went to see her a couple of times in Boston, and here, and Washington. But ballet wasn't good for black people at that time. That was 1958. It's still not that good.

"We came back to New York to do something. We went to the bar next door where the drinks were cheap. I didn't drink, but we used to congregate there."

Lowering his voice, Benny said, "Art was late all the time. He wasn't making any money. There were no uniforms. The guys, the habits were . . ." Again, the ellipsis, and Benny continued: "I said, 'Art, you should be a millionaire, with your kind of talent.' He looked at me with those sad, cow eyes, and he said . . . " Benny's voice dropped to a pathetic hopelessness: "He said, 'Can you help me?'

"I can't believe what I said to him!" Benny laughed at the memory of his own seeming audacity. "I said, 'Yes. If you do exactly what I tell you.'

"He said, 'What shall I do?'

"I said, 'Get a new band.'"

I asked, "Who was then in the band?"

"I'd rather not say," Benny replied.

One of them was Spanky De Brest, like Benny a native of Philadelphia. He died there at the age of thirty-six.

"Art said, 'Well, you tell 'em.'

"I said, 'No! *You* tell 'em.'

"He said, 'Who we gonna get?'

"I said, 'There's a young trumpet player from Philadelphia playing with Dizzy, named Lee Morgan. He's only eighteen years old.'

"He said, 'Can he play?'

"I said, 'Oh yeah, he can play.'

"He said, 'Who you got in mind for bass?'

"I said, 'There's another guy from Philadelphia, named Jymie Merritt.'"

Merritt had played in Philadelphia with Golson, Coltrane, and Philly Joe, and had been with Bull Moose Jackson. At the time Golson recommended him to Blakey, he was out of jazz, working in rhythm-and-blues.

"Art said, 'What about piano?'

"I said, 'There's another guy from Philadelphia. . . .'

"He said, 'What is this Philly stuff? Who is it?'

"'A guy named Bobby Timmons.'

"Then I said, 'Art, Small's Paradise doesn't want you back. You've got to set yourself separate and aside from the other groups that are playing. What's going to make you different from the guy down the street or next door?'

"He said, 'What can I do?'

"I said, 'You've got to get some new material.'

"He said, 'All right.'

"So I said, 'Let me write some things.' So I wrote *Along Came Betty, Are You Real?* I told him he needed a featured number, a number that was his own. 'But you've already played everything there is to play. Except a march!' He started laughing. I said, 'Wait a minute! A march!'

"He looked at me and said, 'Ah, come on.'

"I said, 'No, wait. I've got an idea. Let's have a rehearsal tomorrow.'

"That night I said to myself, 'How can I write a march that sounds military yet doesn't sound like the army? A little something different. Maybe a blues, but not just an ordinary blues. A blues with a different tinge.' I came up with this thing, *Blues March*, just a novelty tune that would be played for a while and that would be the end of it. The next day I brought it in. Nobody has ever played that tune the way he played it. All the world's best drummers have played that song, but to this day nobody ever played it the way he played it. That thing caught on. I couldn't believe it. Until the time he died, that was still part of the repertoire. That and *Along Came Betty* stayed in there.

"Bobby Timmons had a thing he used to play. We were out in Detroit. He used to play this funky lick between tunes, just eight bars. We got to Columbus, Ohio. I called a rehearsal. I'd got in new uniforms. I said, 'Bobby, play that lick that you play. Today you're gonna put a bridge to it.' He said, 'Ah, that's just a lick.' We were at the club. I said, 'We're just gonna sit over here and lollygag, while you're onstage at the piano and putting a bridge to it.' He said, 'How's this?' I said, 'No, that's not the same funky flavor as the outside.' He said, 'Well, you do it!' I said, 'No, this is your tune. You do it, but try to get the same funky feeling that you got on the first eight bars.'

"We sat there, and he did it, and I said, 'That's it.' We rehearsed it and played it that night and laid 'em out in the aisles. *Moanin'*. The rest is history. That's how that came about.

"While I was with Art I wrote a thing—I wrote a lot of things. I laugh about this tune. I was only playing the chords to this tune, and I had three different melodies in my mind, and I couldn't decide which one I was going to use for it. So all day long I'm playing these two chords over and over. That's all my wife could hear, because only I could hear the melody. I finally decided which melody I was gonna use. And then I played it for my wife. It was like she was waiting all day for me to ask her what she thought about it. And before I could get the words out of my mouth, she said, 'It'll never work. It's too monotonous.' That was *Killer Joe*. I've had so many records on that darn thing. And we played that and people ate it up.

"When I first got the new Blakey band together, I called Jack Whitte-more."

Whittemore was Blakey's agent and the agent of just about everybody else of substance in jazz. Benny continued, "I said, 'Jack, get us a concert in Town Hall.'

"He said, 'Why?'

"I said, 'Because we're trying to prove something. Small's Paradise doesn't want the band back ever again in life. One of our first goals is to make Small's Paradise *ask* for us back.'

"He said, 'It'll never happen.'

"I said, 'Trust me.'

"I told the band, 'Fellows, we're going to do this concert black tie. We're trying to make an impression here, and people see you before they hear you.' So we did it and it was a success. Then we started to do some other things. Jack Whittemore called me and said, 'Small's Paradise now wants to have you back.'

"I said, 'Okay, now we're going in the right direction. See if you can get something in Europe.' Art had never been to Europe. 'And,' I said, 'Get in touch with Alfred Lion and let's get an album going.' The album was called *Moanin'* and it had *Moanin'* and a thing I did called *Drum Thunder Suite, Are You Real?, Along Came Betty, Come Rain or Come Shine*. We went to Europe, and we did a moving picture. I was handling the money. I would get the money, pay Art, pay myself, pay everybody, and send the rest over to Jack. So to anybody who wanted money, I said, 'I don't want you drawing money daily at the club. It makes us look cheap.' I would draw a substantial sum, and let them come to me for the draw, rather than going to the club owner, like stumblebums.

"I joined Art in 1957. In 1958, the band came way up. I said, 'Art, you're doing good now. And I'm going to leave you. Because I still want to establish myself here in New York.'

"I left. Wayne Shorter replaced me. Art tried to keep it on a certain level. And he did. Lee Morgan left and Art replaced him with Freddie Hubbard. Many, many people went through the band.

"In November of '89, he made a seventieth birthday tour. Jackie McLean, Curtis Fuller, and I went as a sort of adjunct to his regular band. During the time he was making the announcement, he said, 'This is Benny Golson. He started it all.' And all the guys said, 'What does he mean?'

"Because I hadn't been there all the time. There was Horace Silver, and Kenny Dorham. That was the beginning of the Jazz Messengers, and they knew that I wasn't there. They said, 'What does he mean, you started it all?'

But he was talking about when things started to change for him, and I told them. Art was always appreciative of that. And because of that he always trusted me. He used to call me and say, 'What do you think about this, what do you think about that?' For years."

"I heard he couldn't read," I said, incredulously.

"Are you kidding?" Benny laughed. "He couldn't read a note. But the man was didactic. He taught everybody, including me, in the band. I came in there playing soft and sweet. He used to try to give me a hint, with the loud drum rolls going into the next chorus, and I would disappear. And I didn't get it. And so he did it one night and I disappeared as usual. And to sort of underscore it, he came down with a bang! And then another bang! And he hollered over to me, 'Get up out of that hole!' And I thought, 'Gee, maybe I am in a hole, and I have to start playing differently, a little harder.' And I did, because of him. Yeah, he was a teacher. He taught from the drums.

"And when he died, I said, 'School's out.'

"I asked Freddie Hubbard about it. Same thing. I said, 'When I left Art Blakey, I could not play with another drummer. I was frustrated. I felt like the drummer was tickling the drums.' And Freddie said, 'You too? I had the same problem when I left. And I just took it for granted while I was there.'

"Art Blakey didn't know what it was *not* to swing. Even when he didn't feel good. I really miss him. There was something about him. I loved him, Gene. He was the world's biggest liar, and I didn't care.

"During that period," Benny continued, "Art Farmer and I used to do lots of dates together in town here. He'd left Hamp after I did, came back to New York, and we wound up on the same dates. Jingles and one thing and another. And I loved the way he played. And as it turned out he liked the way I played too.

"I said, 'I think I'm going to put together a sextet. Who do I want on trumpet? I'll call Art Farmer.' And I called Art. He chuckled and said, 'You know, I was thinking of putting together a sextet too, and I had you in mind for the tenor player.' So I said, 'Come on by the apartment, and let's talk about it.'

"He came by and I said, 'Maybe we can get together and have a co-leadership thing. What about trombone?'

"He said, 'Well who've you got in mind?'

"I said, 'Curtis Fuller.'

"He said, 'That's good. I'd like to have my brother Addison on bass. And Dave Bailey, who played with me with Gerry Mulligan. But now what about piano?'

"I said, 'There's a guy I met in Philly when I went over to do a single gig one Sunday afternoon, a jazz concert. This guy can really play and I'd call something in a strange key, and he ate it up.'

"He said, 'Who is he?'

"And I said, 'Name's McCoy Tyner.'

"So I called him and asked him if he'd like to join. He was ecstatic. I said, 'Now, McCoy, we're going to have lots of rehearsals, so you're going to have to be coming back and forth from Philly.'

"He said, 'Well, you know, I'd really like to move to New York.'

"I said, 'Okay, let me see what we can do.'

"And Art and I found him an apartment. The day he was going to move, I got a call from him. The guy who was bringing him and his wife over had broken down on the New Jersey Turnpike. He said, 'Can you come out and get me?'

"I said, 'McCoy, I don't have a car. But tell me where you are, give me a phone number or something.' I called up John Coltrane. He had a car. He came by to pick me up and we went out to get McCoy and his wife. I don't know what happened to the guy. We left him standing out there with his broken-down car. We came in to New York and McCoy started playing with us. A little while later he went with John. And I saw John and said, 'What a friend you turned out to be! You stole our piano player!' But actually it was the best thing for McCoy. He had something else in mind, which was closer to what John was doing at that time."

I said, "It was very hard to keep a group together then—as now, for that matter. I remember talking to J. J. Johnson about it at about the time you and Art started the Jazztet. He was playing the Blue Note in Chicago. He said the Blue Note wasn't making enough money to survive, and the group wasn't making enough to sustain them on the road. Eventually Frank Holzfiend closed the Blue Note, of course."

"The only reason we survived as long as we did," Benny said, "is that the manager we had, Kay Norton, so believed in us and never took a commission. She did a lot for us.

"The Jazztet was together about a year and a half. Then I started working as a single with local rhythm sections. Sometimes I took Blue Mitchell.

"I was writing and doing arrangements for various people, in commercials and stuff like that. And then I began to study again. But not like Howard University. This was on a much higher and deeper level, with a fellow named Henry Brant. He was teaching up in Vermont at Bennington College. He came home every weekend. I would go over to his house in Brooklyn and he would teach me for an hour. Composition, on an advanced level. He taught me so much. It was like I could hardly get it all in, he was teaching me so much.

"Right after that I got a call from Quincy Jones to do a picture, one he couldn't take. I went over to Europe to do it. It was a forgettable picture named *Ski Fascination*. It was all about skiing. I used everything Henry Brant had taught me. I came back and continued to study with him. Now I had all these devices and technical skills at my fingertips, and nowhere to use it in New York. Not the kinds of thing he was teaching me!

"Quincy had already gone to California. Oliver Nelson had gone. Each time one of them went, they would call me back and say, 'Why don't you come out?' Leonard Feather moved to California. *He* called me and said, 'Why don't you come on out?'

"I wisely went out there without moving. Just went out there to survey things. And I got a feeling. I came back, sold what I didn't want, packed up the other stuff, and moved out there. I went to work right away. Quincy got me with his agent, Peter Faith, who was Percy Faith's son. Nice fellow. [Peter Faith died young of a heart attack.] A few months later, I moved my family out.

"I went to work on a William Holden film out at MGM. Alex North was the composer. I did some period music for it. And 'period music' means exactly what it says—a gavotte from the sixteenth century, a George Shearing-style piece, a Dixieland. Period pieces.

"And then through Quincy, I got a call to come out to Universal. Dave Grusin had just done the theme on a Robert Wagner series called *It Takes a Thief*. Very next episode I went to work on it. Stanley Wilson was the musical director. He asked me if I wanted to do another one.

"Then I started to do a variety of things. Ben Gazzara had a series called *Run for Your Life*. I got a call to come over to 20th Century-Fox. And I went to work on a thing called *Room 222*. Then I got a call to do *M.A.S.H.* I stayed with *M.A.S.H.* for three years. And a couple of things that came through. At the same time I got a call from Screen Gems Columbia, and I went over there and started doing *The Partridge Family, I Dream of Jeanie*, that kind of stuff, and I also got calls to come out to Paramount—*Mannix, Mission Impossible*, and some series that really didn't make it. I did quite a few pilots too. I kept pretty busy writing.

"During that time, I didn't play. I put the horn aside in 1964. I had two of every instrument—two clarinets, two flutes, two saxophones. I figured I would never play again. That was it. Then I got the itch again, would you believe it? I came back to do a concert for a jazz society here. And it started to feel kind of good. But I still wasn't going at it full time. I'd pull the horn out when festival time rolled around each summer. But it took me so long to bone up, get my chops back together, y'know, it wasn't worth my while to do it for just one gig.

"So I did that. With more frequency I started to do these things. I eased back into it. But I didn't play the horn from 1964 to about '72, when I really started to get back into it. If I'd known it was going to be so hard, I might not have tried to play again. I picked this thing up and put it together and put it in my hands, and it didn't feel like a saxophone. It felt like plumbing. My chops felt like ripe tomatoes. The mind was going every which direction. My fingers didn't want to co-operate. I didn't like the way I was playing, I didn't like the way I was sounding. I put it down. I felt as if I were recovering from a stroke.

"But when I picked it back up, I didn't sound the way I'd sounded when I put it down. So evidently some processes were going on mentally that I wasn't aware of. But still it wasn't what I wanted to do.

"And I went through, like Picasso, this period and that period. I didn't start to feel comfortable and secure again on the horn until about ten years ago. It took that long. Even then I wasn't playing on a regular basis. It was intermittent until about the last three years.

"And then the Jazztet got together again.

"Around 1981, somebody called me from Europe about putting something together with J. J. Johnson. J. J. was also out in Hollywood then. And he didn't want to leave, because when you move you lose. You're forgotten very quickly. They said, 'What about putting the Jazztet together again?'

"It had been over twenty years. I said, 'Let me look into it.' I called Art, I called Curtis. They said, 'Yeah, maybe do a few gigs.' We were planning to go to Europe but the Japanese, these inscrutable people, somehow found out about it, got on the case even quicker, and we went to Japan before we went to Europe.

"We put the band together with Buster Williams on bass, Cedar Walton on piano, Tootie Heath on drums, Curtis, Art, and me. There were some personnel changes. We worked together, I guess, about three years. It wasn't so stiff, and regimented, formularized, like the first Jazztet. A little looser. And we worked and recorded until about three years ago."

I said, "I had the impression that the years of composition had changed your playing"

"It wasn't the composition," Benny said. "I was consciously trying to change it because I was so unhappy before."

"Whatever it was," I said, "it was a far bigger structure than in the old days. There was something very different about it."

June 1991

The Return
of Red Mitchell

In January 1954, Red Mitchell was on tour in Sweden with, among other performers, Billie Holiday.

"We were all very impressed with the honesty and fairness in Sweden," he said. "I to this day wish that Billie had thought to move over there. I think she would have lived a lot longer. As Ben Webster did, as Dexter Gordon did, as a lot of American expatriates did. Dexter moved to Copenhagen. Ben moved first to Amsterdam and then Copenhagen.

"We were being driven around Stockholm the first day in a stretch limo. Billie thought they were just showing us the nicer parts of town. She said, 'Take us to the slums, I want to see the slums.' Somebody said, 'There are no slums.' And she said, 'What?'

"And somebody else said, 'There's no Beverly Hills, either.'

"And then I reacted to that. I said, 'No slums, no Beverly Hills? Is this just Stockholm you're talking about?'

"They said, 'No, it's like that all around Sweden—every city.'

"I thought, 'Jesus! Dis mus' be de place.'"

And eventually Red did what Holiday did not: he moved there. One of the greatest bassists in jazz became part of that colony of jazz expatriates living and working in Scandinavia, a group that included Edmund Thigpen, Ernie Wilkins, Kenny Drew, the late Sahib Shihab, and the late Thad Jones.

After twenty-four years there, Red Mitchell and his fourth wife, Diane, returned to America, taking residence in what is rapidly becoming a new colony of semi-exiles, the Pacific Northwest. There are jazz musicians living in Oregon and Washington, among them Red Kelly, Bud Shank, Leroy Vinnegar, and Dave Frishberg. Red and Diane settled in Salem, Oregon, Frishberg in Portland. "Dave says," Red remarked, "that it reminds him of San Francisco in the '50s. And Leroy loves it."

Back in the 1950s, two names loomed very large on the bass: Ray Brown and Red Mitchell, idols of other bass players. Mitchell has to be accounted one of the most influential of jazz bassists, in a line with Walter Page, Jimmy Blanton, and Charles Mingus, if only because one of his protégés, Scott LaFaro, influenced just about every younger bass player since his death at twenty-four—almost the same age at which Blanton died. But more bassists have obvious audible debts to LaFaro than to Mitchell, who remains, as Mingus did, a phenomenon of one.

No one sounds like Mingus. No one sounds like Red Mitchell. What makes his playing so really odd is that he developed an approach to the instrument as if it were a saxophone, extracting from it melismatic vocal effects, glissandi that bespeak enormous strength in the left hand. At times he would play bottom notes on the first and third beats of the bar and then strum the rest of the chord on two and four on the top three strings, using the backs of his fingers a little like one of the techniques heard in flamenco guitar.

He developed a huge sound, producing tones that lasted forever, and did things on the instrument that no one else had ever done, and possibly no one else will ever do. He long has been looked on as something of a curiosity because he changed the tuning of his bass from the conventional fourths to fifths. One of the things one would not figure out for oneself is that the tuning actually could affect the sound of his instrument by altering the nature of its resonance.

"With Red's scientific mind," Roger Kellaway said, "that tuning would make perfect sense." I did not at first understand what Roger meant. Kellaway played bass professionally before he played piano. Red played piano before he took up the bass.

Kellaway and Mitchell appeared a great deal together as a duo, in Scandinavia, New York City, and San Francisco, where they recorded an album for the Concord label's Maybeck Hall series. In the spring of 1992, they played two evenings at the Jazz Bakery, a recital series in Los Angeles. I listened to two sets in a state of mind that can only be described as awe. It was some of the most brilliant jazz I have ever heard, a wildly imaginative dialogue between two master musicians at the peak of their inventive powers.

Keith Moore Mitchell was born September 20, 1927, in New York City and raised in New Jersey. He worked with Jackie Paris and Mundell Lowe in 1948. He played piano and bass with Chubby Jackson's big band in 1949, bass with Charlie Ventura, toured and recorded with Woody Herman from 1949 to January of 1951, worked with the Red Norvo trio from 1952 to 1954, recorded with Billie Holiday and Jimmy Raney, and then went with the Gerry Mulligan quartet. He played with Hampton Hawes from 1955 through 1957, then had his own quartet. He played with Ornette Coleman in 1959. For a number of years he was principal bassist in the studio orchestra at MGM, and was, along with drummer Frank Capp, a member of the André Previn trio.

Red and I had been friends by mail and telephone for years, yet had never met. At the Jazz Bakery, I encountered a bearded, red-haired man of mixed Scottish and Irish background who, he said later, always had an affinity for Scandinavia, perhaps because of some dim ethnic memory: The Vikings circumnavigated Europe, leaving a blond strain behind them in Italy, Sicily, and Ireland. They founded Dublin.

I walked up to him as he was setting up before the performance, introduced myself, and drifted into conversation as if we had grown up together.

I asked about his brother, Gordon, long known to jazz fans as Whitey Mitchell, himself a fine bassist. But such was Red's luster in the profession that Whitey hardly ever got a review that didn't mention that he was Red's brother. Whitey, or Gordon, Mitchell, is an extremely funny man. He once had a card printed that read:

> **Whitey Mitchell**
> **bassist**
> **Yes, I'm Red Mitchell's brother.**
> **No, I haven't seen him lately.**

Some years ago I ran into him and said, "Have you still got that card?" "No," he said, "I've got a new one." And he handed it to me. It read:

> **Whitey Mitchell**
> **bassist**
> **Formerly Red Mitchell's brother.**

I effectively destroyed Whitey's career as a bassist. Once while I was editor of *Down Beat*, I ran into him in New York City. Whitey had worked with Gene Krupa, Gene Quill, Herbie Mann, and Oscar Pettiford's big band. Like many jazz musicians, he occasionally worked for Lester Lanin. The music was ghastly but the money was good. He told me some hilarious stories about his experiences with that band. I told him that if he wrote an article about it, I'd print it. He did, and I printed it in 1961 under the title *My First Fifty Years with Society Bands*. Lenny Bruce read it and wrote Whitey a fan letter. Whitey was so astounded and thrilled by the letter (which to this day he has in a frame on a wall) that he became a comedy writer, enormously successful in Hollywood, and a movie producer. "Whenever he gives a seminar for young writers," Red told me, "he tells that story and gives you eternal thanks for starting his career."

I told Red a story I did *not* print. In those days it would not have been possible. Gary Cooper's wife hired Lester Lanin for her husband's birthday party. Lanin brought a few key men to California with him, among them Whitey Mitchell. A contractor put the rest of the band together, no doubt some of those people of the caliber of Mel Lewis and Bud Shank, probably in blue jeans and bright shirts and loafers without socks, and of course the first thing they tried to do was make some of those cornball pieces swing. After the rehearsal, Lanin's road manager found the maestro lying on his back on the bed in his hotel room, hands folded on his chest, mumbling and muttering incoherently. Thinking Lanin was having a fit, the manager said, "Lester, Lester, what's the matter?"

"I'm praying," Lanin said, "to almighty God to save me from these sons of bitches!"

The expression he used was harsher than that.

When I'd finished telling the story, Red laughed, and said, "Do you know how my brother finally left Lester Lanin? Lanin said to him, 'Do you know what the trouble with you is? You're not playing in the middle of the beat.' And Gordon said, 'Do you know what the trouble with you is? You're full of shit.' And that ended the relationship."

Gordon, formerly Red Mitchell's brother and formerly Whitey Mitchell, took to his typewriter and has never looked back.

After the gig with Roger at the Jazz Bakery, Red and his wife spent two days with him, then got into the car and drove up to Ojai and spent two more days here, during which time his marathon eloquence kept me enthralled.

"I was told," I said, "that you left the United States after the Sharon Tate murders." I remembered the period vividly. I was visiting Los Angeles from New York, and everyone in the show-business world was frightened, afraid that the murders had been committed by somebody on the inside. Steve McQueen had taken to carrying a gun. The mood in Los Angeles was eerie.

"It wasn't just the Sharon Tate murders," Red said. "My second wife and I were living in a neighborhood that the Manson Family was working. I think they robbed our garage. They killed an older couple, the Biancas, right across Los Feliz from where we lived. It was just part of the over-all violence that was going on.

"It was really the *institutionalization* of the violence and racism, from the White House down to the subway, that bothered me. I had about six good reasons. About six things happened to me all within a short time. One was the breakup of my second marriage. One of them was the decision not to any longer participate in what I considered to be this vicious cycle, in which the real violence on the street, the violence perpetrated by the government in Vietnam, and all of it, was being reflected in the media. And we were playing this violent music for shoot-'em-ups. Some of us were saying, Oh we're just reflecting reality as it is, all artists have to do that. Others were saying we're contributing to it.

"The truth is, it's a two-way street. It reflects and it causes. And it *resonates*. That's when it really hurts, when it gets into a resonant circuit—when the capacitance is right and the induction is right for a particular frequency, and it builds up to a peak."

Ah. Here was the first hint of the scientific thinking Roger Kellaway had mentioned.

"And I just did not want to be a part of that cycle any more," Red said.

"I had given up on democracy in the United States of America. I had reached the point where I didn't think democracy would ever work here—I didn't think it had ever seriously been tried. It's a republic, after all."

I said, "Ed Thigpen was here for a couple of days recently. He quoted you as saying you didn't think the American public was qualified to vote."

"Yeah," Red said, "I said that. I say the same thing that the white racists say in South Africa about the black majority, that they're not qualified to vote. I think they're wrong; I think I'm right. I don't know about now. We just came back. We'll see. But when something happens like the moving of the venue of the Rodney King case to Simi Valley?"

Red, having lived in Los Angeles, was well aware of the character of the Simi Valley. It's Redneck City, and it is also the bedroom community where several thousand Los Angeles cops, present and retired, live, influence the community, and vote. To those of us who live in the orbit of Los Angeles, the change of venue was shocking. To begin with, did anyone seriously suggest that we in Ventura County didn't see the videotape images of the beating, when we get all the L.A. TV stations and read the *Los Angeles Times*? The population of Ventura County is only two percent black, well below the Los Angeles figure. There were no blacks on the jury and only one Hispanic. Two of the jurors, both women, were from Ojai, one of them a member of the National Rifle Association. I was unsurprised by the verdict.

"And when you see on television," Red said, "that it was Rodney King who was actually on trial, and those people were not his peers, I start to lose faith again. I start to think, 'Well, wait a minute! Even if the government prosecuted all four of these cops on civil rights violations, took it all the way, appealed all the way to the Supreme Court, I'm afraid the Supreme Court might hand down the same decision.'"

"Sure," I agreed. "You have an extremely reactionary Reagan-Bush Supreme Court. The minorities could always resort to the appeal to the Supreme Court and they no longer can, because it is a racist Supreme Court, even with a black man on it."

Red said, "I was going to say, especially with Uncle Thomas sitting there.

"There was another reason I left. I was terrorized by the police, living in Los Angeles. You didn't have to be black to be literally terrorized by the cops in Los Angeles. I was stopped and harassed four times with no reason.

"There were other reasons for moving to Stockholm. I noticed the quality of the jazz players in Sweden immediately. Later on I found it isn't only the jazz players, it's the opera singers, and the choirs, and the symphony orchestras too. The musical standards there are extremely high. As phenomenal as their tennis standards."

"And also visual design," I said. "Why is this?"

"I have no idea. I have really tried to figure that out for twenty-four years now. And I have no idea."

"Equality of opportunity won't do it?"

"I don't think that's *enough*."

"You have obviously retained your respect for the country."

"Oh yes! And I must say, the last few weeks before we left, they showed a lot of respect for me and us. The last week we were there, we were doing a recording at the radio, and we got interrupted just before we were to go into a real heavy blues. Somebody called out from the booth and said, 'Hey, Red, there's a phone call for you.' I said, 'We're just ready for the take!' We'd just drawn in our breath. They said, 'No, it's important, you better take it now.' So I went into the booth, and it was the secretary of the minister of culture saying that the government had voted me a Royal Medal. *Illis quorum* in the eighth degree. I said, 'What is *that*?' I still don't know. I still don't know how and when it's gonna be presented. Usually the king presents it. I found out I was the first jazz musician to get it. What it means roughly translated is: for one who has earned it.

"And then a few days later, a classical composer, Jan Carlstedt, called me and he said he was nominating me for honorary membership in the Royal Swedish Academy of Music. I said, more or less, 'What's that?' He said, 'It's an old society, and we're voting in May. And you shouldn't be disappointed if you're not voted in on your first nomination. Beethoven wasn't voted in till his third nomination.' I said, 'Thank you.'

"I still love the country, and I think they love me there. The last couple of months—I don't know whether it had to do with the announcement that I was leaving—we broke attendance records everywhere we went, with all kinds of different groups. The last month was the busiest I'd ever had in Sweden. Among other things, Joe Pass and I did a live album as a duo in the main jazz club in Stockholm. In September, we had opened a new really first-class jazz club in Copenhagen, called Copenhagen Jazz House in English.

"We had family reasons for coming back, too. My main reason is that we both sensed—and I checked it out with some of my more successful colleagues, like Clark Terry and Dizzy—that there's an increased interest in the music, and love for it, here in this country, and that's gone up from whatever it was in percentage. In 1968 it had to be point zero something, and it's gone up to even three, four, five percent of the population that hears and loves jazz. That's plenty! Out of 250 million people?

"And, finally, I had begun to see racism in Sweden too. The very thing they deplore about America—that Gunnar Myrdal condescension toward our society—was turning up there. They have a word in Swedish for the darker peoples from the Mediterranean. It means 'black heads.' They're having problems with minorities all over Europe, and I don't think they should point the finger at us the way some of them do."

Red and his wife said they had attended a seminar by the writer Toni Morrison at the American Center in Stockholm.

Red said, "Someone at this meeting asked her if, being a black woman in America, she really felt American, and she said, 'Never more than right now.'"

I said, "Benny Golson told me recently that in Italy, an Italian journalist asked him, 'How come you have a white bassist?' And his answer was, 'This interview is terminated.'"

"That's lovely," Red said. "I may have to use that one day."

"I am perpetually astonished by European condescension toward us," I said. "Their assumption they know us because they've seen American movies."

Diane, Red's wife, whose background is in sociology, said, "I realized that within a year after I lived in Sweden. I was a real activist in the '60s. I was upset over the Cambodian invasion especially. I worked eighteen-hour days on committees and all that stuff. And then you get to Europe and you're sitting there, and you're being personally blamed for this Vietnam war. I said, 'Wait a minute, you're just sitting here. I've been working my butt off, taking risks by running up and down the California campuses. I could have gotten picked up by the FBI or whatever. You sit here, self-righteously accusing me of being responsible in this war.' And if you put the United States down, you win points, you win friends. And I got really tired of that. I must say, I very much love Sweden—their respect for education, for culture, and decency."

Red said, "I was prepared for that when I went over to Sweden, but I didn't get draft number one."

"You were putting the U.S. down," Diane said. "More than I was, I think."

Red drew a thoughtful breath. "I wasn't putting the whole country down. I certainly wasn't putting my friends down."

"You were saying the American people aren't qualified to vote," Diane said. "If you say that, they'll *love* you over there."

"I said that the *majority* of American people were not qualified to vote."

"It isn't as good an aphorism," I said, laughing. "But certainly Americans seem less informed than people in other countries. First of all, they've been taught such erroneous history. My baritone player friend Les Rout, who became a historian, put it simply. He said history was not taught in this country to acquaint people with reality, it was taught to instill patriotism."

"That's right," Diane said.

"But that's reasonably true of all countries," I said. "The Russians are just beginning to learn the truth of some of their history, the Germans don't want to know their recent history, and what is taught in Japan is false. But in few countries is this as obvious as in the United States. This country is the only country I know, excepting Japan, that is its own religion."

Red said, "I think the cause of all racism and all war is simply a misperception of what I call Instinct Number 1—the deepest-seated instinct we have, survival of the species. Of course, survival of the individual is linked directly to that. But first things first. I think Instinct Number 1 is the survival of the species.

"And I think individuals will sacrifice themselves willingly if they really think they're doing it for the survival of the species. Unfortunately, it's very easy to misperceive who's in the species and who's not. For example, was Hitler in the species? Was Hitler a human being, or not? Was he outside the realm of humanity or not? You have to accept the fact that Hitler was a human being.

"Unfortunately, we all come from the same gene pool. Sorry about that.

"I hope this doesn't sound like an oversimplification. It is in fact simpler than any answer I've heard from anybody else, and I haven't heard anybody shoot it down yet. If you want the bottom note, ask a bass player. I think the root cause of all racism and all wars is a misperception of Instinct Number 1. I accept the definition of instinct that I read in a book by a Swedish dog researcher. He said that instincts are a priority list reflexively built into a species with preservation of that species in the Number 1 spot. I accept that.

"However, Mother Nature gave us this urge that the species should survive, but she never gave us the information about who's in it, how big it is, who's out of it. That's a matter of our individual perceptions. And it's very easy for us to perceive another group of people whose behavior is not within our ethical code as outside the species. Another species. To be killed at all costs.

"I don't think America could have done what it did in Vietnam if they hadn't been capable of depersonalizing the Vietnamese people and thinking of them as short tan members of another species."

"Gooks, slopes," I said. "And earlier there were krauts, nips, japs."

"Don't forget Commie. We have all those names. Lenny Bruce used to say, 'Let's get together, Jews, Catholics, Protestants, black, white, everybody. Let's get together and beat up on the Puerto Ricans.'"

"And if the cops can call them niggers and Mandingos and gorillas in the mist, they can beat, choke, and kill them without a quiver of conscience."

"I think it starts with the home," Red said. "I was lucky. My father was one of the world's leading opera nuts. He actually studied singing, he had a season ticket to the Met from 1921 to '65 in the best seat in the house, right in the middle of the family circle. He learned some of five or six languages in order to sing the roles right. He learned all the opera roles.

"He had choirs. For quite some years there was a Gilbert and Sullivan company in our town—Radburn, New Jersey. Radburn is part of Fair Lawn, which is outside of Paterson, which is not too far from New York.

"It was an experimental little town founded in 1927, the year I was born, although I was born in New York City. My folks lived in Brooklyn then. Four or five years later they moved to Radburn. It was built for the coexistence of kids and cars. A whole lot of dead end streets and parks. By coincidence, maybe, it was all WASP with a few exceptions.

"I must say there was some strangeness in the town. When I started going into New York as a teenager, going to 52nd Street and to Harlem, meeting some of these giants that I'd heard on the records, they made me feel more welcome there than I had felt in my home town."

One of the finest trumpet players of his time, Red said, was Blue Mitchell. "My brother, Gordon, had picked up the nickname Whitey and also learned bass. Everybody used to say we should get together and make a record, Red, Whitey, and Blue Mitchell. We had a picture taken together in Birdland, Whitey and Blue and me. We just all happened to be there.

"Gordon is four and a half years younger than I am," Red said. "I had taken him in to 52nd Street, even though he was fourteen and I was eighteen. We dressed him up in my father's clothes, which were too big for him. I told him to suck his cheeks in and walk like he was falling asleep and everybody would think he was a junky. It worked, it was okay.

"I didn't start playing bass until I was in the army. He started playing bass in high school at the same time. No direct link. We took up the instrument simultaneously, perhaps by coincidence. I really don't know."

"Why does anyone take up bass?" I asked. "I love the instrument, but it is thankless."

"There are a lot of reasons in my case, a whole lot of reasons. I started on piano, studied nine years of classical music as a kid. Then my teacher died, and I got interested in another kind of music. It was jazz. It was around that time that I heard a Count Basie record on the radio, and that did it. It was a message of love from the whole band. I started dancing immediately. I couldn't dance then and I can't dance now. But I danced all over the living room and I just said to myself: 'I've gotta do something like that.' And by the way, on that record there were two tenor solos. I didn't know at the time that it was a tenor saxophone I was hearing, but I decided immediately that it was the greatest one in the world. And it was Lester Young, I found out later. It was one of those moments of truth.

"That was when I was somewhere between twelve and fourteen. It took me a while to get from there to nineteen, when I chose the bass. But I tried all the other instruments first. I played alto and clarinet for four and a half years, and at Cornell for one year and in the army.

"I took electrical engineering at Cornell. My whole youth I had thought I was going to be an inventor. My father was an executive at AT&T, and he had all sorts of friends in the Bell Laboratories. They took him out of Stevens Tech, a tough engineering school in Hoboken. He finished first in his class. The telephone company grabbed him in 1921, and he never had to look for a job. The only thing is they didn't teach him how to tell people what to do, and that's what the job involved, so he got a real bad case of ulcers. But he was a whiz, and he was a beautiful person. A gentle man. William Douglas Mitchell. A great man. He died just a couple of years ago.

"My father taught me to fix things, and I used to go around in the neighborhood and give people my business card. My biggest hit as an inventor as a kid was a six-shot repeater rubber-band gun made out of coat-hanger wire. All the kids bought them. I sold them for ten cents each. When the teacher would get hit on the back of the head and would look around, there was nobody to blame, because we all had 'em. My father helped me a lot, in a well-intentioned way. He helped turn me off to the profession of inventing. He encouraged me to get a patent on that gun, he took me through the patent-search process, and we got into materials and marketing, and my eyes glazed over and I said, 'Let's talk about something else.' I found out a lot later that the ultimate motivation of an inventor is the Eureka! moment. I've found it! And the ultimate motivation of the jazz musician is exactly the same thing. But in jazz, you don't have to get a patent, you go on to the next moment, and there are a lot more of them.

"I guess you can read between the lines that my parents were supportive."

"Well, Red," I said, "if I have discovered one constant in the lives of scores and maybe hundreds of jazz musicians I have examined, and for that matter artists in other fields, it is parental support. It is critical, and I suspect that this is so in other fields. Sometimes it's a teacher, but by far the majority of musicians, whether from the poorest people or the really wealthy, had parents who encouraged them to study music."

"My father was very supportive of me as an inventor. He helped me get a four-year scholarship to Cornell in electrical engineering. I went the first year and I loved it. I never did my homework; I was trying to figure out how to play bebop on the piano. I played clarinet in the marching band. I had a trio. We played on a local radio station. I was there in '45 and '46.

"One of my friends there was Don Asher, who was taking chemistry. We both played piano and we both had trios. His was patterned after Nat Cole's trio. My trio had piano, bass, and clarinet. The bass player, whose name was Wally Thurell—the janitor at the library, who was African American—was the first person who showed me how to pick a bass.

"I loved engineering and made the dean's list without even doing my homework, but then I was drafted. In the army, they asked me what do you want to do. I put *communications*. So they put me in a band. It was an eight-month comedy of typographical errors before I was finally sent over to Germany. And in Germany there was a big band that played only jazz. This was a special deal of a colonel who was a jazz lover. All the jazz musicians who came to Europe came through our band. If we wanted 'em, we could keep 'em. Jack Elliott, who was then known as Irv Zucker, auditioned me. He knew he would be getting out of the band in two months. And in the army they have no MOS number—military occupational specialty—for piano players or string bass players, because you can't march with them. That makes sense, doesn't it? It's the army way. He said, 'You stay in the band and copy for two months and when I leave you'll be the piano player.' I said, 'Thank you. Amen.'

"We played only jazz. We had several arrangers, two of whom had been with Glenn Miller's band. It was a really good band. We played a half-hour broadcast every Sunday over American Forces Network. I still run into people around Europe who heard that stuff. The singer who got out of the band just before I got in was Anthony Benedetto—Tony Bennett. There was a trombonist named Doc Mancell who was my idol in the band. He's still unknown. He's a giant of a musician. He's still one of my idols.

"When I came home from the army in 1947, and told my parents I was going to be a *jazz* musician, that was something different. I was not going to go back to Cornell, which I could have done free, between the scholarship and the GI Bill. My family and everybody I knew were telling me, If you're going to be a musician, at least go to Juilliard and get a degree, and then if you don't make it you'll have the degree to fall back on and you can teach.

"I went to Juilliard for three months in 1947. I took two courses, music appreciation and bass. Phil Woods came slightly after me. I got A in music appreciation and C in bass. I studied bass for three months with *the* man. If you were going to study bass in New York, who did you go to? Frederick Zimmerman. He was the assistant principal of the New York Philharmonic —which he was very bitter about, having started off as principal, having been Herman Rheinshagen's star pupil. Herman was really the boss in New York, one of the major players in the New York Philharmonic, he had all the good students, all the good jobs. When he retired, he gave it all to Frederick Zimmerman, and they demoted Frederick Zimmerman after a short time because he was not leading the section. He was a pretty good bass player. I heard him play in his apartment. I'd have given him about a C, which is I guess what he gave me.

"You have to understand, I had been trying to play the bass for only three months before that. Having tried all the other instruments and failed, and finding myself more suited to the bass, having a one-track mind, and wanting always to get to the bottom of things. That may sound corny, but it has a lot to do with it. After three months with Frederick Zimmerman, he said,

'Forget it, kid. There's a lot of bass players out there. It's a rough world. What was that other thing you were going to do?'

"I said, 'Inventor.'

"He said, 'Yeah, yeah, be an inventor, you'll make a lot more money.'

"This was 1947. Five years later, in 1952, in Los Angeles, I'm playing with Red Norvo and Tal Farlow, and here comes in this elderly couple, both with white hair, sitting down and listening. Somebody introduced me to them after the first set. It was Herman Rheinshagen and his wife, Muriel. They came to hear me. His wife, who was very nice, said confidentially in my ear, 'You know, Herman is retired now, he's not taking any more students. But I think if you asked him, he'd take you on.' And I said, 'Thank you,' and I did, and he did, and I studied with Zimmerman's teacher for six months. He was inspiring."

Diane said that she recently had come across Red's baby book, in which his father had written about how musical Red was at the age of two.

"I do remember I'd go to the piano," Red said. "I'd make fun of my father's music when I could just barely reach the keyboard. He was into classical music so deep, I used to imitate it. Especially the pompous endings. Tah-dah! He built his own pipe organ. He started out with a reed organ and then a pipe organ in the house, with a low C. I was hearing that from the time I was a kid. I kind of got it by osmosis.

"When I was a very young kid my father turned on the radio one day to turn me onto Jascha Heifetz. My father had hi-fi long before it was called that. This was in the early '30s. It was mono, but it was very good sound. He said, 'This is the man; he's the master.' I said, 'I can hear that he's great, Pop, but I hate to tell you, he's a little out of tune on some notes.' My father said, 'What?' I said, 'That one. That one there.' And he said, 'I'm glad you heard that. You were brought up with the tempered scale and he's using the natural scale.' And I said, 'What's the natural scale?'

"There again I was extremely lucky. My father was actually able to explain to me what the difference was. Heifetz's thirds sounded a little raunchy to me. Later on my father wrote a paper for the American Acoustical Society, which was also presented to the American Guild of Organists, on tuning pipe organs. As far as I know, it's still the definitive paper on the subject. He used his engineering knowledge. He carried it out to four or five decimal places, a degree of accuracy that no one had ever reached before. He explained what was wrong and what was right with previous papers on that subject.

"He was able to explain to me that Mother Nature never promised us a rose garden, that *the* scale, as we call it, is a matter of wishful hearing. It doesn't exist anywhere except within the human race. It doesn't happen anywhere else in nature. It's an acceptance of a series of compromises between the scale you would get if you tuned an instrument in fourths and the scale you would get if you tuned it in fifths. If you tune an instrument in fourths, you get a scale that is shorter physically. The top notes are lower, the bottom notes are higher in pitch. If you tune an instrument in fifths, you get a *bigger* scale. The top notes are higher, the low notes are lower.

"One day I'm going to write a book about this. One chapter will explain why some bass players and some cellists get along like some cats and some dogs. They could all get along just fine, except they tune their instruments differently. All the other stringed instruments are tuned in fifths. As a matter of fact, that's the tuning the bass started with.

"The 'normal' tuning today, which is causing this war between the bass players and all the other string players in the symphony orchestras—*every* symphony orchestra—is this difference in tuning. The 'normal' tuning of bass is fourths. It was a catastrophic mistake. I believe it started gradually around the 1700s. The bass originally had only three strings, tuned exactly as I have them tuned, from the top down, A D G.

"They couldn't make a C string in those days without its being as thick as your thumb, because they used only gut. They didn't have wrapped strings. So the low note was G, a seventh above the lowest note on the piano, which is an A. It's that G. Then a fifth up to D, and then a fifth up to A. That's the way the bass started. Then some smart-asses—I think Bottisini was one of them—found that if they lowered the top string a whole tone, from A to G, they could do finger tricks across the strings and play faster, because speed was a problem on an instrument that big. For a long time the bass was tuned G D G. It was a fifth on the bottom and fourth on top.

"As a matter of fact, there are still different ways of tuning the bass, and the symphony players haven't straightened it out yet. Three times now the Royal Philharmonic in London has been in New York when I was working at Bradley's, and six of the eight bass players have come down to hear me. Partly because they're jazz fans, but partly because they're interested in the fifth tuning. And the last time, they invited me to a concert of theirs at Lincoln Center. It was a very good concert, a very good orchestra.

"They had eight basses tuned four different ways. The principal and assistant principal used what most jazz players use, E A D G from the bottom up. The next two bass players had five-string basses, with B, not C, on the bottom. I remember because they played Brahms' First Symphony, and he wrote a low B. Only two of the bass players had it, but it sounded great anyway. From the bottom, B E A D G. And the back row, the first two had extensions—that piece of ebony that goes up beyond the fingerboard. They have to cut the scroll to put it on. The low string goes on up over a pulley and down to the tuning peg. There are two kinds of extensions. Two of the guys had the one, and the other two had the other.

"The one extension is without metal fingers. There's a clamp that goes over where the low E normally is. If you want to use that, you have to open that first, and you get a loud Clack! And then you have to finger the whole scroll. Bass players with large hands can in fact play certain limited passages on that—Ron Carter, for example, and Rufus Reid. But it's not really practical. You can't just play a walking bass line down there and back up. You can't use it in a solo as Zoot Sims used to use his low register. You remember Zoot going down to his low register, and right back up as though it wasn't low? Zoot could do that, and Zoot has always been one of my idols.

"The other two guys had the metal fingers on 'em. That's even worse. With the metal fingers, which clamp down on the strings and are connected through telescoping tubes to four metal knobs that stick over the top of the neck, you can at least attempt to play classical music on the bass. There's no way you can play jazz on it, but you can at least try to play classical music that is written down there—but with a *lot* of problems.

"During my years as the first bass player at MGM, it wasn't because I was the best of the bass players around—it was about flexibility. I could play rock-and-roll—I played the electric bass for ten years—and I had studied enough to play the classical music that we got to play.

"But when we would turn the page and see a cue like that, depending on how many bass players we had, I would hear 'Sh-sh-sh-shit' right down the line. Those guys learned to hate those low notes, because they were a big problem when you had those extensions.

"There are a lot of other ways to tune the bass. Glen Moore, the Oregon bass player with the group Oregon, has several tunings. His main is high C, which Chubby Jackson and Eddie Safranski used to have on their five-string basses, down a seventh to D, down a fourth to A, and down a sixth to C. The two C's on the outside are two octaves apart, and he calls them his melody strings, and the D and A in the middle he calls his harmony strings. And he has a lot of music he can play on that bass that nobody else can play.

"There's a particular phenomenon on a stringed instrument when you get a perfect fifth, and that is that you get a crescendo when you let it ring, instead of a diminuendo—you play two strings, in my case, the top A string and the D, and it'll get gradually louder over a period of about ten seconds.

"I was extremely lucky when I was a kid. My father was one of the few people in the world who could have explained it to a kid. If you started with the low A on the piano and then measured the frequency of it, it would be 27.5 cycles. If you double that, it's 55, and you get a natural octave, and if you double that it's 110, another natural octave, and if you double that 220, and if you double that 440—that's where A is supposed to be, most of the time—880, and on up. And you get a certain number at the top. If you start with the low A and take three halves of that, that's the ratio that a fifth is. Think of the open G string, whatever that frequency is, you've got a D harmonic, which is a matter of dividing the string in thirds. The D harmonic is an octave and a fifth above the open G. If you divide that in half, you'll have a fifth. So that's three halves, that's where the interval comes from. My father was able to explain to me that if you started with the low A, 27.5, and took three halves of that and three halves of that and so on up until you get to the next A, you'd have a completely different number—higher than if you went up by octaves. Audibly higher. You'd hear it in a second. Anybody except somebody who's tone deaf.

"When I started playing bass, I asked several people how do you tune this thing? They said, 'In fourths, E from the bottom.' That makes it quite different from cello, which is in fifths. All of the nineteen years I played that way, I had a lot of problems, most of which disappeared when I changed the tuning. It's exactly like the cello, C G D A, but an octave lower. The bottom string is a major third lower than the normal E."

"Did you have trouble getting strings?" I asked.

"I experimented from '66 to '71 with all the strings in the world that I could get hold of. Hampton Hawes was particularly tolerant in that period. It was when I was with him, at Mitchell's and Donte's, that I made the change. I had piles of strings on the piano. I would change every set. After five years, I had gone through all the strings in the world, and it was close but no cigar. So in 1971, I called the Thomastik company, which makes the best bass strings, and that's when I got this young renaissance man who was head of the company. He was twenty-nine, was a jazz fan, and knew who I was. He said, 'Of course we'll make strings for the fifth tuning. It's a great idea.' And they did.

"Now they make four types of fifth-tuned strings, three-quarters bass, four-quarters, normal and soft, more gut-like. It took them a year and a half to get the first batch right. They made three batches. The third batch was okay, and they've gone from there.

"When I made the change in '66, I took my second wife and her son down to the beach near San Diego and practiced for nine days around the clock over the sound of the surf. There's a motel that goes right out over the surf."

(Red's brother has an interesting comment on this transition in Red's life and work. "By begging, lying, and cajoling," Gordon said, "Red created a ten-day gap in his schedule, went to that motel, restrung his bass, unlearned the old system, invented a new one, learned it, and went right back into the studios ten days later as if nothing had happened. Astonishing! It's like learning oboe over the weekend.")

"Legend always had it," I told Red, "that you changed the tuning and played a gig two days later."

"That's a little exaggerated," Red said. "It was nine days. I came back to Los Angeles, and the first job I worked with the bass now tuned in fifths was with André Previn. I was playing first bass with sixty-five men at the Sam Goldwyn studio. I figured: Okay, André Previn with a big orchestra. If I can fool André, with his elephant ears, I can fool anybody. I didn't tell André I was doing anything different. About twenty minutes into the session, I made a gross mistake. I pushed my finger down on the first string, and it would have been right if I'd had a G string. But it was a whole tone high. André stopped the orchestra. He didn't usually do that. This time he looked over at me and said, 'Red, really. If it weren't you, I'd say that note was out of tune.'

"I said, 'Thank you, André, it was a whole tone out of tune. It will happen again, and I'll explain to you on the break.'

"I explained to him what I had done.

"He said, 'You mean, I can think of the bass the same as I think of cello? It looks the same on paper, but it sounds an octave lower?'

"'Yes.'

"He said, 'The same string crossings?'

"I said, 'Yes.'

"'The same flageolets?'" (Flageolets are the harmonics of stringed instruments.)

"'Yes."

"'Same bowings?'

"'Yes.'

"And he slapped his forehead and he was the first of a long line of composers who said, 'Damn! Why doesn't everybody do that?'

"I asked, 'Well? Why don't they?'

"Dizzy Gillespie said the same thing. Dizzy understood it immediately. I didn't find out until fifteen years later that it started with that tuning. Gary Karr in New York has a bass built in 1611 by Amati. He started playing seriously when he was eleven. When he made his debut in New York at, I think it was Town Hall, he got a phone call the next day from a woman who said she was Serge Koussevitzky's wife, and she loved his playing and was going to give him Serge Koussevitzky's Amati. He laughed and said, 'Who is this?' It was her, and she gave it to him. He paid $10,000 for his bow, but he got his Amati free."

"Is there such a thing as a $10,000 bow?" I asked, naïvely.

"Oh boy!" Red said, raising his eyes. "I'll give you the same answer I gave my son when he asked, 'What is it with women?' I said, 'You must keep it in mind that all women have one thing in common, and that is that each one is unique.' And it is exactly the same thing with bows. Two bows made by the same maker—forget it, they're going to be different. I finally found the bow of my life in 1972. It was a French-style bow made by a German maker, Pfretschner, and I was playing all my solos with the bow, and finally getting the bow to sound like I always thought it could—like Gene Ammons a couple of octaves down. I was not out after that classical sound at all. I was after Gene Ammons' sound specifically.

"It started to sound that way. And then a customer came into a little jazz club in Stockholm, a young guy who was totally drunk. This guy took the bow and started conducting us with it. I took it away from him. It happened three times. I said, 'Look, I'm not angry at you at all. But if you do that one more time, I'm going to kill you? You got it?' He laughed, ha ha ha, and sat down. I thought I had cooled him out. We took a break. We came back, and he was gone, and the bow was gone and I haven't played with the bow since. That was the bow of my life. That was twenty years ago. It may sound a little childish.

"After two or three years, I realized that not having that resin on the strings allowed them to sing much longer. And I could get all the colors out of the strings that I couldn't get when that resin was stuck on 'em."

"Can you get a sound without resin on a very good bow?" I asked.

"The best players use the least possible amount of resin," Red said. "Gary Karr, after a concert, wipes the resin off the bow. The less resin you use, the better it sounds, right down to zero. I had always preferred my pizzicato sound to my arco sound. That's not about anybody else, that's just about me."

"John Heard," I interjected, "says that there are all sorts of techniques of bass playing, including harmonics, that have not been fully explored by jazz players."

"He's right," Red said. "And there are all sorts of tricks and techniques used by cellists. When I made the switch to fifths, I got together with Fred Seykora, who is now working with Roger Kellaway's new cello group. He was the second cellist at MGM, and one of my best friends. Fred and I got together every day for a week at my house. He wanted to learn how to improvise. I had been teaching that. I wanted to learn how a cellist thinks with this fifth tuning. I think we helped each other. I think he's the only cellist in Los Angeles now who can improvise, unless Fred Katz is still around. He blew my mind with his explanation of the tricks and physical things cellists have to go through that bass players never even think of.

"To get from one note to another note on the same string, let's say from F to B-flat on the D string. You have four fingers up there to start with, not counting your thumb, and your nose, and your elbow, and anything else you might be able to get up there. You should be able to go from any of the four fingers on the one to any one of the four fingers on the other note. That means you've got sixteen ways to get from one note to the other, and you've gotta know all sixteen ways. It's gotta be in your muscle memory, you can't be thinking about it. And they all sound different, and each one has a different function. Especially as a jazz player, you need to know those alternatives, because you don't know where you're going from the second note.

"One of my favorite tricks—I got it from Charlie Christian—is like false fingering on saxophone, to go back and forth to the same note on different strings. You get a bloop-blop bloop-blop effect.

"My idols are not all bass players. Zoot Sims was one of them, and Sarah Vaughan for her intonation, among her countless other qualities. She could land on a note perfectly and then it would get better. How in hell did she do that? She'd land right in the center of the bull's-eye and then go deeper into the middle of the center of the middle of the bull's eye. That alone could give me goose bumps and make me cry."

"Sahib Shihab said you could listen to her just for her use of vibrato," I told Red.

"That too. I usually advise my students to emulate horn players, not bass players, and I recommend most heartily Miles Davis from the '50s and '60s. First of all, because he was not a natural trumpet player, he had to fight for everything he got out of the trumpet. So he thought and thought. He both fought and thought. And what he came out with was so simple and so deep that any bass player could play it. So if you're going to emulate a horn player, emulate Miles Davis. A couple of octaves down it sounds even deeper.

"I think Miles used his problem as an instrumentalist to the nth degree. He thought hard and fought hard behind every note he played. He never *ever* played thoughtlessly."

Back in the 1960s, when I was in Paris translating some of the Charles

Aznavour songs into English for his first Broadway appearance, he made a comment that I would never forget. He said that the artist builds a style not on his abilities but on his limitations.

I told Red about that and then recalled an evening I spent hanging with Miles at the Cloister, a basement club of fond memory in the Maryland Hotel in the Rush Street area of Chicago, some time in the early '60s. After a set, Miles slipped onto a stool beside me at the bar and ordered drinks. He liked to drink champagne from very small glasses. I told Miles that the group sounded exceptionally good tonight. And Miles rasped, "Maybe you're just listening good."

Red chuckled and said, "When you reach the fourth state of consciousness and you're in tune, within yourself, with your fellow players, with the audience, with the entire universe, and it's perfect, afterwards get a copy of the guest list. Remember who was there. For whom were you playing? That's one rule I will never back down on—when it is happening, get a copy of the guest list.

"I have two basic physical problems that should almost have made it impossible for me to become a bass player. One of them is that I'm very right-handed. And when you play the bass the normal way, the left hand does 80 or 90 percent of the physical work. The left hand has to be like a flexible vise, and the right hand has to be like a freshly caught dead fish. The answer has to do with the left and right brains.

"How do you make your much stronger hand much looser than your weak hand? I have to think about this consciously every time I play the bass."

"Why didn't you reverse it?" I asked.

"I tried it, and I could not do it. But when I found out a little about the right and left brains, then I realized what we do is correct. There was a trombonist named Hoyt Bohanon. He was right-handed. He played the trombone normally, and he never liked his vibrato. And then one day at a party he got drunk, turned the slide around, played it left-handed, and he loved his vibrato for the first time in his life. So he relearned the trombone. It was the limp wrist of the left hand of a right-handed person that did it.

"It is in fact the left brain that controls articulation. The right hand. That's what the right hand does—articulate. The right brain controls spacial visualization, fantasy, forms, abstraction. That's what the left hand has to do.

"Gary Peacock and Scott LaFaro were both protégés of mine. I remember one session particularly in East L.A. when I showed them both this two-finger technique, which I had worked out in 1948 in Milwaukee, on a job there with Jackie Paris."

Red was referring to the alternating use of the index and middle finger on the right hand to pull the strings.

"It's a little harder than patting your head and rubbing your stomach," he continued. "But it's the same kind of problem. You have a tendency, if you go one-two one-two one-two with your fingers, and you want to go two-one two-one on the other hand, they hang up. So you have to develop the independence. So that you can go one-two one-two one-two, or, even better rhythmically sometimes, two-one two-one two-one with the right hand and then random—you have to practice!—fingering with your left hand so you can keep the right hand consistent and the left hand can go anywhere and not be hung up. When you get it down, the one hand doesn't know what the other hand is doing.

"And then you use your weaknesses. As Miles and Dizzy both used their pauses between phrases. You use the unevenness of it later so that the accents are where you want them. The loud notes are where you want the accents."

Red and I talked late that night.

Next morning I asked what was the biggest shock on returning to America after his twenty-four years in Sweden.

"On the one hand, finding that so many of my friends have died," he said. "Of course I was aware of it in most cases. On the other hand, finding that some people I haven't thought of for thirty years are alive and well.

"For all the problems, I have the feeling that we *are* going to muddle through. I am not an optimist, but basically in my gut I feel that if you view the world from the point of view of the astronauts—I keep writing things like this into songs. . . .

> A small distant ball
> with some swirling weather,
> well, whatever we call ourselves,
> or this place,
> we're all on this thing together.

"I have a feeling it'll be the genius of nature—I don't use the word God without qualifying—Mother Nature, whatever. If you take the step back and call it World or Earth, you must kind of accept that everything that happens on it is natural, even the violence, even the violence in language, the violence people do to each other, the violence species do to each other, is all beyond our ken, in some way.

"We came back with our eyes open. We know who's sitting on the Supreme Court. We saw Uncle Thomas and his confirmation. The riots in Los Angeles didn't surprise us at all. It was a shock, of course, but it wasn't surprising after the verdict, and the verdict wasn't even surprising after the shift of venue to Simi Valley.

"Yet it was totally understandable. The reaction of the government was exactly the same as Lyndon Johnson's reaction to the Kerner Commission's conclusion that it was white racism that caused those riots in '65. In this case, the racism—unfortunately being a contagious disease—has spread. You can nail that jury for white racism. The decision they handed down was typical, glaring, blatant, obscene white racism. They actually were persuaded that Rodney King was *in control* of the situation while the shit was being beaten out of him and the whole world saw it. That's astounding. It can't be anything but outrageous white racism, and our government hasn't faced that fact yet, and they're not about to.

"So we're coming back to America with our eyes open. But! What we're coming back to is America, more particularly to Oregon, and more particularly to Salem. There is a native American word that Jim Brown filled me in on. Jim and Mary Brown are the people who put the Oregon Jazz Party on. *Salishan* means a coming together from diverse points to communicate in harmony. They had one word for that. Don't we need that word? Isn't that a bull's eye? Isn't that what jazz is all about? I think more *salishans* is what the world now needs more than ever.

"We're supposed to be healers. In Bradley's in New York, Kirk Lightsey and I knew three very well-paid psychoanalysts who told us they came to us for their therapy.

"In one episode of a Swedish TV detective series, they had a murder in a subway station in Stockholm. In fact there had never been a murder in any subway station in Sweden. One week later, there was a murder in the same subway station. And, dig this, the guy who committed it apparently had not seen that show. Maybe somebody told him. Who knows? I think there is some kind of cosmic relationship.

"I just read a couple of days ago that we actually have magnetic crystals in our brains, and it might be why people who live near high-tension power lines develop sicknesses. It might be why some people lose their sense of direction. It might have something to do with how the sense of direction works in the first place. I have no suggestion as to how we're going to fight this thing. My brother and I were talking about it, and he said there's only one thing worse than all the violence on television and in the movies and that's censorship. I don't think censorship is the answer, but I think there's going to have to be some kind of peer pressure.

"I hope America some day catches up with Sweden on the issue of freedom of speech. They have a lot more of it there than we have. They don't know what a bleep is on television. They don't have the dot dot dot in the press. They do have the blue blob on television if it's going to protect someone's physical existence. But they have far more freedom of speech than we do—more than we've ever had here. They have laws against what they call *hetsmotfolkgrupt*. It means baiting or persecution or agitation against 'folkgroup,' any ethnic group, or it could include the police. It's illegal to agitate, incite people, work people up and into a frenzy against any group, understood that no freedom is absolute. And as surely as you can't scream fire in a crowded theater, you can't go on the radio or television or in press and do what Hitler did. It's against the law over there.

"I'm almost sixty-five," Red said. "I am thrilled and delighted to still be alive, and I've been thinking about starting a group soon called The Grateful Living."

Later that morning he and Diane left for Oregon.

Although he did not mention it to me, Red had been suffering angina pains for more than a year. In late October, 1992, he was hospitalized with a mild heart attack. He voted by absentee ballot for Bill Clinton—the first time he had voted in twenty-eight years. On Tuesday, November 3, he learned the results of tests on his heart. They were favorable, and his spirits soared. And that night his candidate, Bill Clinton, erstwhile musician, lover of Charlie Parker and Zoot Sims, was elected president of the United States. Red's brother, Gordon, called from Los Angeles, and they laughed and exulted over Clinton's victory and, as Gordon put it, told the joke of the week. Red went to sleep happy.

Sometime that night he had a stroke. The next day, Wednesday, November 4, Gordon spoke to him again on the phone. "It was like talking to Rain Man," Gordon said later. "There was nobody there." Red lapsed into a coma, and on Sunday, November 8, he died. Pianist and author Don Asher, Red's friend since their student days at Cornell, sent me a card. It said, "I just heard about Red. I don't have to believe it if I don't want to."

Two weeks and a day after Red died, on Monday, November 23, 1992, Nazi swastikas were painted on fifty-two gravestones overturned in a Jewish cemetery in Stockholm.

December 1992

Three Sketches

1. The Lion in Denver

"The way they do things in Dallas, Texas!" said Cedar Walton, who was born there January 17, 1934. "You talk about conservatism! They suspect anything from outside Dallas. Even when Duke Ellington used to come there when I was a kid, the attitude was: 'We've got our own bands here. Who is this guy?' They believed him once they heard him, but they suspected him. Unless it's made in Texas or grew up there, they're suspicious. That's the attitude.

"The whole state is like that. They believe they can live without anything from outside Texas. It's incredible, man. I got a booking in Austin. It was like pulling teeth until they found out I was from Texas. They need to be really convinced."

Cedar is a quiet man, a powerful pianist and a very good composer. He went to Lincoln High School in Dallas and then to Dillard University in New Orleans, where he and Ellis Marsalis were freshmen together. After Dillard, he transferred to the University of Denver and majored in music. "I just liked the campus, quite frankly," he said. "I was on summer vacation with my parents. We were on our way out to California, but we just got as far as Denver. We stayed there, and I visited the campus, and I said, Wow! Nice! So for no other reason, I picked it. It was new. The dormitories were new. And they had co-ed dormitories! I thought: Maybe I can meet somebody.

"They had a good music department, too. Denver's quiet; it's not like Texas. There was a pressure lifted. Ethnic. It's not as blunt as in Texas. I grew up with the sign on the bus. You know, you had to sit behind it. Me and my mother would go shopping and . . . . So that was something I found removed.

"By this time I had learned to be terrified by white people, in a sense. But I worked it out. I'm talking about 1951 or '52. 'Afraid' isn't entirely accurate. But there was a hesitancy on my part, simply because I wasn't used to it. It's like going into a cage of lions. You're a lion yourself, but you've never been around that breed of lion.

"But I got used to it. I could relate to the instructors. It turned me, I think, into a fanatic student in terms of trying to keep up. I zeroed in on my music. We had a nice curriculum. We covered all the instruments. We had to play them all. That gives you a great insight on writing because you've actually played them. Some of them will make you faint, like the oboe. I blacked out once. I learned the flute. It was fun. Here was a band full of people who didn't play those instruments. It sounded horrible, but it was good for you."

He stayed there three years, dropping out for a while when his after-hours jazz activity started to pick up. "I had this gig starting at midnight," he said. "It was the drummer's group. The other guys were in their thirties. I was under twenty. I was just a student. I met people like Charlie Parker. He came and sat in. Jerome Richardson came through with Earl Fatha Hines. I met everybody who came through Denver, because I was playing the gig at the place they'd go to after playing a concert. It was a nice experience. I met Richie Powell. I remember staying up all night with him. He showed me some things. He was with Johnny Hodges. So was John Coltrane at that time.

"It was a good experience. I saw Charlie Parker and Dizzy Gillespie playing chess on their intermission at the Rainbow Ballroom. I remember how impressed I was. Wow! Dizzy with his pipe, looking at the chess board! By the time Charlie Parker came down to our club, he had had a few drinks, and his sound wasn't clear. But his ideas were flowing, he just couldn't manipulate the sound I was used to hearing on records. But I thought he played brilliantly. For some reason he played everything in C. *Dancing on the Ceiling, What Is This Thing Called Love?*, and I think a blues. Then he fell asleep. It was a high bandstand. He asked for a chair. He was sitting right by me. I looked over and he had dozed off, in deep sleep."

Then, with a college friend, Cedar drove to New York, sharing the expense. "We had about $75 each, and my Chevrolet, and we made it, and still had some change left over. This was in 1955," he said. "We checked into the Sloane House YMCA. Rooms were about $11 a day, and I looked for day work right away. I had a variety of jobs, including stock boy at Macy's, Horn and Hardart dish guy. I just wanted to stay around New York and see what I could do.

"My mother kept saying, 'Come home, son! You've got no business up there!'

"I started to get a few gigs, though. After a year of that, almost to the day, April 1956, I let Uncle Sam catch me. I went to Fort Dix. I ran right into Wayne Shorter. He was stationed there. He was playing weekends with Horace Silver.

"And then Duke Ellington came to Fort Dix. He actually let me sit in! Can you imagine? I said, 'Do you think it's possible for me and my friend, who is a singer, to do *What Is This Thing Called Love?*' He said, 'Yeah.' I couldn't believe it. I thought he'd say, 'Not now, son.' We went up and did it, just me and the rhythm section. Duke said, 'Go easy on those keys, young man!' Jimmy Woode swears it was him on bass. Sam Woodyard on drums. And the whole band joined in on the last chorus, like a clambake ending. I said, 'I'll be . . . . This must be a dream.'

"And when Duke came back, he said, 'I thought I told you to go easy!' I've got that in my memory to keep on track for a long time.

"I was at Fort Dix six months. Then I got into a special service unit, entertainment unit, at Seventh Army in Stuttgart. The Seventh Army Symphony was there too. Leo Wright was there, Don Ellis, Eddie Harris, and Don Menza. They had a band called Jazz One, and we had Jazz Two. We did a nice tour. Our duty for the first couple of weeks, once we got transferred into that unit, was just to go into the room and write music, go to lunch, come back, write music, go to dinner. Me, and Leo Wright, and whoever else we could grab. I was there eighteen months, playing jazz and touring around, until April of 1958."

I remembered that there was a jazz club in downtown Stuttgart, a little dark place in a basement.

"That's right," Cedar said. "The Atlantic Bar. That's where I first heard the Modern Jazz Quartet. Or maybe it was Frankfurt. I met Milt Jackson at that time. We went out after the gig and jammed. He played the piano too. We've been friends ever since, very close.

"When I got out of the service, I *dove* back into New York activity, since I'd done all this practicing in Stuttgart. I gigged around, with people like Gigi Gryce, Kenny Dorham. Just nice gigs. I was still only twenty-two, twenty-three. There were jam sessions Monday night at Birdland. J. J. Johnson heard me. By the time I was twenty-four, I was with J. J. That was my first traveling gig. Tootie Heath was the drummer. I replaced Tommy Flanagan."

"You came through to the Blue Note in Chicago," I said. "Because that's where I first met J. J."

"I seem to remember that's when I first met you," Cedar said.

I said, "I remember Frank Holzfiend was having trouble keeping the Blue

Note going. I had a conversation with J. J., who said, 'I can't pay the guys in my group what they're worth, and Frank Holzfiend isn't making any money, and this just isn't practical.' Or words to that effect."

"He kept the group together for a while," Cedar said. "Tootie Heath and I decided to defect, so to speak, to the Jazztet. We played Bird House in Chicago. We recorded live at Bird House. Curtis Fuller had gone by then. Tommy McIntosh had replaced him on trombone. We were almost a new group, me, Tootie, Tom McIntosh, Tommy Williams on bass. Only Art Farmer and Benny Golson remained from the original group.

"Later on, Benny and Art agreed that there was too much *music* in the sextet. Sitting there reading, it was unnatural: you needed to just come out and play. There was not that much room for solos. There was so much other work to do. But Benny realized that later. He threw away the book, in essence. It was a nice musical experience. Benny Golson, I think, is one of the world's most patient musicians in terms of getting what he wants out of people. That helped me a lot. It's a good memory. And it really prepared me for my next gig, which was Art Blakey. The horns were Wayne Shorter, Curtis Fuller, and Freddie Hubbard.

"You couldn't write enough music for Art. You'd write it now, you'd get it played now, and you'd get it recorded now. You can't ask for anything more, being an instrumentalist. A lot of people walking down the street regard music as something that's sung and instrumentalists as people in connection with a singer. Have you ever met people like that?

"Art Blakey was an education. You could apply everything you'd ever known about music. He would beg you to write, he would insist on it, he would hire you because you were a writer. The group played my music fast! They played it faster than I could. I said, 'Wait a minute. I wrote this thing.' People used to attend our rehearsals in New York. Word would get out that the group was rehearsing and you'd have an audience sitting there. It was nice.

"Art's dynamics! I watched him in amazement. We did a date for Riverside. I was just amazed how he, practically the first time through on a tune, memorized all the dynamics. That press roll of his. All these things. Then he'd be quiet. I just couldn't believe this guy."

I said, "Buddy Rich also had a phenomenal memory. He once told me he thought it was because he couldn't read."

"Out of necessity," Cedar said. "Blakey too. Art would say, 'Go ahead and play it.' And he'd memorize it. It was the first time I had run into that kind of intelligence, without it being that kind of formal intelligence from books. That's another kind of intelligence. He was a great bandleader. It was with him that I first went to Japan, and we went to Europe. We worked and recorded all the time.

"After that tenure, I opted to stay in New York. By then I was married and had a family starting. I took a gig at the Five Spot on Eighth Street opposite Charlie Mingus. The trio opposite had been led by Roland Hanna. He left, so I came. Reggie Workman came in on bass. It was a permanent gig. Art seemed disappointed that I left, which was flattering to me. I was tired of the traveling. Now I don't mind traveling.

"After that, I just freelanced. A nice period, freelancing, recording. I think I got my first recording contract during that time, with Prestige. I would travel then, but just little things. Slowly but surely I started to get my own gigs. That was a good feeling. I continued to record for Prestige."

A lot of time had passed since then, Cedar mused. "My son is thirty years old. He's married and lives in Jersey City with his family. My other son is twenty-eight and lives in Connecticut, and my daughter is twenty-two and lives in Manhattan. My wife and I got divorced. I remarried and had another daughter, who is now fifteen.

"I came out to California in February of '88. I was coming out here all the time, and sort of unconsciously deciding to make the move. I like to go in to New York, but I like it out here."

Cedar made the European festival circuit with Dizzy Gillespie a few months before Dizzy's death in January 1993. He said, "Every night, it was Phil Woods and Dizzy. Phil knows Dizzy's music about five times more than I do, because he's played with Dizzy a lot. A lot of those things, most of us know about 90 percent. But there are little things in them. With Dizzy you got the refined versions. That was fun, because we could have rehearsals in the dressing room without really playing. We could talk through these things and go out and play something new every night. It was great, with Mickey Roker, Rufus Reid, Bobby Hutcherson, Steve Turre.

"I just made a record with Phil Woods and Jackie McLean, produced by Bill Goodwin."

An album he said he particularly likes is one called *Cedar Walton Plays*. "I'm very proud of that one, because I used a horn ensemble. It has an orchestral sound. It's not a lot of writing. Just little hits.

"My most enjoyable work, though, is with the trio. I like trio work. I have a delightful combination of gigs, assignments, projects."

He has also done a couple of small stints of movie acting, the first of them in the film *'Round Midnight*.

"That was a nice experience," he said. "Dexter Gordon picked me for that scene where the character comes back to Birdland. It's ironic. I just did one day's work in a movie directed by David Lynch called *Wild at Heart*. I'm doing the same thing, on the bandstand and looking around occasionally. Same role. Maybe I'll get a career in that kind of role. It's a hard thing to show to your mother, saying, 'Mother, I'm in a movie,' and she has to wait all this time to see you."

Cedar is one of the few musicians who says he liked the film *Bird*. He said, "They weren't aiming at people who know something. I don't mind any movie. It's just a movie. A movie has to be about *something*. And it has to be through somebody's eyes. We can't help it if we know better. The truth is not as movie-like. Movies are a special medium. I just like movies, the way they're made and everything."

Cedar, who lives in a pleasant apartment not far from the sea, had just appeared in a concert in Japan presenting ten jazz pianists.

"I love orchestration. I just don't get a chance to do much. But I did on that project there. I'm fifty-six years old. I probably won't be a great conductor. But that's one of my dreams."

Cedar was playing a steady circuit of festivals and concerts throughout the United States and Europe, and seems quite content with life. "The scene seems to have improved," he said.

2. Kenny, Mel, and the Roots

Benny Golson prepared me for Kenny Washington. Benny said, "Unless you're ready to listen for three hours, don't ask him anything about jazz history, especially drums. He'll start probably with Baby Dodds and take you up to Tony Williams and beyond."

Benny was right. I asked a question or two and found that Kenny—aside from being a highly admired drummer in the bebop tradition—is a formidable scholar of the music's history. Living in a small apartment in Brooklyn, he was surrounded by his huge record collection, whose contents he knows thoroughly. You can't mention a record without his knowing the label, date of issue, and personnel.

Kenny, who was born in Brooklyn, May 29, 1958, is one of the most respected drummers of his generation. He has recorded with Kenny Burrell, Benny Carter, Betty Carter, Ron Carter, George Coleman, Johnny Coles, Walter Davis Jr., Tommy Flanagan, Johnny Griffin, Lena Horne, Milt Jackson, Lee Konitz, Hod O'Brien, Mingus Dynasty, Cedar Walton, Frank Wess, Phil Woods, and many others—about a hundred albums in all.

"My father turned me on to record collecting," Kenny said, with a warm, embracing, off-center smile. "He was the first cat to tell me, 'If you want to be a great player, you've got to listen to the people from the past.' He had a big record collection. His name was Charles Washington. He was an IBM computer operator—before IBM got big. He didn't have as many records as I have, but man, he had a great cross-section. He had everything. He had Dixieland. He was a Duke Ellington freak. He was a Count Basie freak. He was a monster when Duke Ellington or Count Basie came to the Apollo. The family went to see them. I saw Duke when Clark was with the band, and Cat Anderson and Johnny Hodges. I saw one of the sacred concerts, too. They did one of the sacred concerts here in Brooklyn. So my father was very much into music. He turned me on.

"I must have been about five or six years old when I started playing drums. I studied with Rudy Collins, who used to play with Dizzy Gillespie in the mid-'60s. Actually, I learned from the records. I had a number of teachers. I grew up in Staten Island. I had a teacher named Dennis Kinney. I went to the High School of Music and Art, which at that time was on 135th Street, across the street from City College. I went up there and studied with Justin Di Cioccio. After that I went on to play with Lee Konitz. In fact, it was Jimmy Knepper who got me that gig with Lee. I played with Betty Carter. After that it was like a snowball, working with all kinds of different people.

"I was always interested in finding out why somebody plays like they play. I was always interested in checking all kinds of music out in all kinds of different styles. The problem with most young musicians now is that they never do that. Most of the tenor players are into John Coltrane, but they don't really know anything about Coleman Hawkins or Don Byas.

"The drummers are too much into Tony Williams and Jack DeJohnette. And nobody knows anything *really* about Jo Jones or Shadow Wilson. Or even Mel for that matter."

The reference to Mel Lewis echoed a special and lovely relationship. "Well," I said, "if that's so, what they're missing is that Jack DeJohnette *does* know about the older people."

"Right," Kenny said. "And Tony Williams too. And Elvin also. Those guys know all about the roots. They couldn't play as good as they play if they didn't. But some of the young guys now, they don't *have* to look back, see. That's the frightening part about it. Like, a young guy now that gets a recording contract, he doesn't have to go back and check those guys out. They get so much press play and what have you, they figure, 'Why the hell should I go back and check out all these old guys? I'm making all this money.'"

I said, "I was talking the other day with Chris Potter, the tenor player, who's now working with Red Rodney. He's only twenty, but he has an enormous sense of history, as you do, and he made exactly the same point you do. He says there's a generation of people in the middle, in their thirties and forties, who have been ignored in all the publicity over the new young people."

"Oh sure!" Kenny said.

"People like Brian Lynch and Dick Oatts," I said.

"I first met Dick Oatts with Mel Lewis," Kenny said. "When Mel started getting sick, I used to sub in the band for him. I did a record date the other day with Dick Oatts.

"And I met Mel through Lee Konitz. Lee said, 'Gee, Mel, I've got this young drummer, man, he can play.' I was working this place called Stryker's Pub. Lee said, 'He can really play, but he plays too *loud*. Maybe you can come down and sort of give him some *advice*.' So then Mel came down, right? I didn't know he was there. We were all hanging out outside, because it was warm. Lee said, 'Okay, time to play. Mel Lewis came in to check you out.'

"I played a set. First thing Mel said: 'I don't like your cymbals. I don't like those cymbals at all. And you're playin' too goddamn loud! You could bust out the windows in this place!'"

We laughed. I said, "Mel was never exactly tactful."

"Oh buddy! Man. I knew he had a lot of hip cymbals."

"Yeah, you know where he got that big crash cymbal, I'm sure. Dizzy gave it to him."

"That Chinese cymbal," Kenny said. "That cracked, though, man. That broke. 'Cause I asked him about that cymbal. What I said to Mel, not out of disrespect, man, or being a wise guy, was, 'Well look, Mel, do you have any extra cymbals you could lay on me, or I could buy from you?' He looked at me. He wrote down his number. He said, 'Come on over to my house.'

"He was living right across the street from Ron Carter—74th or 75th, something like that. I get up to his place. Doris, his wife, lets me in. Mel's sitting there. He says, 'Have a seat.' He says, 'How old are you?' I told him. I was about twenty.

"He said, 'Are you married?'

"'No.'

"He said, 'Good! Stay that way! Because, man, you can really play, and I've seen that kind of thing mess up a whole lot of potentially great musicians.'"

I said, "Since you knew Mel so well, I'll tell you a story. The other day Connie Kay said to me that he thought Mel was maybe the best big-band drummer he ever heard. I mentioned this last night to Roger Kellaway, who worked with Mel a lot, and he said, 'Yeah, and if Mel were still alive, he'd be the first to tell you.'"

"That's *right*!" Kenny said, laughing.

"Modesty was not his style."

"Oh man! But Mel was just great for me. We sat and talked. He says, 'But you play too goddamn loud. And another thing, you young drummers, you never use your bass drum. Now if it was a funk record, and there was no bass drum, you'd think something was wrong, now wouldn't you? And you play too loud. The band doesn't come up to the drummer, the drummer adjusts to the band.' He says, 'You remember that, man.' And so from then on, man, I used to come and hang around with him, and listen to the band. Or he'd come around where I was working to check me out. He'd come down any old time, unannounced. One time, I was working the Vanguard or somewhere and Mel says to me, 'Damn, Wash! Those drums sound like shit! Man, tune 'em, damn it, tune 'em.' Next night he comes back. He taps on my drums, he says, 'That's much better. Man, I knew you could tune your drums better than *that*.'

"And about the bass drum. One of the last times that I saw him, I was working up at Bradley's. So I'm playing. I'm sitting up there playing. I don't see him walk in. I'm looking someplace else, looking straight ahead. And all of sudden I see Mel! He's down there *under the piano*! All of a sudden he pops up his head. He says, 'Yeah, man, you're using that bass drum.' He was down there listening to see if he could hear the bass drum or not.

"Mel was beautiful to me."

"Dizzy makes that same point," I said, "about young players not using the bass drum."

"Oh yeah," Kenny said. "Mel used to get on me about that. Miles got on me about it. Miles came down to hear Johnny Griffin one time." Kenny slipped into the whispered rasp that almost everybody uses when telling Miles Davis stories. "Miles says, 'Yeah, man, you're playin' you' ass off, but if you don't use that bass drum by the next time I see you, I'm gonna kill you. Come on, man, put a weight on that right foot. That's what I used to tell Tony [Williams] to do.' They were right.

"Mel was great. I used to come and play when he couldn't make it or if he had another gig. Or when he got sick. Especially during his last year. I used to come down and sub for him. I used to watch him. He was incredible.

"When he was going through chemotherapy, they had a big tribute concert, the American Jazz Orchestra. I used to play in that band. When Mel couldn't make it, he'd send me in as a sub for the concerts at Cooper

Union. They decided to do a tribute to Mel. They played all his music, a retrospective of his career. They got a Johnny Mandel thing that Mel did with the Gerry Mulligan Concert Band back in the '60s. They got some Terry Gibbs things. Some Stan Kenton stuff, all kinds of pieces. Mel was worried about whether he was going to be able to remember all that stuff, because of the chemotherapy and what it does to your brain. By then he was completely bald.

"I came in. I said, 'Man, can I sit behind you so I can read the charts?'

"He said, 'Sure, man.' They called this tune off quicker than he could get the music out. He just started playing. There was this place where the band stopped and started, and he was catching everything. Bam, bam! And he hadn't played this, man, in thirty years. There was a place where he came in on the down beat instead of on the and, a half a beat off. He said, 'Damn, Wash. I don't remember this stuff.' And he was, bap, bap, bap-di-bap-bap, swingin' his ass off. And so after the tune was over, I said, 'Right, Mel. Right! You don't remember this stuff! You came in a half a beat early a couple of times, and you don't remember the stuff. Riiiight, Mel.' And the band started cracking up.

"I had never seen anything like that. He was an amazing cat, man. The best thing for me is, like, he was able and willing to show me anything I wanted. Just to be able to sit there and talk to him. That first night at his house, I sat there from seven in the evening until three in the morning. He was playing all these different records he had made, showing off his own talent and what he had done all these years. But! I learned a whole lot. He was showing me about adaptability. He said, 'Listen to what I played on the Barbra Streisand record *Color Me Barbra.*' He fit into every one of those situations. I learned *a lot* that night.

"Any situation Mel was in, big band or small band, he took care of business. He didn't *make* any bad records. At all. Period."

"You remember the Mulligan big band record *News from Blueport*?"

"Yeah, yeah."

"Gerry and Clark Terry are trading fours and eights, and Mel and Bill Crow get a groove going that is scary!"

"Yeah." Kenny said. "You know, that just came out again, on CD. I must get that from Polygram."

I mentioned that I had just put together a two-CD retrospective package for Polygram on Oscar Peterson, and of course Kenny knew about it. He said:

"Yeah. I see that you included *Con Alma* from the big-band record. That's a *mean* record. That was one of the first Oscar Peterson records I ever heard."

"Ed Thigpen is wonderful on that," I said.

"Yeah," Kenny said enthusiastically. "He's got the six-eight time thing, with the mallet on the cowbell." Kenny sang Ed's figure. "I learned how to play six-eight time from that record. From that and Rudy Collins, who learned it from Dizzy.

"That Oscar Peterson Trio with Ed Thigpen was a big influence on me. Learning how to play trio. Between that trio and Ahmad Jamal's trio with Vernel Fournier and the Jo Jones Trio with Ray Bryant and Tommy Bryant, Ray's brother. There was one record on Vanguard and one on Everest. Man, Jo's brushes. That record *Affinity* by Oscar Peterson, I tell all my students, 'If you can find that record, buy it.' I have students come in to America from Germany and different places. They take a couple of lessons. They've heard me on records. I don't have a lot of steady students.

"But I'm telling you, those Oscar Peterson records of that period. *West Side Story?* Man, that's how I learned to play ensembles. How to play in a piano trio situation. Listening to those records."

"Thigpen is such a lovely colorist."

"Yep."

"And there's always Elvin, when it comes to color. That guy moves around a top cymbal like it's a melody instrument."

"Elvin's *mean*, boy."

Kenny's conversation ranged over Will Marion Cook, the sharp-key writing of Fletcher Henderson, the playing of Roy Eldridge, and what he sees as an injustice in the record industry—the emphasis on youth, to the detriment, the ignoring of a generation of players in their thirties and forties who have reached their prime.

"You know what happens, man," Kenny said. "The best players are the best-kept secrets. To me, there's a lot of musicians out here who have all this name, but they don't play that well, man. It's all hype. I mean, the guys who are getting all this press play. They're supposed to be this, that. But they don't play that well.

"They think they're getting away with it. They *are* getting away with it. But the real people that know, they know what's going on. To me, the hype and publicity are unbelievable.

"What I see is that the more you play, the better you try to play, the less you're recognized for it. I really believe that. I know some guys who don't have *anything* together, y'know, and there they are, they're stars. Certain guys I know who talk all this stuff! Certain musicians I won't mention. It's all Park Avenue. But when you get down to the brass tacks, and really start talking about history and facts, you find that they know a doughnut hole. Zero. Really, man! It's amazing."

3. Jack in the Woods

"You spend half your life tryin' to get to the big city," Ben Webster said to me one night at the bar in Jim and Andy's, "and the other half tryin' t' get out." It was one of many bits of lore I absorbed in that unforgotten hostelry.

The younger jazz musicians, like younger artists of all kinds, keep arriving in New York to make their mark, for even today it's in the Apple that one has to do it. To be sure, as a cultural entity New York today encompasses much more than Manhattan, and there is a significant enclave of young jazz players over in Brooklyn.

In the old days, even the established jazz players lived in or near Manhattan, because they were busy in the daytime playing studio gigs. But those days are gone. There are no more big-orchestra dates with people such as Tony Bennett and Sarah Vaughan and Marilyn Maye. And the jingles dates are gone with the arrival of synthesizers.

So there is little reason for the established jazz musician to endure the pressures and frustrations of life in Manhattan—or for that matter Los Angeles—and so the last decade has seen a dispersal of jazz musicians from the major centers. Now they can live quiet lives in quiet places and, in our post-railway age, fly to the festivals and concert dates and occasional night-club gigs. Bud Shank lives in Port Townsend, Washington, Gene Harris in Idaho, J. J. Johnson in Indianapolis, and Herb Ellis in Arkansas (near a golf course, of course). Hank Jones lives a few hours out of the Apple on a farm near Cooperstown, New York.

In a little closer, perhaps an hour and a half out of New York City, there is a little community of jazzmen in the Catskills, in the general vicinity of Woodstock. Warren Bernhardt, Jimmy Cobb, Dave Holland, and Jack De-Johnette live nearby.

Jack lives in a house you'd never find unless he met you with his car near the highway and guided you up winding graveled roads through the wooded hills. It is near a small community with the rather sweet name of Willow. The house is modern, but rustic, built of bare wood. Jack's two dogs rushed to meet me. A winter thaw was in progress, and sun was on the snow.

The living room is large, and high, with a peaked wooden ceiling and large expanses of glass. It was washed in light that afternoon. Jack's wife, Lydia, an artist, who did the paintings on two of his album covers, including *Special Edition*, was not home. It startled me to think that Jack was nearing fifty. (He passed that date August 9, 1992.) I still think of him as one of the young fellows. Inspired by Max Roach, Philly Joe Jones, Elvin

Jones, and Tony Williams, he assimilated all the sources he admired and has become a powerful influence himself.

I met Jack in Switzerland in 1968, when he was with Bill Evans. I arranged that booking of Bill's trio at the Montreux Jazz Festival, then a charming and intimate event, not the gaudy circus it became and remains. I can pin the date down because the trio recorded at that time, and I took the photo of the castle of Chillon that is used on the cover of the resulting album. Bill was standing with me. The session was June 15, 1968.

I suggested to Jack that since he was himself a pianist, working with Bill must have been a particular pleasure, and for Bill, in turn, it must have been a joy to work with a drummer who was a pianist. (Another of Bill's favorite drummers, Philly Joe Jones, also played piano—and well.)

This prompted Jack, sitting on the piano bench with his back to the keyboard of his own grand piano, there in the woods near Willow, to slip into an effortless dissertation on the Bill Evans Trio—Scott LaFaro, Paul Motian, and Bill—when Jack was coming up in his native Chicago. His voice is low and almost diffident, soft and a little froggy. Jack is a handsome man, with a round and youthful face.

"I guess the concept of the bass the way Scott played it was not so much unusual—people like Mingus were playing with the fingers before Scotty was discovered," Jack said. "You had Jimmy Blanton. I think had Danny Richmond been a different kind of drummer, he might have had the kind of interplay with Mingus that you got with Scott LaFaro and Paul Motian. People like Gary Peacock might have pre-empted that. That combination of Bill, Paul, and Scotty shifted the emphasis of time from two and four. The way Paul broke up the time. He played sort of colored time rather than stated time. As opposed to what Miles would do. So that they made it in such a way that when they did go into four-four, it was kind of a welcome change. Then they'd go back into broken time.

"I remember the effect it had on rhythm sections in Chicago, because I was at the time a pianist, playing with a bassist who also played cello. We would sit up nights late, listening to the trio records. I noticed the rhythm sections in Chicago started playing that way. So I saw that influence start happening, where the time was broken up.

"I had a drummer with me named Art McKinney, who was doing things like Paul and Tony Williams were doing. This whole concept of broken time freed up the rhythm sections. It created a dialogue in rhythm sections as opposed to just the solid rhythm section like Wynton Kelly and Paul Chambers and Jimmy Cobb. Then you had Tony Williams, Ron Carter, and Herbie Hancock.

"After that everybody followed that concept.

"It affected me on piano. Especially the voicings. If you listen to how Wynton Kelly played after Bill left Miles, he's playing those voicings like Bill. Because Miles wanted those voicings. Those pastel, transparent chords brought light into the music. Everybody—Keith Jarrett, for one—was influenced by that spirit of the way Bill would voice things."

I told Jack that Larry Bunker had said that when he first joined Bill and would try to play figures that would fit what Bill was doing, probably in the heads and out-choruses, Bill would immediately change it.

"I never had that problem," Jack said. "I always played against the music anyway. Because, being a pianist, I always hated drummers who got on top of a rhythm. If you repeated a phrase, they'd answer you back. I don't like that call-and-answer kind of response. I played my own ideas, which is what Paul did. And you have a dialogue. You play your own personality, you play your own ideas. That's what Eddie Gomez and I did, and Tony Williams, and all the drummers and bass players who participated in the freer aspect of the interplay between drums and bass and the soloist."

I asked about Jack's parents and family.

"My mother was a poet," he said. "She wrote songs. My uncle was a jazz deejay named Roy Wood, who became president of the National Association of Black Broadcasters. He was my influence into jazz. My father wasn't living with us. He was in California and just provided financial support. And I went to visit him. I had a half-sister. So I was the only kid.

"The piano was one of the things they gave you—piano and violin. My first experience with a piano teacher was horrific. It's a wonder I still had a love for music. This was an old fogy guy. If you didn't play the right notes, he'd smack your hands. He was crazy. I'd be in tears. I told my mother I didn't want to take piano. I was about four.

"My grandmother had a friend who lived around the corner who was a graduate of the American Conservatory of Music. She had at that time a real innovative, state-of-the-art way to teach kids where it was fun and interesting. She'd have little recitals at her house, give you gold stars and incentives. That got me turned onto playing the piano.

"I got into drums in high school, because we didn't have a piano in the marching and concert band. I played bass for a semester and then switched to drums. I started playing both of them around Chicago, I worked on piano and drums. I came to New York in 1966 with the idea of playing both of them. But I got hired on drums, so I decided to make that my forte and bring out the piano later. I was in my early twenties. My first job in New

York was with John Patton, and my second job was with Jackie McLean. I free-lanced around. My first international job was with the Charles Lloyd quartet. I was with him about two years.

"I worked with Stan Getz for a while. Between the times I worked with Stan and with Miles, I worked with Bill. I know because I left Bill to go with Miles. I joined Miles in '69, and I was on the *Bitches Brew* album. Then I did a lot of free-lancing. I worked with Betty Carter, I worked with Abbey Lincoln, Joe Henderson, McCoy Tyner. I worked for a week with Monk, which was a great treat, at Club Baron uptown in Harlem. I worked there with Walter Booker, Charlie Rouse, and Monk. That was great. I had a good time."

I told Jack I was intrigued that anyone who plays piano so well would switch instruments. "I would think the piano would be such a great love," I said.

"Well it is," Jack said. "It still is. I still maintain it. But I felt that I had more to contribute as a drummer at that time. I still intend to contribute to the piano aspect of it, in terms of composing. I'd like to make some more piano records, and maybe do some special performances at some time when I've been able to woodshed and get it the way I want it. I haven't regretted making the drums the main instrument.

"It was almost a prophecy come true. When I was in Chicago, I worked with Eddie Harris. I filled in with Eddie once when he had the *Exodus to Jazz* record. Harold Jones played drums in the piano trio with me. So I had both references. I've played with a lot of drummers, so I know from the aspect of a soloist what a lot of different drummers do. I worked for a week with Eddie, filling in for Harold. Eddie always liked my drumming. I went out on the road with him a few times. We played a week in Philadelphia, at the Show Boat lounge, I think it was. Eddie was a multi-talented person himself. Eddie is more intelligent than a lot of people give him credit for. He's very intuitive. He understands the business end of it. He wouldn't keep me steady with him, because he said, 'Well, man, you gotta make up your mind which one you're gonna play.' He said, 'I play piano, I play French horn, I play vibes, I play everything else, but you've gotta make your mark on one. Yeah, you play good piano, but drums, I'll tell you, if you stick with drums, you're gonna make a lot of money.'

"I said, 'Nah, I want to play both.' And I continued. And then when I got to New York, something just said, 'You're gonna make your mark as a drummer.'

"Now Eddie plays the piano and the saxophone and he's singing—after telling me to stick to one instrument! Eddie's always complaining about something. He complained about New York and the hostility of New York. He said, 'What do you want to go to New York for? The people are so *cold* there.' I think he's not happy unless he has something to moan about—but a talent! He just had a natural knack for all the instruments. There are just some people who can do that. Like Ira Sullivan. Ira is another genius. I saw him with Red Rodney. Red Rodney said to me, 'We'll be playing these things, and I'll look over at Ira, and he's playing the wrong fingering, but the right notes are coming out! It just blows me away.'"

I told Jack about a semi-mythical incident in which some musicians took Ira into a pawnshop and turned him loose on all sorts of instruments, all of which he would pick up and immediately play. It is part of the jazz folklore of Chicago, but I've never known whether the story is true.

"He's just gifted, very gifted," Jack said.

"It was always said he couldn't read," I noted.

"I think Ira can read a little bit. I don't think he's ever been a fast reader. He knows notes. He teaches down in Florida."

I said, "In those cases where they say someone can't read, it usually turns out that they can read but can't read fast."

"Well, I'm one of those!" Jack said, laughing.

"Bill Evans was a *freaky* reader," I said.

Jack said, "Oh yeah. I saw him look down a whole score and play it. Herbie Hancock does that too. Some guy had written a piece, all sorts of clusters, Herbie played it first time down. Classical complex stuff. Bill was amazing. Stan Getz was another guy. Stan read, but he claimed he didn't know anything about changes. But he had a natural ear! Stan heard the melody of something and played off the melody, but what he played is amazing. I heard a tape of Stan with [drummer] Terri Lyn Carrington and [bassist] Anthony Cox. There was a young pianist on it, and his youth was pushing Stan, and Stan was playing stuff like Wayne Shorter, unbelievable stuff at breakneck tempos. And Stan was just floating through it. And Stan jokes with me. He says, 'Jack, you never played for me, you were just there for the money!' And I say, '*What* money?'

"Gene Ammons was an amazing sight-reader. He'd see the music, look at it, and throw it on the floor.

"The thing I loved most about Stan was the sound. All those guys who came out of Lester Young. Stan came out with his own originality. Stan moved with the times. He kept young people with him. But his lyricism was the most beautiful thing! Like Bill! They had this thing, this ability to play and interpret a melody. Play a ballad, and play delicious stuff, and just play the melody, play the song, tell the story of the song!"

"I remember long ago in Chicago," I said, "Donald Byrd and I used to hang out a lot and he said, 'After fifteen years in this business, I've come to the conclusion that the hardest thing is to play straight melody and give it feeling.'"

"Yeah!" Jack agreed. "That's what the young, especially the young black musicians, are now discovering—all of a sudden. They have all the chops they need, they can play as high, as fast, as low, as they want, and especially trumpet players. I was watching this program on television on black entertainment. Ramsey Lewis has a show. It's a half-hour format. It's one of those things where, again, they cram everything into this half hour. You have to come on the show and bring a clip of your stuff, because you don't actually get a chance to play. So Ramsey interviews these players. They had the Harper Brothers on, they had Marlon Jordan, Kent Jordan, these young New Orleans new breed of musicians. He was playing a ballad, and he was saying, 'You play a ballad, and you see people go *Aaaaah*, and that's what I want to do—move people.' The younger kids have the chops, but now they're not so much trying to show it off but to go inside and dig. Draw something out of the music."

"Speaking of guys who play several instruments," I said, "I was talking last week in Toronto to Don Thompson . . . ."

"Oh, he's amazing!" Jack interjected.

"Well, apropos of your point about young people who can play all the notes in sight, Don said he thinks a lot of the young bass players did not really learn the lesson of Scott LaFaro. Don said they're playing high on the instrument, and fast, but they forget, he said, how melodic and how supportive he was . . . ."

"Yes!" Jack affirmed. "That's important! To learn to be supportive! When it's time to fly, you fly!"

"Jazz is unusual in the arts since it's a co-operative."

"Well it's supposed to be," Jack said, laughing. "That's not always the case!"

"How long have you been working as a leader?"

"I guess my first album as a leader of a group was in 1975, with a group called Directions, on Prestige. The group included Alex Foster, Peter Warren, and John Abercrombie.

"I did a lot of traveling last year because I was on tour with an all-star band I put together with Herbie Hancock, Pat Metheny, and Dave Holland. Prior to that I made an album called *Parallel Realities,* which was my biggest seller—I guess it was the most accessible record I'd recorded. I had a group called Special Edition, which is my present band, with people like David

Murray and Arthur Blythe, along with Peter Warren. I had Howard Johnson and John Purcell. And Rufus Reid joined the band. I had Chico Freeman also. The current group, which has been together for the last three years, has Greg Osby, a fine pioneer of the alto and soprano saxophone, and Gary Thomas, who is a young giant of the tenor saxophone and flute. Before Special Edition, I had an all-star group with Eddie Gomez, Lester Bowie, and John Abercrombie, called New Directions. We recorded two albums for ECM, one of which won the Grand Prix du Disque in France. The *Parallel Realities* record won the album of the year last year in Japan.

"I've been doing a lot of recording, touring, and writing. I want to get more involved in producing.

"Johnny Griffin said that jazz is not a trend, jazz is a life-style. You have to live the life, whatever that consists of. Doing it full time, you're constantly living on the edge. That's changed now that we're in recession. People who had corporate and white-collar jobs are now finding themselves out of work. If you're fairly successful, and it seems like I am, you're free-lancing. I think jazz is suffering quite a bit in the United States, but it's doing very well in Europe and Japan. So a lot of the musicians record for European and Japanese labels, and are actually being supported and working in the other countries.

"The work is minimal, harder, here because the emphasis is on commerciality. The instant return, rather than looking over the long haul. With the Gulf war, the recession, and the savings-and-loan business, America is learning the hard way. They have to experience it.

"But the American spirit is resilient, and people will learn by their mistakes and start to plan for the long haul rather than the short gratification. I think it was necessary to go through that period of greed. It's yin and yang. The universal sequence of life is that, pushing and pulling. Good and evil, good and evil. We have free will to distinguish between good and evil. We're the only species that has to learn from its mistakes. We have to learn by doing. That's the only way we grow. And jazz is the perfect example of that, because a lot of mistakes of jazz have become the catalysts for innovation. Things that weren't intended. Mistakes can have a positive effect on things. There's a price to pay for them. But if the lesson is learned and you build off those mistakes, build a stronger foundation to counteract the mistakes by taking stock, you go forward."

I told Jack that Max Roach seemed curiously optimistic these days. "I don't mean unrealistic, because he's perfectly aware of what's going on in the country. But I've never heard Max in quite that mood. Max seemed to feel a little as you do, that the country may have learned something."

"Yes," Jack said. "America, with all its bulk and greed and bigotry—there's something about this experiment that still hasn't reached its fruition. The experiment has a potential. The potential is here in America. That's why everybody looks to it. You still have the right to make a decision that people may not have in, say, China. Russia has to go through the same thing that this country went through—the Civil War, with all those states seceding and then becoming a united states of their own. They all have to get their nationalism together and then come together. They've got to work that out. Here, we're ahead of that. It's very complicated to get all these nationalities in one country and try to address all those needs. But they will be addressed. It's just hard to deal with masses of people and make sure every person is taken care of. It's still an experiment in America, but it has the potential to lead in a positive way: to learn from the mistakes and greed, to learn to help the less fortunate. And to learn a spirituality, which has been missing for the last ten or twelve years.

"After 'Trane died, the spiritual aspect of the music went out the window. We have this commercial radio format. Coltrane put the spiritual aspect into the music. That's the element I hope we get back to, because we do need a spiritual renaissance, not necessarily from a religious point of view, but from a cosmic point of view. Not going to some retreat and meditating and talking about peace and love. We have *work* to do. *How* we work is what matters. I think we need to learn how to work less and produce more, so we're not doing this workaholic thing. You can test yourself in a way that is not stressful. We need to lighten up on the stress and learn that we can have more power with ease, with more relaxation, with more concentration, and get the job done more thoroughly and much faster, even though it might seem slower.

"In our computer information age, we have to learn to sort it out from nonsense, from the trivial. We have to learn how to slow down and let things take their time to build—like, young musicians or writers or poets or playwrights or dancers, who haven't had time yet to build. Flowers. I think it's very important to learn how to let time do the growing, let some things age. You get wisdom."

I mentioned something Max Roach had remarked to me: "If we can't make it here, we can't make it anywhere."

"The American experiment," Jack said, "cannot be said to have failed, because it hasn't been completed."

1992

Jazz Black and White

Part 1

On April 12, 1991, a remarkable interview with Sonny Rollins appeared in the *New York Times*, remarkable because it was a highly visible public admission by a major black artist that there exists a substantial anti-white racism in jazz.

The occasion for the interview, with Peter Watrous, was a Carnegie Hall reunion concert with guitarist Jim Hall. Thirty years earlier, Rollins had made the album *The Bridge* with Hall.

Rollins told Watrous, "In 1961 I had been off the music scene for a while, so in contemplating my return . . . I thought it would be good to have a band without a piano to make an impression, get a little different sound. Jim had an incredible harmonic sense; he's such a sensitive player. So to me, he was the perfect guy to play with."

Rollins continued: "As I recall, we got very good response, it was a big story and the group was great. But there was some controversy about the fact that Jim was white. After *Freedom Suite*"—an album Rollins recorded in 1958—"some people expected me to behave in a certain way and wondered why I would hire a white musician. I took some heat for that. I thought it was a healing symbol, and I didn't have any qualms about doing it. Social issues didn't have anything to do with hiring white musicians who were qualified; it was that simple. And it was a great group."

The job had a salutary effect on the career of Jim Hall. He had been patronized as a mere white west-coast player when that style of music was denigrated in New York as effete. Since Rollins was seen as a black militant, his approval opened doors for Hall, who was forthwith accepted as a major guitarist. The association with Rollins validated Hall, as the period with Miles Davis gave a sort of Good Housekeeping Seal of Approval to Bill Evans and other white musicians Miles hired, including Chick Corea, Dave Holland, Dave Liebman, John Scofield, John McLaughlin, and the saxophonist Bill Evans.

Quiet as it's kept, anti-white bias has existed in jazz for a long time. Oscar Peterson encountered opprobrium when in 1953 he hired Herb Ellis as the guitarist in his trio. "We," he said, meaning himself, Herb, and Ray Brown, "really became a close-knit unit. Our friendship became even tighter, and we were criticized for having a white person in our group.

"I would get hate letters in Chicago about Herbie Ellis being in the group—from both races, by the way, just so everybody gets their rightful recognition. I'd get hate letters about, 'What is that white cat doing in the band? He can't play nothin'—he's white.' Whatever that had to do with it, I don't know."

Another black musician who will talk openly of anti-white bias is Art Farmer.

"This whole racial thing," Art said, "is a lot of shit, from all the way down all the way to the top. And the closer you get to the top, the more it disappears. But I used to think that way too.

"After Miles Davis made that nonet record for Capitol, what they called *The Birth of the Cool*, he came out to Los Angeles. I'd known him for years. That was a great record, with Gerry Mulligan and Lee Konitz and the others. I said to Miles, 'Man, why have you got those white guys on your gig?' Miles said, 'I don't care what color they are. As long as they can play the music the way it's supposed to be played, that's what it's all about.'

"It made me re-examine my thinking.

"Where I grew up, Arizona and California, you were damned sure that white people couldn't play jazz. The situation was so divided. Your ears would be closed right from the beginning. You just wouldn't listen to some white person playing jazz, just wouldn't give a damn. It went on and on and on and on and on. White people playing jazz, it didn't make any sense to me at all.

"I don't apologize for my ignorance; I was a young kid. But, man, look, if you were a black kid coming up in L.A. and went through all the shit out there, I didn't want to hear about no white people playing jazz. You'd go out and play in a club that drew a mixed audience, and the police would come in and close it down. That kind of thing closed my ears, man. I couldn't give credit where credit was due, because of the social scene.

"After I got away from that, and was able to be more objective about it, then I could hear what people were doing. And then it seemed to me the most stupid thing on earth to think that just because somebody is white they can't play, and vice versa—that just because somebody is black, they can play.

"Years ago, Dizzy Gillespie was on the Mike Wallace television show.

Mike said something like, 'Is it true that only black people can play jazz?'

"And Dizzy said, 'No, it's not true. And if you accept that premise, well then what you're saying is that maybe black people can *only* play jazz. And black people, like anyone else, can be anything they want to be.'"

Yet another black musician who will talk about the issue is Clark Terry. But first let me tell you a harrowing story that Clark told me some years ago.

Soon after high school, Clark traveled with Ida Cox and the Darktown Scandals in the Reuben and Cherry Carnival. After finishing a tour, the group went south from Pennsylvania to its winter quarters in Jacksonville, Florida. Clark said, "I was hanging out with William Oval Austin. We called him Fats Austin. He was a bass player. We had no warm-weather clothes. We went to the five and ten cent store to buy some T-shirts. They cost about fifteen cents in those days."

The store was crowded, and Austin accidentally bumped into an elderly white woman carrying a cane. She started screaming, "That nigger tried to knock me down. Kill him, kill him!" Clark and his friend edged their way to the door, and, as soon as they were outside, ran. A screaming mob pursued them. The two musicians came to a site where an office building was being erected. Fortunately for them it was a Saturday and the site was deserted. They ran into it. Clark pulled Austin down into an excavation and the two young men covered themselves with mud and debris. They could hear the crowd running above them. At last a silence descended. "But we stayed buried in that mud till dark," Clark said. Then, cautiously, they crawled out of the excavation and left.

It is one of numberless incidents of that kind I have heard, variations on an ugly theme. But it remains especially vivid in my mind, and it is one reason Clark's magnanimity of spirit amazes me. It amazes me that men like Clark can even speak to whites, let alone rise far above racism. Clark despises racism both black and white.

Some years ago he formed a big band to teach music to boys in Harlem. "I started that band out of my own pocket," Clark said. "It was the forerunner of what turned out to be the Jazzmobile. I got all those little kids together and bought instruments for them. One of those kids is now head of the jazz department at Boys High School in Brooklyn.

"We were rehearsing at this little cold-water walkup flat on 125th Street. There was a very talented kid named Fred Wayne, who wrote me about sixty charts. We had a full big band, and I was teaching these kids how to read.

"Don Stratton at the Manhattan School of Music made it possible for us to use the school. Here we've got kids coming off the corner, and for the first time they've got access to classrooms, to blackboards, to music books, to tapes—real college atmosphere.

"After a while I had to go out a lot. I had Don and a few other people to help me teach the kids while I was away. Attendance started falling off. I found out that one kid was a sort of ringleader in the hate-Whitey movement. He had instigated the kids to not pursue the program any more.

"I came back. Don Stratton said, 'Things are not going too well, Clark. I kind of suspect what it is, but you'll find out.'

"I called a little meeting and came to find that that's what it was. One of the little dudes had the nerve to say to me, 'Man, we don't want Whitey teaching us about *our* music.'

"There they were with university facilities, instead of climbing up those damned stairs, five flights to rehearse in a cold studio.

"I just gave it up. I just completely forgot about it, I got so disgusted.

"A long time ago, I had a problem with this when I had a big band at Club Baron. The band was about 50-50. I had people come up to me and say, 'Man, what kind of shit is this, bringing Whitey up to Harlem?'

"I'd say, 'Well, man, Harlem is known as the home of good jazz, and I thought it was up to somebody to bring good jazz back here. In doing so, I picked the best cats I can get, and I don't listen with my eyes.'

"My theory is that a note doesn't give a fuck who plays it, as long as he plays it well."

Once upon a time, jazz was considered popular entertainment, though from its earliest days it had champions who perceived it as high art. In due course, it achieved the wide recognition so many writers and musicians and lay admirers have insisted it deserved, with full degree-granting courses in the playing of the music at universities all over the United States and Canada, commissions for composition, and awards for merit. But as this process progresses, anti-white racism is showing increasing signs of being institutionalized. Two examples are the American Jazz Masters Fellowship Awards given by the National Endowment for the Arts, and the Jazz at Lincoln Center program conducted by trumpeter Wynton Marsalis and writer Stanley Crouch, both black.

Three Jazz Masters Awards, giving recipients $20,000 each, are made each year by the NEA. Between 1982, when the awards were instituted, and 1993, only one of the thirty-six awards went to a white musician, Gil Evans, who, perhaps significantly, was a Canadian. In 1994, when drummer Louie Bellson received one, the proportion of the awards rose to two white musicians out of thirty-nine awards. Some of the awards went to players whose contributions to the evolution of the art would be deemed by most informed people as marginal; and the omissions from the list included Woody Herman, Benny Goodman, and Buddy Rich, all of whom were alive when the awards began, and Red Norvo, who still is.

The inverted racism in later years has been reinforced by the need to be politically correct, turning up all over the country. For example, in 1991 pianist John Eaton, from Washington, D.C., was engaged to give a recital at the Museum of Natural History in Denver, Colorado. He was asked by the museum staff to play a program that was politically correct. They asked him to perform only music by black composers. Eaton dismissed this "impertinent proviso" as "a new version of an old practice dormant since the McCarthy years." He told the museum staff he would play what he felt like playing or not come to Denver. The museum staff relented—a little. He arrived in Denver. The emcee at the museum made what Eaton considered a "bizarre request."

The emcee asked, "Would it be all right if we put a portrait of Duke Ellington on the stage while you're playing, Mr. Eaton?"

Eaton, amazed though he was, agreed, noting in passing that the painting was "the most grotesque likeness of anybody I've ever seen," although Ellington, as he put it, was "an excruciatingly handsome" man.

Eaton played his recital, which in fact ended with a selection of Ellington pieces. It was not enough. He was accused after the performance by a museum staffer of not appreciating "adequately the importance of Afro-America in the music you played tonight."

Eaton was sufficiently disturbed about the incident to write an article for the *Washington Post* about it; and the *Rocky Mountain News* was embarrassed enough for Denver to carry an editorial about it.

Hank O'Neal, who heads the small Chiaroscuro record label, said, "These matters are becoming increasingly serious, and I see nasty little examples all the time in New York. When I first started Chiaroscuro a zillion years ago, the primary idea behind the company was to document mainstream musicians, usually black, who were being ignored by the majors and what few minors existed in 1970. It is now a few years later and we are still doing this but at least half the things we have done over the past year or so have been devoted to outstanding young musicians who can't get arrested by a big company simply because they are white."

Anti-white bias does not come only from black musicians. Many white critics (and even some white musicians) have abetted it. Some European jazz critics use it as an entrée in courting black musicians (not all of whom are taken in by it) and in venting a strong if muted anti-Americanism.

It has long been manifest in the myth that the first serious appreciation of jazz occurred in Europe in a time when jazz was held in contempt in the land of its birth, which overlooks the immense popularity of Louis Armstrong and Duke Ellington by the end of the 1920s and the body of intelligent American critical writing on the subject by that time. The legend persists despite extensive research by James Lincoln Collier, and to a lesser extent by me, that shatters it. When anyone questions it, some British writer is certain to fly into fulminations bordering on apoplexy.

The politics of it are as follows:

The United States is a backward and uneducated nation that never could have appreciated the great art form it spawned. We Europeans had the aesthetic sensitivity, cultivation, and intelligence to write "seriously" about jazz before you ever understood its worth. You are a land of racists; your failure to appreciate jazz is proof of it.

My father, who was English, very early made me see that, obviously, you did not encounter racism where there were no racial minorities. Even small minorities did not inspire racism, since a small group was seen as a faint threat, if that. Only when the minority had reached a goodly size, a sort of critical mass, did racism begin to show itself. He said there was little racism in England because it had no large visible ethnic minorities. If there ever should be, he said, you would see racism in England. He lived to see the influx of population from the West Indies, India, and Pakistan—and the rise of a vicious English racism, graphically described to us by my sister, who lived there with her Chinese husband, a physician, and experienced it firsthand. A survey done some years ago found that something more than 60 percent of the white English population admitted to being racist. At least the general run of white American racists have the grace to be hypocritical about it.

The French version of the anti-American malady is manifest in the film *'Round Midnight,* although you may not detect it unless you have lived in France.

'Round Midnight is insulting to white Americans and patronizing to black. Its essential message is: We French are able to appreciate the great art of your noble savages, your naïve but talented singing-and-dancing darkies. You do not appreciate them; you kill them.

A quality of parody is implicit in the film's main character, a compound of Lester Young (his idiosyncratic argot) and Bud Powell (his voluntary exile in France, where of course he is loved and appreciated). The protagonist supposedly is a great and innovative musician. Dexter Gordon was not playing well by the time the picture was made, and thus the film misrepresents what greatness in jazz really is. Ironically, in view of the movie's essential thesis, it was during his sojourn in Europe that Gordon's playing declined.

A clear example of the French attitude to jazz came in a conversation I had in a sidewalk cafe in Paris with André Hodeir, the French composer and jazz critic. He said, "No white man ever contributed anything to the development of jazz." The English critic Stanley Dance has taken the same position, and the late Ralph J. Gleason wrote, "It is possible to speculate that all the white musicians could be eliminated from the history of the music without significantly altering its development." The avowed Marxist critic Frank Kofsky wrote that jazz "is first and foremost a black art—an art created and nurtured by black people in this country out of the wealth of their historical experience." This is in spite of Lester Young's openly acknowledged debt to Frank Trumbauer and Bix Beiderbecke, to cite one example.

This is not a debatable point. These influences on Young are well documented, both in his own statements and those of his friends. In a biography titled *Lester Young: Profession Président* by Luc Delannoy, published in French in 1987 by Editions Denoel and in English as *Pres: The Story of Lester Young* by the University of Arkansas Press (1993), the author notes:

"Two recordings fascinated Lester: *I'll Never Miss the Sunshine*, containing a breathtaking chorus by Tram and recorded in Camden, New Jersey, on June 14, 1923, by the Benson orchestra of Chicago, and the first recording made by Tram and Bix with the Sioux City Six on October 10, 1924. . . .

"At the beginning of 1927, Trumbauer signed a contract with the OKeh company for a group formed around the nucleus of the Jean Goldkette Orchestra, with whom he had been performing for three years. A first record was cut in New York on February 4. . . . That recording and the many that followed it formed the basis of Lester's record collection."

Another saxophonist who attracted Young was Jimmy Dorsey.

Young repeatedly attested to the influence of Trumbauer and Beiderbecke, though he was initially interested in Red Nichols. In 1959, not long before his death, Prez was interviewed by François Postif in Paris. The interview is on tape. Young told Postif:

"I had to make a decision between Frankie Trumbauer and Jimmy Dorsey. I wasn't sure which direction I wanted to go, you dig? And I had these . . . records and I'd play one of Jimmy's, I'd play one of Trumbauer's. . . . I don't know nothin' about Hawk then, you dig? But I can see the only people . . . telling stories I liked to hear were them. So I'd play one of his, one of them, you dig? So I had both of 'em made, you dig?"

Postif asked: "Do you think your sound is close to the Trumbauer sound?"

Prez answered, "Yes."

The influence of Lester Young in turn on Charlie Parker is also well documented. On November 3, 1993, the *International Herald Tribune* published an interview by Michael Zwerin with photographer William Claxton, famous for his brilliant visual documentation of jazz. Claxton recalled a weekend Charlie Parker spent with him at the home of Claxton's mother in Pasadena, California, at a time when Parker was appearing at the Tiffany Club. Chet Baker was playing trumpet in Parker's group. Claxton asked Parker why he had hired Baker. "He plays pure and simple," Parker said. "I like that. That little white cat reminds me of those Bix Beiderbecke records my mother used to play."

The statements of both Lester Young and Charlie Parker make mockery of an English writer's assertion that Beiderbecke "made history but didn't influence it."

Statements by Benny Carter of his debt to Trumbauer, and any number of other examples of white influence in jazz, not the least of which was Jack Teagarden's expansion of trombone technique, refute Hodeir. Indeed, at the very time Hodeir made that statement—it was in 1958—Bill Evans was revolutionizing jazz piano in New York, bringing into it voicings and an approach to touch and time that would influence hundreds, perhaps thousands, of pianists, black and white alike. Hodeir's statement was made, of course, with the complacent confidence with which so many Europeans express their insights into a country they do not know and, in many instances, such as that of the British critic Max Harrison, have never even visited.

Since 1959, I have known most of the major writers about jazz in America. I have never known a white jazz critic who was racist, excepting in that sense that a few have been anti-white. I have read perhaps three black ones who aren't.

Leroi Jones (Amiri Baraka), in his 1963 book *Blues People*, argued that jazz is not merely black music but is the music of rebellion. He defined jazz as "Negro music," saying it "drew its strength and beauty out of the depths of the black man's soul . . . . "

Baraka described Benny Goodman as "a rich Jewish clarinetist." Anti-Semitism seems to be an integral part of the anti-white racism.

The pianist Joe Zawinul, in a 1992 interview with the European magazine *Jazz Forum*, was asked, "Do you agree that, as some black musicians say, only black musicians can play jazz?"

He replied, "You ask Miles Davis. He always says I'm the only one." In view of remarks Miles made, including expressions of admiration for Bill Evans, Miles may have been shining him on. Farther along in the interview, Zawinul said: "The Jewish people took away a lot of the black music and made it sound like itself. The black musician was supposed to be working in the kitchen, cleaning the dirt. That's the Jewish system. That's the way it is."

Considering the relationships of Joe Glaser with Louis Armstrong (Armstrong even wore a Star of David on a chain around his neck); Martha Glaser with Erroll Garner, Artie Shaw with Hot Lips Page, Roy Eldridge, and Billie Holiday; Benny Goodman with Teddy Wilson, Lionel Hampton, and Charlie Christian; Norman Granz with Ella Fitzgerald, Oscar Peterson, Count Basie, and more; Orrin Keepnews with Thelonious Monk, Cannonball Adderley, and more; Alfred Lion and Francis Wolff with Art Blakey, Horace Silver, and more; Bob Weinstock with Miles Davis, Red Garland, John Coltrane, and more, not to mention the work of such writers as Leonard Feather, Nat Hentoff, and Barry Ulanov on behalf of black artists, the remark strikes a strange note. Zawinul was born in Vienna. Vienna is widely known as the anti-Semitism capital of the world.

Wynton Marsalis too has expressed anti-Semitism. During an appearance on the TV show *Tony Brown's Journal*, he said blacks have been held back for so many years because the music business is controlled by "people who read the Torah and stuff."

He continued: "Every idiom of black music, be it jazz, rhythm-and-blues, or whatever, has declined in its negroidery and purpose. It became more whitified. It's not the white people's fault. The white people, they do what they do to support the misconceptions that they started when they brought the brothers and sisters over here as slaves. We are, in effect, in a state of war. . . .

"The documents of this country, which are noble, (have been) misrepresented and compromised to the point of absurdity by so-called white people who were Europeans, people who functioned as Negroes in European society. They came over here and said, 'We're not the lower class of European society now, because we have these black Americans that we can dog and mess over.'" There was no mistaking his meaning.

Nor that of Stanley Crouch, whom Marsalis acknowledges as his friend, teacher, and mentor, in a liner note to the Marsalis album *The Majesty of the Blues*: "But we must understand that the money lenders of the marketplace have never EVER known the difference between an office or an auction block and a temple, they have never known that there was an identity to anything other than that of a hustle, a shuck, a scam, a game."

One of the most interesting examples of black bias in writing about jazz occurred in an article by Herb Boyd, published in the February 1991 issue of *Crisis*, the magazine of the National Association for the Advancement of Colored People. The general import of the article was that jazz has survived despite the white society and the dilution of it by white players.

Boyd writes that "Wynton and Branford Marsalis were given the red carpet and Miles popped up in ads and a sound bite or two, but these affairs have leveled off and much of the media clamor over jazz is now focused on Harry Connick Jr., Geoff Keezer, Benny Green, Joey DeFrancesco, and a gaggle of other young white hopefuls. Rushing them to center stage while hundreds of black musicians hover in the shadows is not a new development; the pattern for this is as old as American greed and was evident at the very dawn of the Jazz Age.

"Jazz was hardly baptized when it was expropriated by white musicians. The first jazz group to make a name for itself through recordings was the Original Dixieland Jazz Band (ODJB), a white band from New Orleans. After several black bands refused to record, fearing their ideas would be stolen, the ODJB leaped at the opportunity, cut a disc and sold a million copies in 1917. As they gained fame and fortune, such stellar performers as trumpeter Freddie Keppard, Papa Celestin and Doc Cook labored in comparative obscurity.

"During the next decade when Louis 'Satchmo' Armstrong had no peer on trumpet or cornet, Bix Beiderbecke, a white cornetist from Iowa, was heralded and feted as if he were the second coming of Buddy Bolden. A quiet, unassuming artist, Bix was nevertheless the darling of the flappers and his acclaim soon rivaled, and among many listeners, eclipsed Satch's. . . .

"Even more so than during the so-called Jazz Age, white musicians ruled the roost, commanding the spotlight, and went to the rank; for every Tex Beneke and Charlie Barnet that was featured in the movies and on radio or headlined a show at a major ballroom, there were dozens of black bands, even including such illustrious royalty as Duke Ellington and Count Basie, dodging the nightriders on the 'chitlin circuit.'"

The theme that "the white man stole the black man's music" is reiterated by Spike Lee in an interview with *Los Angeles Times Magazine* of June 2, 1991. "There is definitely a black aesthetic in music, art and dance," Lee said. "For me, black culture is a lot more interesting. I know whites think that, too, because they try to steal everything they can and make money off it, and then have the audacity to call it their own. . . ."

Saxophonist Archie Shepp said, "We are not angry men. We are enraged. . . . I can't see any separation between my music and my life. I play pretty much race music; it's about what happened to my father, to me, and what can happen to my kids."

Amiri Baraka wrote that whites won almost all the jazz polls in the 1930s and '40s. But Duke Ellington had one of the most popular bands of the swing era and for some time after 1940 won more polls than any other bandleader. Anyone who has copies of the *Metronome* All-Star Band records made in the 1940s knows that the personnel of those records was quite mixed. Dizzy Gillespie won the *Metronome* poll in 1946, when bebop still was new. In June 1946, after an Ella Fitzgerald performance at the Apollo, *Metronome* called her "the greatest singer of them all." By the end of the 1950s, the balance had shifted even further toward black players. As Stuart Nicholson points out in his biography *Ella Fitzgerald* (Victor Gollancz, London, 1993), she had an almost unbroken run of winning the *Down Beat* poll from 1937 until 1971 when she was displaced by five votes not by a white singer but by Roberta Flack. When I was editor of *Down Beat*—from May of 1959 to September of 1961—part of my job was to conduct those polls. In the 1959 Readers' Poll, 32 of the 62 winners were black, and as for press opinion, in the 1960 international jazz critics poll, the discrepancy was larger: of 61 winners, only 12 were white.

It is true that John Maher, the owner of the magazine, tried to keep black musicians off the covers, but my colleague Chuck Suber, the publisher, and I fought him with every weapon up to and including threats to resign, and won. But the battle grew exhausting and Maher's bias was one of the reasons I quit. Thus I know from personal experience that bias existed at the business level but not among the musicians and not among the writers, all of whom were passionately liberal and pro-black on social, political, economic, and aesthetic issues. And there was disparity in the polls.

But from the earliest days of jazz, white writers fought against bias, none more energetically or with a greater sense of fairness than Leonard Feather. In the 1940s, when he and Barry Ulanov ran *Metronome* magazine, one of them—Leonard can no longer remember which—coined the term Crow Jim for anti-white racism. Leonard was incensed by the Herb Boyd article.

"Two wrongs don't make a right," Leonard wrote in a letter to me. "That rather obvious truism comes to mind.

"Before dealing with the second wrong, let's look back at the first wrong—the exclusion or downgrading of great African-American artists who suffered humiliation, denial of jobs, segregated musicians' unions, and innumerable other problems. The cause was very obvious: racism.

"It infuriated me to see capable but hardly earth-shaking white musicians winning *Down Beat* and *Metronome* polls while the true giants were relegated to lower places. Big Sid Catlett never won a *Down Beat* or *Metronome* poll; neither did Jimmy Blanton. At a time when Billie Holiday was at her peak, the *Down Beat* winners for female vocalist were first Helen O'Connell, later Helen Forrest and Dinah Shore. True, some of the white musicians won deservedly: it was logical for Benny Goodman to earn first place, but it was frustrating to see Louis Armstrong all but ignored while the trumpet winner in 1937, '38, and '39 was Harry James. During the early 1950s, when Louis Armstrong was by no means past his peak, this honor went to Maynard Ferguson and then Chet Baker.

"I fought this racism tooth and nail. In the belief that carefully selected experts would make more representative choices than magazine readers, I worked with Robert Goffin, the Belgian jazz critic, and Arnold Gingrich, then editor of *Esquire*, to assemble an interracial board of experts. This resulted in the magazine's publication of poll victories in which 20 of 26 winning musicians were black. The winners were presented in a concert at the Metropolitan Opera House. The New York *Amsterdam News*, the *Pittsburgh Courier*, and other African-American publications hailed this unprecedented acknowledgment of the true heroes of jazz.

"In 1956, Stan Kenton fired off an angry telegram published in *Down Beat* complaining about the jazz critics' poll. 'It's obvious,' he wrote, 'that there's a new minority group, white jazz musicians.' He expressed 'complete and total disgust' at the results of the poll.

"In a long letter attacking Kenton, I pointed out the triumphs of black musicians, most of whom inspired the members of the Kenton band.

"Meanwhile, however, the first wrong has given way to the second. As a life member of the NAACP, I receive its *Crisis* magazine every month and was shocked to see in the February 1991 issue the laughably inaccurate article by Herb Boyd that turned the truth upside down: Bix Beiderbecke was acclaimed while Louis Armstrong was in eclipse, etc. . . ."

Any statement that jazz is "black music" and only black music is racist on the face of it. In the first place, the description of jazz as something invented in a cultural vacuum solely by blacks is simplistic at the least. New Orleans, where jazz emerged, was a complex society of many peoples. The term Creole originally meant anyone of European ancestry born in the New World, including Spanish America. In New Orleans there were white Creoles, black Creoles descended from Haitian immigrants, and Creoles of mixed blood. (The word's roots are Spanish and Portuguese.) By a stroke of the legislative pen, the mixed-blood Creoles were classified as black, despite their French ancestry, French language, and European culture. This was a boon to jazz in that they brought to the black community a great deal of musical knowledge and European musicianship.

It is of course insane to classify someone who is seven-eighths white as black. It was a fiction by which white racists kept light Creoles in their place. It is a fiction by which black racists maintain the definition of jazz as "Negro music."

Herb Boyd resorts to the kind of slanted language that intends to destroy by innuendo: phrases such as "a gaggle of young white hopefuls." The language itself is contemptuous.

"Rushing them to center stage while hundreds of black musicians hover in the shadows" is another such phrase. It is a willful, deliberate lie. On February 24, 1992, *Newsweek* magazine carried a two-page story on a generation of musicians caught in the middle. Of saxophonist Bobby Watson, it said, that "just as he struck out on his own, the rules changed. He suddenly was too old to be promoted as a 'young lion' in the mold of Wynton Marsalis. . . . Yet he was too young to be marketed as the kind of 'living legend' the industry soon began to champion." (The record industry's emphasis reflects its usual venality; about half of its jazz output comprises reissues, which cost virtually nothing.) Besides Watson, the magazine cited Mulgrew Miller, Victor Lewis, Kenny Barron, Tony Williams, Sonny Fortune, and Ray Drummond. The article prompted saxophonist and composer Bill Kirchner to write the magazine a letter saying, "One could conclude from Tom Masland's otherwise creditable article that 'jazz's lost generation' consists entirely of black males. As I'm sure that profilees Bobby Watson, Ray Drummond, et al., would readily confirm, there are dozens of seasoned white jazz artists (male *and* female) who likewise deserve wider recognition, and black females as well. Masland does not mention that any such people even exist. What's his problem?"

The magazine didn't print the letter.

As for pianist Keezer, his career was pushed forward not by a white establishment but by Art Blakey, Benny Golson, and Art Farmer, all of whom hired him when he was unknown. At the time Boyd wrote that, Keezer had yet to play in a white group, and he still records with such colleagues as Christian McBride. Joey DeFrancesco worked for Miles Davis. Benny Green is a member of the Ray Brown Trio, a role in which he succeeds Monty Alexander and Gene Harris. Oscar Peterson recently was asked by the Glenn Gould Foundation to choose a promising young pianist as a protégé. He selected Benny Green. Oscar has been a staunch activist for minority rights in Canada.

Leonard Feather noted, "Mr. Boyd's ignorance was such that he included

Lionel Hampton and Teddy Wilson as members of Benny Goodman's band. They were not. As anyone with a minimal knowledge of jazz history knows, Teddy Wilson played only with the Goodman trio and Hampton with the quartet. The first real mixed band was led not by Goodman but by Benny Carter, whose international interracial orchestra was heard in Europe in 1937."

If the Original Dixieland Jazz Band was the first to be recorded, it was not because of white exclusion. By Herb Boyd's own statement, it was a matter of default. He says that several black bands refused to record. Then it was their fault, not that of an "establishment", that they were not the first on record. Again, the language is slanted: the sneering "the ODJB leaped at the opportunity . . . ." Could it be that they were smarter than their black colleagues? Boyd would be enraged by the very suggestion; but the thought is implicit in his accusation. But again, Boyd is ignorant or willfully dishonest. Black entertainers were being recorded before, during, and after the ODJB. As James Lincoln Collier put it, "The record industry, venal as always, would record anybody they could make money with."

Whether Boyd's next paragraph about Beiderbecke and Armstrong is the consequence of ignorance or willful mendacity is impossible to say. Armstrong was the most powerful influence in jazz, the man who defined its future as the art of the soloist. Armstrong became rich and famous, one of the best-known Americans in the world. At the time of Beiderbecke's death in 1931, Armstrong was appearing in a Broadway show and starring at Connie's, one of New York's leading cabarets. Bix, by contrast, was an obscure figure, unknown to most Americans and admired mostly by a small cadre of musicians—including, incidentally, Armstrong, who is on record as bitter about Bix's so-called friends who kept tempting him to drink. He received almost no press exposure in his lifetime, and it was not until 1936 that Otis Ferguson took an accurate measure of his music in the *New Republic*. Sales of his recordings were small, whereas many of Armstrong's were hits.

As for the mocking "second coming of Buddy Bolden," nobody knows how Bolden really played. The testimony that survives holds that he played loud and stayed close to the melody, inserting at most small embellishments. He was not a great improviser, perhaps not an improviser at all. Bix was a great improviser.

"Almost every jazz buff," Boyd wrote, "knows that Fletcher Henderson, Sy Oliver and Edgar Sampson scored the hits made famous by the likes of"—note the choice of words again—"Benny Goodman, 'the King of Swing,' Glenn Miller and Tommy Dorsey."

None of those writers wrote for Glenn Miller. But Boyd is apparently ignorant of one black arranger who did write for Miller: Eddie Durham. The more significant point is that white arrangers were writing for black bands before black arrangers wrote for Dorsey and Goodman. Bill Challis wrote for the Fletcher Henderson band when Henderson was still finding his voice as an arranger. They were, furthermore, close friends. It is likely that Henderson learned much from Challis. Benny Carter, one of the important figures in developing big-band writing, was emphatic in telling me, "Bill Challis was my idol."

Another white writer for the Henderson band was Will Hudson, who also contributed to the books of McKinney's Cotton Pickers and Erskine Tate around 1931, Cab Calloway in 1932, Henderson and Jimmie Lunceford in 1933 and '34, and the Mills Blue Rhythm Band in 1935. Two of Lunceford's big hits, *White Heat* and *Jazznocracy*, were Hudson compositions.

"Hudson," Gunther Schuller wrote in *The Swing Era*, "had a particular flair for the fast riff instrumentals popularized by the Casa Loma band, especially in their first hit, *Casa Loma Stomp*. Mills, a shrewd businessman" —he refers to publisher Irving Mills, Duke Ellington's partner—"felt that what Lunceford needed was a couple of 'hot' instrumentals à la Casa Loma in his repertory. Indeed, the Casa Loma's success in the early '30s had a widespread effect to which no band was impervious." In other words, the Lunceford hits echoed the style of the Casa Loma.

Russ Morgan, a white trombonist, also wrote for Henderson, and the arrangement of *Body and Soul* that Louis Armstrong recorded in 1930 is his. Van Alexander wrote extensively for Chick Webb.

Taken in sum, Fletcher Henderson probably played more charts by white arrangers than Benny Goodman played charts by Fletcher Henderson.

Part of the mythology holds that Tommy Dorsey "stole" Sy Oliver from Lunceford in order to get some soul into his band. Recently I had a number of conversations with Lillian Oliver, Sy's widow, whom he met when she was singing with one of the Dorsey vocal groups, the Sentimentalists.

Oliver was twenty-three when he joined Lunceford in 1933, playing trumpet, singing, and writing. Oliver told Dempsey J. Travis, who quotes him in *An Autobiography of Black Jazz* (Urban Research Institute, Chicago 1983), "I loved Jimmie, but at the same time I resented him. I had a love-hate relationship with him that until this day I have never fully understood, and yet he's one of the few guys that I can recall that I always respected. Of course I recognized that he was the world's greatest square."

According to Lillian Oliver, Lunceford paid Oliver $2.50 for his arrangement of *Margie,* and he had to do his own copying. Nor was the salary good. "Sy wanted to go to university," Lillian said. "He had already given Jimmie Lunceford his notice when Tommy Dorsey's manager told him Tommy wanted to talk to him. Tommy told Sy, 'Whatever Jimmie Lunceford is paying you, I'll pay you $5,000 a year more. And if you'll give me a year, I'll rebuild the band any way you want it.'" This was in 1939, and Dorsey was as good as his promise.

Furthermore, Lillian said, Dorsey was the first bandleader to give his writers full credit for their compositions. And he set up a publishing company to protect their copyrights and incomes. Thus Lillian still receives royalties from such Oliver compositions as *Well, Git It; Yes, Indeed;* and *Opus No. 1.*

Oliver got along well with Dorsey, Lillian said. "And he just loved Buddy Rich."

Finally, the Boyd article's special pleading that Duke Ellington had to work "the chitlin' circuit" is ludicrous. Boyd apparently doesn't know much about Ellington. Duke was a national celebrity before the '20s were ended, was invited to the White House in 1931, and traveled to engagements by private railway car. By 1937, Chick Webb had eight radio broadcasts a week, more than any big band, black or white. His fan letters numbered 5000 a week.

We can only guess at the excellence of the Jean Goldkette band out of Detroit, for its record company insisted on recording its more commercial pieces. The only way we can judge the Bill Challis charts is by some recent reconstructions of them.

What we do have is the testimony of Rex Stewart, who was playing cornet in the Henderson band when the encounter by the two bands at Roseland occurred. In *Hear Me Talkin' to Ya,* the invaluable 1955 compilation by Nat Shapiro and Nat Hentoff of interviews with jazzmen, Stewart is quoted as follows:

"About that time Fletcher inaugurated one-night stands . . . and each year we went further afield. . . . In 1930 we opened at the Greystone Ballroom in Detroit. Charlie Horvath and Charley Stanton were in charge and they said there were only two great bands in the country, Jean Goldkette's Victor band and us. Well, we scoffed and took it very lightly. After all, men like Buster Bailey, Don Redman, Hawk (Coleman Hawkins), Big Green, Russell Smith had been everywhere, and if this was such a hell of a band, they would have known about it. As I recall it, we closed the Greystone on a Sunday and had a few days off until Friday to open at Roseland in New York. Most of the guys came right back to Harlem, but Redman went to West Virginia to see his people and didn't make it back to New York.

"Opening night and no sign of Don, but Smack"—Henderson's nickname—"had a boy from Harlem, Benny Carter, to sit in until Don returned. We thought it strange (that) we were to open because we always were the featured band and played last. We had no idea of who was to be our relief. We finished our set and went outside for some air, but I was wondering who the other band was, how did it sound, and could I learn plenty with a Capital P. It was that Victor band with all those never-to-be-forgotten names, but my special kick was Bix, whose work I have always admired. . . .

"We were supposed to be the kings, the greatest thing in New York. We had the best men, the best arrangements. Then suddenly up pops this band of Johnny-come-latelies out of the sticks—white boys on top of it—and they just *creamed* us. It was pretty humiliating. And Bix—that *tone* he got! Knocked us all out."

The influence of Bix would soon show up in Stewart's own playing. In the mid-1930s Duke Ellington recording *Kissin' My Baby Goodnight*, the Stewart solo is a direct and obvious imitation of Beiderbecke's. Revisionists have never been comfortable with Stewart's admiration for Beiderbecke, and it has been said, and written, that he later repudiated this early admiration. Not so, according to his daughter Regina. "When I was a little girl," she told me, "my father talked about Bix, Bix, Bix. I didn't know who Bix was."

Another witness to the Goldkette band and the admiration it generated was Cuba Austin, who played drums with McKinney's Cotton Pickers. The Cotton Pickers and the Casa Loma Orchestra (at first known as the Orange Blossoms) were managed by Goldkette, whose base of operations was the Greystone Ballroom. In *Hear Me Talkin' to Ya*, Austin recalled his first encounter with the Goldkette group. The McKinney group arrived in Detroit to play the Arcadia Ballroom.

"Detroit was a wide-open town in those days and the great Goldkette band and the Orange Blossoms were also in Detroit," Austin said.

"We played a season at the Arcadia and moved to the Greystone. . . . All the boys around Detroit at that time loved to jam and it wasn't a surprising sight to see Bix Beiderbecke, Don Murray, Hank Biagni, Joe Venuti, and others all on our bandstand jamming.

"Goldkette used to have a sort of music school in a locker room at the Greystone, and he and Don Redman would take turns at the blackboard, explaining arrangements and teaching us to read better."

The headwater of the style of orchestration that became a river in the swing era goes back not to Fletcher Henderson or even Don Redman and Challis, although they all were major contributors to its evolution. The structural format of the big swing bands is the invention of Ferde Grofé.

Grofé had excellent credentials and, as James Lincoln Collier notes in his book *Jazz: The American Theme Song* (Oxford University Press, New York, 1993), around 1915 "was probably the only man in the world versed in jazz and classical music." Working in dance bands, Grofé developed a system for coaching musicians who couldn't read or at least not well. He would play on the piano the line assigned to each one "and bit by bit put together a complete arrangement, a scheme Duke Ellington would use to great effect ten years later."

Leading a small dance band in San Francisco in 1913 was drummer and sometime pianist Art Hickman. A newspaperman who wrote a little story about the group referred to its "pep" and "enthusiasm," calling it a "jazz" band—the first known use of the word in print. Hickman was asked to bring a band into the St. Francis Hotel's Rose Room; Hickman wrote the tune *Rose Room*, later a jazz standard, for the occasion. By then, Collier points out, New Orleans black musicians had been playing in San Francisco for at least five years. Collier thinks Hickman was probably playing some sort of raggy version of New Orleans jazz.

Hickman engaged Grofé to write for the band. At that time, the saxophone was an instrument that no one took seriously, although it had been developed by the Belgian Adolphe Sax more than seventy years before. Excepting the use of an alto by Bizet in the *Arlesienne Suite* and occasional employment by Ravel and Debussy, the classical-music world had almost totally ignored it and to a large extent still does. Probably the first musician to record on saxophone was Rudy Wiedoeft, a vaudeville performer who did so on C-melody sax in 1916.

"The critical moment," Collier writes, "came in 1918 when somebody heard a vaudeville saxophone team, Bert Ralton and Clyde Doerr. . . . Hickman no doubt was aware of the novelty value of the saxophone, but Grofé saw that saxophones could be used as a small 'choir' in the dance band. Doerr and Ralton were hired. This was the beginning of the saxophone section, which would become the heart of the modern dance orchestra."

The band was a sensation in San Francisco and, in 1919, at the Biltmore Hotel in New York City. Interest in the saxophone exploded. Collier writes, "According to Abel Green, dance band correspondent for the New York *Clipper*, Hickman, with his New York exposure, was the start of the new dance band. Joe Laurie, in his memoir of vaudeville, said, 'The guy who started all the dance bands' was Hickman. The jazz writer Charles Edward

Smith said, 'Contrary to the widespread misconception, inspiration in swing bands was inspired not by jazz, but by popular dance bands, such as that of Art Hickman.' And James T. Maher, an authority on early dance bands, said that Bob Haring, Jr., whose father arranged for Hickman for a time, said, 'Everybody—all the players, and the arrangers, and even the bandleaders—the saxophone playing (of) Bert Ralton and Clyde Doerr . . . completely changed the way the New York musicians thought about the saxophone."

The New Orleans clarinetist Sidney Bechet heard the instrument about this time, and began playing soprano saxophone. The soprano would remain his principal instrument for the rest of his life.

The spread of the idea of the saxophone section must have been rapid. In Wilkes-Barre, Pennsylvania, the young Bill Challis took up the instrument and began arranging for bands. I have examined early Challis arrangements in Wilkes-Barre, where they are kept by his brother Evan in what years ago was their father's barbershop. Aside from noting that Challis had been using the trumpet-trombone-saxophone choirs in 1920, I was startled to see that the charts were written on commercial score paper set up for that instrumentation and rhythm section. (The paper provided for three saxophones.) I realized instantly that the gospel of the evolution of the swing bands that I had read and never questioned was false.

One of the first bandleaders to take note of what Hickman and Grofé were doing in San Francisco was Paul Whiteman, who hired Grofé to play piano in his band and write for it. He took the band to New York, becoming such a success that he had to set up farm-team bands; he sold records in the millions. He hired Challis out of the Goldkette band to expand his book, which at some points contained parts for six saxophones.

Another significant figure, according to Artie Shaw and others who survive from that era, was Paul Specht, who claimed to have made dance-band broadcasts as early as 1920. This is credible. We have no date for that Specht broadcast, but on May 20, 1920, station CFCF in Montreal, which had gone on the air in early 1919 to become the first regularly operating radio station in the world, originated a broadcast with full orchestra.

"What is important about all of this is the fact that Don Redman, later to be Fletcher Henderson's musical director, was for a period a factotum in the Specht office," Collier writes.

"Jazz writers have for decades been claiming, on the basis of little evidence, that Henderson and Redman together invented the formula for the swing band. It is clear, however, that the bigger dance band playing arranged jazz had been around for several years before the Henderson band began to make its mark. Henderson presumably brought Don Redman in as musical director precisely because of the dance band experience he had gotten with the Specht office. The Henderson band, of course, went on to become one of the pre-eminent hot dance bands of the time, while the Specht band is today forgotten—although it could play surprisingly hot when it wanted, as the records attest. . . .

"The point is that the great success of Hickman, and especially White-man, drew all the other bands in after them. The Dixieland group playing unwritten music began to fade away. As we have seen, after 1923, the Henderson, Ellington, Armstrong, Oliver, and Nichols groups were re-shaped to conform to the new 'symphonic' style of jazz. . . ."

(In the early 1940s, Benny Goodman donated his record collection to the Widener Library at Harvard. It was collated and catalogued by Grover Sales. "I found a lot of very well-worn Art Hickman records," Grover said.)

Paul Whiteman has been subject to decades of opprobrium by jazz critics. He hired fine writers and let them do their work, and he employed some of the best jazz soloists he could find, including Frank Trumbauer and Bix Beiderbecke, who, as we have noted, exerted far wider influences than they are given credit for.

There is a curious inner contradiction, in our age of affirmative action, in these complaints by black writers about Goodman, Dorsey, and Shaw hiring black players and writers for their bands. They are accused of stealing the music because they hired these men. They would be accused of racism if they had not. To anyone whose purpose is to make a case, not to uncover truth, this kind of circular reasoning is useful.

Supposedly these white musicians hired blacks to give "soul" and swing to their bands. Is that why Count Basie hired Buddy Rich, and said later that Buddy was the best drummer the band ever had? And why Duke Ellington hired Louie Bellson and Dave Black?

The influence of Bix shows up in the exquisite, spare, spaced, selective choice of notes in the work of Miles Davis, the almost sculptured character of their lines. I told Miles it seemed as if there were a link and asked whether he had listened a lot to Bix. He said, "No, but I listened a lot to Bobby Hackett, and *he* listened to Bix."

That my memory does not play me false is attested to by Miles's auto-biography.

On page 8, he writes that Dizzy Gillespie was his idol. "But I liked Clark Terry, Buck Clayton, Harold Baker, Harry James, Bobby Hackett, and Roy Eldridge." On page 28, he recalls listening to a radio show called *Harlem Rhythms*, saying, "Most of the time they played black bands, but sometimes when they had a white band I would cut it off, unless the musician was Harry James or Bobby Hackett."

Miles is often cited as the archetype of the black racist. At one time he was widely quoted for the statement, "I want to kill just one white man before I die." When I heard it, I laughed, knowing that Miles loved saying things for shock value, and I mused, "I wonder who was the white idiot he said it to." For one of the unpublished stories about Miles concerns a jive black record producer who made the mistake of assuming a chummy intimacy on grounds of color. Miles gave him the glare and said, "You're the right color but you're still a stupid motherfucker."

Miles was aware of the mythology that had grown up around him and in a strange sort of way, I think, hurt by it. He once said to me, almost poignantly, during a period when we used to hang out a lot, "Gene, why do they call me a racist when my best friend is Gil Evans and my manager is Jack Whittemore?"

Another of his friends was Bill Evans. Miles also remained on good terms with Gerry Mulligan and was planning to go on the road with Gerry in the band the latter put together to play the Birth of the Cool music. His failing health precluded it.

Miles's relationships with such people seems to bother Stanley Crouch. I do not think Crouch sees himself as a racist. I even think he tries to be fair and believes that he is. His inner character, his life experience, however, makes this impossible, as one sees on reading *Sketches of Pain,* a piece he wrote attacking Miles in the February 12, 1990, issue of the *New Republic.*

Crouch says that Miles "was never of the order of Armstrong, Young, Parker, or Monk." Miles, like Bill and Gil Evans, was of exactly that stature, though Armstrong should not be on that list. Like Tatum, his accomplishment put him in a class of his own. But Miles was a major figure.

The first hint of Crouch's racial bias in the piece comes in his reference to the Birth of the Cool as "the highly celebrated but essentially lightweight nonet session that Davis steered. . . ." But of course: those sessions were built out of an experiment, led by Gil Evans, in getting with the smallest possible number of players the sound of the Claude Thornhill band. To grant its importance would be to admit that a major movement in jazz came from Thornhill and Evans, both white. Crouch can't handle this, and thus dismisses it with an adjective.

Crouch says that the group inspired what became known as "cool" or "west coast" jazz, "a light-sounding music, low-keyed and smooth, that disavowed the Afro-American approach to sound and rhythm." Jazz, then, is a black music and a black music only.

"Heard now," Crouch writes, "the nonet recordings seem little more than primers for television writing. What the recordings show us, though, is that Davis, like many other jazzmen, was not above the academic temptation of Western music. Davis turns out to have been overly impressed by the lessons he received at Juilliard when he arrived in New York in 1944."

The Western musical tradition, then, is to be rejected. Out with that bath water go the scale and harmonic systems, the arpeggios, the notation, the left-hand patterns from Beethoven and Chopin in which stride piano is rooted, the instruments themselves, Czerny, Arbens, even the I IV V I chords of the blues.

Later in the piece, Crouch praises Monk's piano work on a Davis album as being "as far away from European convention as bottleneck guitar work."

Of *Miles Ahead, Porgy and Bess*, and *Sketches of Spain*, three brilliant albums to come out of the friendship and collaboration between Miles and Gil Evans, Crouch says that "those albums . . . reveal that Davis could be taken in by pastel versions of European colors (they are given what value they have in these sessions by the Afro-American dimensions that were never far from Davis's embouchure, breath, fingering); if Davis's trumpet voice is removed, in fact, a good number of Evans's arrangements sound like high-level television music."

Crouch then goes on to denigrate the other Evans, Bill, in the *Kind of Blue* album, saying, "On the one piece where straight-out swing was called for, Davis used Wynton Kelly instead of Evans; but on the softer pieces the things that Evans had learned from Debussy, George Russell, and Mingus issued in voicings of simple materials and intricate details."

Like Herb Boyd, Crouch is either ignorant or consciously mendacious. Bill left Miles in November 1958 to develop his own trio. Miles hired Wynton Kelly to replace him, and as Jack DeJohnette has pointed out, he expected Kelly to use some of the style of voicings Bill had pioneered. *Kind of Blue* was not recorded until March and April of 1959, and Miles asked Bill to come *back* to the group for the recording.

Crouch suggests that whatever small ability Bill had came from two black musicians. Although George Russell did much for Bill's career, there is little if anything of Mingus in Bill's work. There is, however, much of Ravel, Chopin, Poulenc, and Scriabin. And if Crouch wanted to cite the real black models in Bill's work, he should have mentioned Red Garland, and by Bill's own statement to me, Sonny Clark. (Bill's composition *NYC's No Lark* is an anagram on Clark's name.) The self-revelation of Stanley Crouch in his inability to reconcile Miles Davis's admiration and indeed love for Bill Evans and Gil Evans must be added to the alloy. His private feelings about Bill Evans seem to amount not to indifference but hatred.

Writer Eric Nisenson, author of two books on jazz, including a study of John Coltrane titled *Ascension* (New York, St. Martin's Press, 1992), describes being a guest at a colloquium of jazz critics. "Before the colloquium began, Crouch held court backstage," Nisenson said. "His topic was 'Bill Evans was a punk,' which he repeated over and over. Evans, you see, didn't understand jazz rhythm, wasn't playing within 'the tradition.' . . . Crouch's attack on Evans was so vindictive that it almost seemed as if Evans had personally insulted him in some way."

But when Crouch encounters Helen Keane, Evans's manager of eighteen years and producer, he smiles ingratiatingly and wags an index finger and tells her, "I'm listening! I'm listening!"

The fact—and it is a fact—that a white musician could have a major influence on jazz, on black musicians as well as white, simply does not fit the political agenda of writers like Herb Boyd and Stanley Crouch. Neither, of course, does the image of Jean Goldkette, who was not only white but also a European, born in France, coaching the Cotton Pickers, or the fact that Ferde Grofé and Art Hickman developed the sax section and the antiphonal groupings of the dance band. So all of it is ignored.

The Crouch bias turns up everywhere. In a 1985 article in the *Village Voice* in which he excoriated the movie *Cotton Club*, he complains that a white musician, Bob Wilber, was hired to reconstruct the Ellington scores from that period. Then he refers to the music on the sound track being "played by a band whose timbre and attack identify it as white." Roy Eldridge said he could tell by listening whether a musician was black or white. Leonard Feather put him to a blindfold test. It established conclusively that he could not; indeed his score was well below the 50 percent he could have achieved by the law of averages.

Nowhere in his piece about *Cotton Club* does Crouch mention that many of the songs written for the real Cotton Club were by white composers, particularly Harold Arlen, and lyricists, including Ted Koehler and Dorothy Fields.

Cannonball Adderley told me an instructive story. When Bobby Timmons left the piano chair in his quintet, Cannon made a decision on the man he wanted for his replacement. He played some records by this pianist for the other members of his group. Only when he had aroused their enthusiasm and had their firm support for the hiring did he tell them that the pianist was white, English, and Jewish: Victor Feldman.

Miles Davis for a long time wanted Bill Evans to come back to his group. His love of Bill's work may have been one reason he hired Herbie Hancock, although Hancock had validity of his own. Crouch does admit that "Hancock [was] developing his own version of the impressionism that Evans was making popular."

It is a grudging and small concession.

Part 2

It was long a belief among blacks that they understood white society, because they work in it, serve it, cook for it, wait on it, carry its bags, know its kitchens and parlors and porches, but white society does not understand them. The last is largely true. White society does not know black society. But the rest is not true; seemingly most blacks do not understand white society either.

This becomes evident when you read the book *Notes and Tones*, a series of interviews compiled by drummer Arthur Taylor, published in Belgium in 1977 and reprinted by DaCapo in New York. The first significant thing one notices is that not one of the jazz musicians Taylor interviewed was white. He evidently was not interested in what white musicians think, perhaps does not even consider them jazz musicians. He repeatedly asks the subjects if they are more comfortable being interviewed by him, a black musician, as opposed, we must presume, to some journalist, probably white. Predictably, they all tell him what he wants to hear: yes.

A certain frustrated bafflement infuses these interviews. Musician after musician thinks the white business world is wicked, exploitative, corrupt. But many of them do not begin to grasp the scope of the evil, and the book reveals nothing so much as the width and depth of the chasm between white and black society in America.

Randy Weston tells Taylor, who has just referred to jazz as "our music":

"We don't control anything. We should control our own press. We have to depend upon the white status quo to judge us and gauge us with everything from polls to popularity contests to decide who gets this, who gets five stars, who gets one star. I mean it's a combination of all these factors. And again, the reason behind it all is racism."

Weston too is proprietary about jazz. He says, "I look upon this music as our folk music, as the folk music of the Afro-American, this music we call jazz."

And then the paradox: He is proud of being an American, calling the United States the greatest country on earth.

The sense of alienation is most poignantly expressed by Johnny Griffin who by then had, like Taylor, moved to Europe. He tells Taylor, "I'm here in Europe because it's lighter on me than it is in America. You don't have 35 or 40 million black have-nots over here like you have in America. But you [do] have them here because I see them sweeping the streets of Paris and Holland. It's the black man's ass up in the air. He's stooping down picking up the dirt everywhere. The main thing is I'm here because I did something wrong on my planet and they sent me here to pay my dues. I figure pretty soon my dues should be paid, and they're going to call me back home, so I can rest in peace."

Taylor says, "You're not serious about that, are you?"

"I can't be from this place, Arthur," Griffin says. "There is no love and I love people. All I see is hate around me, except for a few of my friends. That's what's wrong with the earth today. Black and white on this planet, there is no love; there is only hate. . . . These governments drawing lines between men, between tribes. Yellow people against brown people against black against Moslems against Christians against Hindus. What is all of that? I know I'm not from this planet; I can't be. I must be from some place else in the universe, because I'm a total misfit. I can't get with none of this."

Taylor asks, "What do you think of protest in music?"

Johnny says, "I learned how to play music for the beauty that I could derive from compositions and for the catharsis that it gives me when I am able to express myself. That's why I study my instrument so I can play it better and I am better able to express myself. For me to take my saxophone and make squawks like chickens, or elephant sounds, is the worst thing I could do. I would stop playing. I'm always talking about using my horn like a machinegun but not to kill anybody. I want to shoot people with notes of love. I want them to laugh. I want to give them something positive. I'm not playing music for a negative purpose, 'cause that's like a cancer. I'm not studying music to give myself cancer. I'm playing my horn to bring out the positive things in people so they can enjoy what I'm doing. Actually, if I'm too negative, I can't even play. I can play actually because as soon as I start playing, music takes me away from this b.s. around me. In fact music is the thing that saves me. It's my relief."

Taylor asks Miles Davis, "Do you have any particular hobbies?"

Miles says, "Making fun of white folks on television."

Then Miles gets to the effect of ubiquitous imagery on the psyche. He says, "I can't stand those white movies about white problems. I'd like to see a movie dealing with Negroes as human beings, not just a black maid and a doctor. I'd like to see one in everyday life . . . like an executive, or the head of a company. One who falls in love and out of love; one who drives a sports car; and one who acts like me or like you; who has girls, white girls, colored girls, Chinese and Hawaiian and German and French, you know? They don't have that in the movies, so I don't go. . . . I have a funny feeling all day after I've seen a movie with the same white problems. You know, full of girls with long hair and where everybody's having a lot of fun, and we don't have any fun. You don't see any Negroes. It makes me feel funny. . . ."

When the book was published, Miles was at the peak of his power and talent and fame, one of the great artists of jazz, and he could have all the girls he wanted, including French: he had been through a love affair with Juliette Greco. But the movies still made him feel funny.

Miles: The Autobiography (Simon & Schuster, New York, 1990) is a disturbed, and disturbing book, absolutely harrowing in places.

Miles Davis was born into a wealthy and educated family, his father an East St. Louis dentist and horse breeder. Miles lived a comparatively sheltered life in a manse on a ranch, riding horses for a hobby. One can only speculate on the extent of the emotional damage done when he was beaten by a racist cop outside Birdland in New York.

Miles projected a tough-guy image, and he was tough. There were affectations about it, however. I once heard him say to a girl making a pass at him in the Sutherland Lounge in Chicago, "I ain't got no free fucks to give away." But it was a rehearsed line, a lick he had worked out to enhance his image as a bad-ass: I heard of him using the self-same line on a girl in New York. I think Miles was a frightened man, always aware that because of his color he could be beaten and, in some parts of the United States, killed with impunity. The tough image was armor, a persona carefully created to intimidate whites and hold them at a safe distance.

There was a great sensitivity in Miles. I do not know how it could have been otherwise. Those gorgeous melodic ideas, that rich and individual tone, did not come from nowhere. I once was hanging out with him in a now-vanished club called the Cloister in the basement of the Maryland Hotel in the Rush Street area of Chicago. Business that week was not good. In the office, the club owner or manager was paying Miles. Miles always insisted on cash. He counted the money carefully, peeled off a number of bills, and handed them back to the man, saying, "You didn't make any money with us this week." That's not hearsay; I was there. The club operator was white.

The autobiography reveals the inner conflict with which Miles lived because of race. This is evident in contradictions in the book, sometimes on the same page. On page 58, he (or his collaborator, Quincy Troupe) says of his studies at Juilliard, "The shit they were teaching was too white for me." On page 74 he says, "I took some lessons in symphonic trumpet playing. Trumpet players from the New York Philharmonic gave the lessons, so I learned some things for them." On page 60, he says, "They weren't teaching me nothing and didn't know nothing to teach me because they were so prejudiced against all black music." Only two paragraphs later, he says, "Another thing I found strange after living and playing in New York was that a lot of black musicians didn't know anything about music theory. . . . A lot of the old guys thought that if you went to school it would make you play like you were white. Or, if you learned something from theory, then they would lose the feeling in your playing. I couldn't believe that all them guys like Bird, Prez, Bean, all them cats wouldn't go to museums or libraries so they could borrow those musical scores so they could check out what was happening. I would go to the library and borrow scores by all those great composers, like Stravinsky, Alban Berg, Prokofiev. I wanted to see what was going on in all of music. Knowledge is freedom and ignorance is slavery, and I just couldn't believe someone could be that close to freedom and not take advantage of it. I have never understood why black people didn't take advantage of all the shit that they can. It's like a ghetto mentality telling people that they aren't supposed to do certain things, that those things are only reserved for white people." (Later in the book he tell us that Bill Evans turned him on to Khachaturian.)

There is something wrong with this passage. Since Miles admired Prokofiev, it is inconceivable that he did not know that Charlie Parker did too; in at least one instance Parker was listening to the *Scythian Suite* in Gil Evans's apartment during the period when Miles was constantly there. Parker wanted to study with Edgard Varèse. Coleman Hawkins had a great taste for classical music and was known to haunt museums, particularly art galleries, and many of the founding pianists in jazz, including Willie "the Lion" Smith, James P. Johnson, Fats Waller, Earl Hines, and particularly Teddy Wilson, had considerable knowledge of the classical piano literature. Sidney Bechet was a great lover of Beethoven. Don Redman had two conservatory degrees. I have previously documented (*Meet Me at Jim and Andy's*, Oxford University Press, New York, 1988) the extent to which many significant founding figures in jazz had solid academic credentials, including Jimmie Lunceford, who had a bachelor's degree in music and taught the subject.

Marc Crawford, a black journalist from the *Ebony* staff who wrote an article for me about Miles at *Down Beat*, described Miles listening with fervent admiration to the Italian pianist Arturo Benedetti Michelangeli in a recording of the Ravel G-major Piano Concerto. And finally, I recall my own conversations with Miles about classical music. Indeed, during a period when he lived three or four blocks from me in the West 70s in New York, he learned that I owned a complete set of recordings of the contemporary music commissions of the Louisville Orchestra. He pressed me to lend them to him, which I did. (I never got them back.)

Miles attests to the anti-white racism in jazz on page 231 of the book: "Some of the things that caused Bill [Evans] to leave the band hurt me, like that shit some black people put on him about being a white boy in our band. Now, I don't go for that kind of shit; I have always just wanted the best players in my group and I don't care about whether they're black, white, blue, red, or yellow. As long as they can play what I want that's it. But I know this stuff got under Bill's skin and made him feel bad. Bill was a very sensitive person. . . ."

Then on the next page, 232, he says, "It's a strange thing about a lot of white players—not all, just most—that after they make it in a black group they always go and play with all white guys no matter how good the black guys treated them. Bill did that, and I'm not saying he could have gotten any black guys any better than Scott (LaFaro) and Paul (Motian), I'm just telling what I've seen happen over and over again."

But that's nonsense. All of it. Bill did not come to prominence with the Miles Davis group: he was first discovered in Louisiana by Mundell Lowe and Red Mitchell, and worked with them. He began to cause a stir in New York with Tony Scott's group, and then he electrified the jazz world with solos recorded in two George Russell compositions, *Concerto for Billy the Kid* (1956) and *All About Rosie* (1957).

Russell was in fact responsible for Bill's joining Miles. George told me in 1994:

"Miles called and said he needed a piano player. He said Red Garland was fucking up. He asked if I knew a piano player. I said, 'Yes, I know a piano player. He's a killer. His name's Bill Evans.'

"Miles said, 'What does he look like?'

"I said, 'He's white and he wears glasses.'

"Miles said, 'Yeah. I heard that motherfucker at Birdland. Bring him over.'

"I took Bill to meet Miles. Cannonball and Coltrane were with the group.

Bill sat in and Miles hired him on the spot. The next week they went to Philadelphia."

Bill made his first album as a trio leader in 1956, two years before joining Miles. His next trio album was made not with white musicians but with Sam Jones and Philly Joe Jones. The latter remained Bill's close friend, and was part of the road group at various times. Jack DeJohnette was also with Bill for a time and recorded with him. Miles hired him away from Bill, and so could hardly have been unaware of Jack's time with Bill's trio. Over the years, Bill recorded with Cannonball Adderley, Percy Heath, Connie Kay, Freddie Hubbard, Harold Land, Kenny Burrell, and Ray Brown.

Eddie Gomez, Bill's long-time bassist and probably the first Puerto Rican to emerge as a major jazz musician, told me that once, when Miles was without a bass player, he called Bill to ask if he could borrow Eddie. Since the trio was on a two-week layoff, Bill said of course he could. Eddie recalled driving with Miles to a job. All the way, Miles talked of his love for Bill and admiration for his musicianship. Bill's sight-reading was legendary, and, Eddie said, as he and Miles passed a big billboard, Miles said, "Bill could read even that."

So. I simply cannot understand that passage about Bill in the book.

The book's veracity is questionable. Clearly Quincy Troupe did outside research on it and added passages to it. When Miles was asked on a television show a question about the book, he said, "I haven't read that far yet." Nonetheless, the book is a potent contribution to the mythology of jazz, the more effective for being a strangely moving (to me at least) chronicle of the torture of a brilliantly gifted American. And its inaccuracies and lies will be repeated.

But of all the myths used to justify and reinforce reverse racism in jazz, none has been as effective and ubiquitous as the story that Bessie Smith died of loss of blood outside a white hospital that would not admit her after an automobile accident. Though it has been completely discredited, the story keeps turning up and even formed the basis of the Edward Albee play *The Death of Bessie Smith*.

The story that she expired outside a white hospital that would not admit her was perpetrated by John Hammond.

Hammond was born to wealth. He was a Vanderbilt on his mother's side. He early manifested a staunch racial liberalism, but it was not wedded to a concern for facts. Indeed, *Down Beat*, one of the publications for which he wrote, was in those days cavalier with facts, and Hammond was by no means a scrupulous journalist.

A month after Bessie Smith's death, he wrote an article in *Down Beat* under the headline:

Did Bessie Smith Bleed to Death While Waiting for Medical Aid?

The piece read in part:

"A particularly disagreeable story as to the details of her death has just been received from members of Chick Webb's orchestra, who were in Memphis soon after the disaster. It seems that Bessie was riding in a car which crashed into a truck parked along the side of the road. One of her arms was nearly severed, but aside from that there was no other serious injury, according to these informants. Some time elapsed before a doctor was summoned to the scene, but finally she was picked up by a medico and driven to the leading Memphis hospital. On the way this car was involved in some minor mishap, which further delayed medical attention. When finally she did arrive at the hospital she was refused treatment because of her color and bled to death while waiting for attention.

"Realizing that such tales can be magnified in the telling, I would like to get confirmation from some Memphis citizens who were on the spot at the time. If the story is true it is but another example of disgraceful conditions in a certain section of our country already responsible for the killing and maiming of legitimate union organizers. Of the particular city of Memphis I am prepared to believe almost anything, since its mayor and chief of police publicly urged the use of violence against organizers of the CIO a few weeks ago."

It was hardly a piece of solid reporting. The hospital where she died wasn't even in Memphis. *Down Beat* later printed a story saying that the singer had been taken to a black hospital.

The facts of the case were thoroughly investigated by Chris Albertson for his biography of the singer. After the car in which she was riding struck the truck, a physician named Hugh Smith, on his way to some early-morning fishing with a friend, Henry Broughton, came across a car lying on its side on the highway. The truck it had hit was gone. In his headlights the doctor saw Bessie Smith. The driver of her car, Richard Morgan, was unhurt. Dr. Smith found that her forearm had been almost torn from the upper arm. The doctor and his friend moved her to the grassy shoulder of the road, and the doctor asked Broughton to go to a farmhouse and call an ambulance. By the time he returned, about ten minutes later, the singer was in shock. When no ambulance arrived, Dr. Smith decided to drive the woman—he had no idea who she was—to Clarksdale, Mississippi. When he and Broughton were moving their fishing tackle from the car's back seat to the trunk, to make room for her, they heard a car approaching at high speed. The doctor stood on the left running board of the car and reached into it to blink its headlights. At the last minute he jumped free and the car smashed into his, wrecking both vehicles. The young couple in the other car were badly injured. Dr. Smith now had three patients on his hands and no car to drive them anywhere.

Just then two ambulances arrived; one had been summoned by the driver of the truck that had caused the first accident.

Years later, when the myth had taken hold, Dr. Smith, a past president of the American Academy of Orthopedic Surgeons, was asked whether the singer had been refused admittance to a white hospital. He answered:

"The Bessie Smith ambulance would not have gone to a white hospital—you can forget that. Down in the Deep South cotton country, no colored ambulance driver, or white driver, would even have thought of putting a colored person off in a hospital for white folks. In Clarksdale, in 1937, a town of twelve to fifteen thousand people, there were two hospitals, one white and one colored, and they weren't half a mile apart. I suspect the driver drove just as straight as he could to the colored hospital."

The driver of that ambulance, Willie George Miller, later affirmed that he had done exactly that. There was no such thing as blood plasma in those days, nor were there blood banks. Dr. Smith later observed that in that era, it took an hour to draw a pint from a donor. And, of course, a donor with matching blood type had to be found.

Bessie Smith expired, according to the death certificate, at 11:30 a.m. in Ward I of the Afro-American hospital in Clarksdale, Mississippi, of shock and possible internal injuries.

Twenty years after the accident, the late George Hoefer noted in *Down Beat* that the truth about the accident still was being ignored by writers.

Further testimony to the incident is that of Lionel Hampton, who described it in his autobiography. The driver of Bessie's car, Richard Morgan, was Hampton's uncle, and the two men were close. Hampton wrote:

"It was in the fall of . . . 1937 that one of the biggest tragedies that ever happened to my family took place. Bessie Smith was killed in a car accident, and my uncle Richard was driving the car. . . .

"Later on there was a big scandal about how Bessie had first been taken to a white hospital and they wouldn't admit her. John Hammond wrote that in a story for *Down Beat*. But it later turned out that she was taken directly to the colored hospital. By the time they got her it was too late to save her. No reporter ever asked Richard what really happened, or if anybody did, they never wrote the story."

Even Hammond recanted. Chris Albertson wrote:

"Thirty-four years later John Hammond admits with some embarrassment that his article was based entirely on hearsay and that a few phone calls, made at the time, might have curbed the circulating rumors. Once the article appeared, however, it was too late to change the story; people refused to accept any other version."

Why?

When you wish to foment hate, you must dehumanize the object of it, and myth is a valuable tool to do so. The Bessie Smith legend is a bloody shirt to be waved to that end. It doesn't matter whether it is true.

One of the most widely disseminated myths in jazz is that Dizzy Gillespie, Charlie Parker, Thelonious Monk, and their associates invented bebop to keep "the white boys" off the bandstand at Minton's in Harlem.

The myth is silly on the face of it. To suggest that men of such genius would devote their energies and thought to so small and negative a purpose is a confession of ignorance. Parker was quoted as saying that he and his associates were not revolting against anything; they were only taking the music in the direction in which they thought it should go. The early jazz musicians, including Earl Hines and Louis Armstrong, thought they were in the entertainment business. It was writings about the music that gradually convinced them they were developing an art form, after which the music became in varying degrees self-conscious. The beboppers were aware of the scope of their skills. But the idea that bop was invented to exclude "white boys" is refutable on at least three counts besides the foregoing:

1. It was not in the great and glorious heart of Dizzy Gillespie to do something so mean.

2. If white exclusion were the purpose, why did Parker and Gillespie adopt young white disciples, such as Stan Levey, Red Rodney, Al Haig, Gerry Mulligan, Phil Woods, Dodo Marmarosa, George Wallington, and others and facilitate their growth in the evolving new style? Throughout his life, Dizzy was, like Miles, color-blind in his hiring practices, and so was Charlie Parker. Asked for his idea of the perfect pianist, Bud Powell said, "Al Haig."

3. The myth rests on an ignorance of the way musicians hear. Competent arrangers and players could sit at a front table at Minton's and tell you exactly what Parker and Monk were doing: some of the "new" harmonic

practices had been around in classical music for nearly half a century. Parker, Gillespie, and company didn't use altered and substitute chords to keep anybody off the bandstand; they used them because they were interesting. To be sure, they did not suffer fools gladly, and anyone who wanted to sit in with them and could not cut it was encouraged to leave. Dizzy used to recall with a chuckle a very bad tenor player who was importunate enough to try to play with them. Dizzy called him Demon and said, "He was the original freedom player. Freedom from melody, freedom from harmony, and freedom from time."

Demon (and many musicians remember him) was black.

Yet the myth about Minton's persists. Myth has incredible power. The myth of Nat Turner, for example. Little is known about him, but in the late summer of 1831, in Virginia, Turner led "the only effective, sustained revolt in the annals of American Negro slavery," as William Styron put it in the author's note to his novel based on the incident. During this insurrection, Turner and his followers killed fifty-five white persons. Turner and seventeen of his followers were captured and hanged. His body was delivered to doctors, who skinned it and made grease of the flesh. For some years, at least one man carried a money purse made of leather tanned from the skin.

While he was awaiting trial, Turner made a 7000-word confession that was published in a pamphlet of twenty pages. The man who took the confession, a lawyer named Thomas R. Gray, and the six Virginians who verified it and passed sentence of death on Turner seemed completely baffled by the revolt. Gray wrote of the confession:

"It reads an awful, and it is hoped, a useful lesson as to the operations of a mind like his, endeavoring to grapple with things beyond its reach. How it first became bewildered and confounded, and finally corrupted and led to the conception and perpetration of the most atrocious and heart-rendering [*sic*] deeds. It is calculated also to demonstrate the policy of our laws in restraint of this class of our population, and to induce all those entrusted with their execution, as well as our citizens generally, to see that they are strictly and rigidly enforced."

There is dark irony in the condescension of the comment that Turner endeavored to understand things beyond his reach. For it is Gray who endeavored to grapple with things beyond his reach; it escaped his comprehension that Turner and his followers and their ancestors had endured torment and provocation enough to drive anyone mad. Further, Gray's comment reveals that attitude on which slavery was based and justified: the unquestioned belief that blacks were some sort of higher form of ape. He wrote, "No acts of remembered kindness made the least impression on these remorseless murderers."

Acts of remembered kindness? When one is in no position to refuse it, even a kindness is condescension.

The idea of inherent genetic difference was one of the cornerstones of slavery. The English political economist and statistician Sir William Petty (1623–87), one of the founders of demographic and economic statistics and also of the Royal Society, hypothesized gradations among human groups. Petty's background was amazing. He'd studied medicine at Leiden, Paris, and Oxford, and had been a seaman, physician, a professor of anatomy at Oxford, a professor of music, inventor, surveyor, and member of Parliament. His views were taken seriously. He was an advocate of religious toleration, yet emphasized physical differences of the races according to anatomy, paying particular attention to the hair, lips, noses, and bones of black Africans. He said that they differed in their "naturall manners" and the "internall qualities" of their minds.

Another Royal Society member of that time, a surgeon named Charles White, took note of ways in which, he said, blacks resembled apes. He wrote of their skull capacity, length of arms and legs, body scent, and shorter life span, and suggested that, like some animals, they had superior hearing and sense of smell and, interestingly, better memory.

Growing up in Tidewater Virginia, the future novelist William Styron was troubled even in boyhood by the racial division of Southern society, its incomprehensible contradictions, injustices, repression, and cruelties. He was drawn to and fascinated by black culture, including its music, as many Southerners have been. He wrote, "I felt [an] anxiety about my secret passion for blackness; in my closet I was fearful lest any of my conventional racist young friends discover that I was an unabashed enthusiast for the despised Negro. I don't claim a special innocence. Most white people were, and are, racist to some degree but at least my racism was not conventional. I wanted to confront and understand blackness."

So, curiously enough, did I, but for a completely different reason. Growing up in Canada, on the Niagara Peninsula, where there was almost no black population, my only perception of blacks and blackness was jazz, and the only blacks I ever even saw were men with shining musical instruments whose autographs I shyly but very determinedly sought—the gods of my private pantheon. My fascination with jazz contributed to an interest in the United States and to my decision to move there. Thus it helped determine the direction of my life. Styron's interests led to his writing his novel *The*

Confessions of Nat Turner, one of the most remarkable works of imagination in American fiction.

By the time it was published, in 1967, I had many black friends, most but by no means all of them musicians, and felt I had, for a white, a much more than ordinary insight into the American black culture, including its comedy, which at that point was completely unknown to the vast majority of Americans. I remember nights of seeing Moms Mabley from the wings of the Regal Theater in Chicago; an evening in a South Side nightclub watching Nipsey Russell and Redd Foxx exchange hilarious insults while Art Farmer explained those references that were outside my experience. Yet the Styron book came as a shock. The persons we know in life, even our most intimate associates, are always to some extent opaque, but those we encounter in fiction are transparent. We can enter by imagination into their lives and for a while even live them.

As Styron himself says, his Nat Turner is a fiction. He says the book is "less an 'historical novel' in conventional terms than a meditation on history."

The horrors of slavery, and of the forms of discrimination that succeeded it, are dramatic and obvious enough: the packed slave ships, the floggings, brandings, casual mutilations, the hangings. One becomes, in Shakespeare's term, "supp'd full with horrors." Horror compounded becomes abstract, as in the fire-bombing of Dresden. Like huge sums of money or the distances to the stars, it becomes incomprehensible. We are incapable of understanding, much less accepting, the millions of Cambodian deaths resulting from the United States effort to get out of the morass of Vietnam. The photos of great piles of skulls tell us nothing of the lives and final agonies of those who inhabited those crania. What Styron did in the book went far beyond making the reader aware of the physical enslavement of its protagonist: he evoked his emotional and spiritual subjugation, debasement, and humiliation, and ultimate consequent dementia, and yet failure of the surrounding society to conquer character. He did this by an ingenious device, one that at one point would influence my own writing.

He juxtaposed the thinking of his character with the speech in which he hides, the "Yes, marse" posturings of a man who does not dare reveal his intellect. Styron's Nat Turner has, in contravention of the law, learned to read. His thinking is literate and lyrical. Thirty-one years old, he says to a pimply-faced white guard of nineteen in his jail cell: "Marse Kitchen, I'm hungry. I wonder if you could fetch me a little bit to eat. Kindly please, young mastah. . . . Just a little piece of pone."

Twenty years after Styron wrote the book, when I was researching *The*

Will to Swing, my biography of Oscar Peterson, I came across tapes of radio broadcasts Oscar made in Montreal when he was nineteen. Slavery may have been gone, but its legacy was not. The Uncle Tom language Oscar was forced by the script to use sickened me. I took an interview Oscar had done in later years in which he described, in specific and eloquent terms—and Oscar is nothing if not eloquent—the training and mental processes he was going through at that time and I intercut it with the script materials of those broadcasts. The effect jolted people. One of Oscar's close friends, who is black, and who was reading the manuscript for me as the book unfolded, said, "It's awful, it's embarrassing, and don't change a word." Oscar said that the scripts were more than humiliating—they were insulting. But he had a goal, a determination to achieve some real clout, and he put up with them. I have seen his eyes mist as he remembered those days. To some extent he was going through an experience like that of Styron's Nat Turner: the true life of the mind and the false life of the mask. That's how valid Styron's novel was—and is.

The Confessions of Nat Turner got glowing reviews, and Styron received an honorary degree from Wilberforce University, the black university in Ohio that Benny Carter once attended. The president of Wilberforce thanked Styron for the book, and the author gave a brief talk at a ceremony in his honor. He had no hint of the calumny about to be heaped on him. Within a year, a book appeared bearing the title *William Styron's Nat Turner: Ten Black Writers Respond*. Styron was said to have "a vile racist imagination," to be a man "psychologically sick" and "morally senile."

In essence the attacks asked how a white dared to write intimately of the black experience, even to put himself inside the protagonist's skin by doing so in the first-person singular. The fact that all art is artifice, a series of devices and accepted conventions, didn't enter into it. The first-person singular is commonly used. In real life, people rarely think through or set down on paper clear and structured narratives of their experiences, but that never bothers us when we read tales thus told. Nor, for that matter, are we disturbed when we read fiction in the third person in which the writer presumes to tell us the thoughts of all his characters. Fiction is by its nature an act of narrative intimacy, whether in first or third person. The irony is that it was the black writer James Baldwin, a friend of Styron who had made his notes for *The Fire Next Time* while living in Styron's home, who had urged him to make the leap of imagination and write the Turner story in the first person.

In an afterword to a 1992 paperback edition of the book, Styron wrote, "Baldwin was wrestling with his novel *Another Country*, which deals intimately with white characters, and we both ultimately shared the conviction that nothing should inhibit the impulse that causes a writer to render experience which may be essentially foreign to his own world: it is a formidable challenge and among an artist's most valuable privileges. Baldwin's determination to pursue this course aroused the ire of many militant blacks, who saw such a preoccupation as frivolous and a betrayal of a commitment to the black cause. He stuck to his belief though his conscience and his persistence brought him rebuke and bitter alienation. My attempt, of course, was an even greater effrontery, and after *Nat Turner* was published, Baldwin told an interviewer most accurately: 'Bill's going to catch it from black and white.'"

In other words, a white man should not write about a black man because the former has no soul and cannot understand one who does; the black man should not write about the white man because the latter has no soul and is not worth the waste of time required to comprehend him. If such views were universally held among blacks, this would amount to an astonishing resegregation of the country, this time not of schools, soda fountains, and buses, but of the mind.

More than twenty years after it appeared, *The Confessions of Nat Turner* has gone largely unread by blacks. Some of the attacks on it sound as if their writers had not read it. Indeed, when in the mid-1980s, the *New York Times Book Review* asked a number of writers to make a list of "Books I Never Finished," Paule Marshall was quoted as saying she had never even started *Nat Turner,* having been assured that it was racist.

There is one major point that all these black writers overlooked or were incapable of seeing. They did not examine, perhaps could not examine, the effect of the book on a white audience. Black writers are preaching to the choir; Styron is not. No other work of fiction has ever so illuminated the horrors of chattel slavery in the United States to a white reading audience.

High on the list of white works that attempt to come to terms with the black experience only to encounter obloquy are *Porgy and Bess* and *Show Boat.*

I first became aware that at least some blacks are hostile to George Gershwin's *Porgy and Bess* when, during an evening in the company of the late pianist Calvin Jackson, I asked him to play one of the songs from it. With a meaningful chill in his voice, he said, "I don't play anything from that score."

A commonly encountered attitude is that George and Ira Gershwin and Dubose Heyward had no business writing an opera about blacks because they were not black. Yet many black jazz performers, singers and instrumentalists alike, have found the score a rich source of material. Gershwin's compositions are probably played by jazz musicians more than those of any other composer. Miles Davis, whom no one ever accused of being a Tom, made a magnificent album with Gil Evans from the *Porgy and Bess* score. Ella Fitzgerald and Louis Armstrong recorded the songs from it in a memorable album, and various other black singers, including Sarah Vaughan and Nina Simone, have made selections from it powerful elements in their repertoires, particularly *I Loves You, Porgy.* (Few persons know or have even heard the full score. They know songs from the score, but not the score, which is a work of genius.)

Show Boat preceded *Porgy and Bess.* First presented in 1927, it was based on a novel by Edna Ferber. It had a magnificent score by Jerome Kern and Oscar Hammerstein II. Revolutionary for the time, with an integrated plot and a serious, indeed tragic, story, it was closer to opera than to the strings of light sketches that had characterized the New York musical stage until then. And some of its characters were black.

In 1993, *Show Boat* was revived in a production directed by Hal Prince at a new performing arts center in North York, a city contiguous to Toronto. It caused a storm of controversy; or more precisely a single woman caused the storm. A Jamaican named Stephanie Payne, a trustee of the North York school board, vowed to destroy the show, calling it racist. She apparently had never seen a production of it. Almost immediately the newspapers devoted huge amounts of space to the controversy. On March 19, 1993, the *Toronto Star* gave nearly a full page to it, under the general heading "Is 'Show Boat' racist hate literature?" with pro and con views.

The producer of the new *Show Boat* was Garth Drabinsky. And on a nationwide television news show, Payne finally said, "Most of the plays that portray blacks or any other ethnic group in a negative way is always done by a white man; and always usually a Jewish person is doing plays which denigrate us."

The *Toronto Sun* carried an editorial condemning Payne. On March 10, she made an apology of sorts. "My purpose . . . is to try and apologize for remarks that I made, which can be correctly construed as anti-Semitic," she said, but vowed that she would stop the staging of *Show Boat.*

She and perhaps 150 other persons, many of them the children of the real protesters, picketed the opening night in October. Crossing the picket line was Lincoln Alexander, then lieutenant governor of the Province of Ontario. Alexander is black. The show was given rave reviews, and the newspapers received letters from Canadian blacks praising it, saying there was nothing racist about it.

Payne and the other pickets faded away.

The conclusion to be drawn from *Show Boat, Porgy and Bess*, and *The Confessions of Nat Turner* is that no white man can or should even try to write about black characters, since whites lack the intellect, sensitivity, talent, and "soul" to do so effectively.

By this logic, Shakespeare shouldn't have written *Romeo and Juliet* because he wasn't Italian, and Aaron Copland should not have written *El Salon Mexico*. And then by projection, Jessye Norman, Kathleen Battle, and Leontyne Price should never essay European opera or lieder, since they are not white Europeans. André Watts should never play Rachmaninoff or Debussy, nor should any black American write string quartets or symphonies or any other music in European forms, and they most assuredly should not ask for jobs playing in or conducting symphony orchestras. Finally, Wynton Marsalis should never have recorded the Haydn and Hummel trumpet concerti, since black Americans did not "invent" that school and style of music. The absurdity of this reasoning is patent. But it is precisely to this absurdity that the policies and statements of Wynton Marsalis, Stanley Crouch, and others of their persuasion lead.

The inversion of all this, the idea that white musicians should not—indeed, cannot—play jazz, growing in virulence in recent years, is one of the most pernicious in the history of American aesthetics. The writer W. Royal Stokes refers to it as "the separatist school of thought that has been making its way into jazz." James T. Maher, one of the elder statesmen among the writers about American music, refers to it as "genetic jazz."

One of the most articulate black commentators on the subject is the bassist Anthony Jackson. He is not only a good writer, but he is, apparently, also one with courage. For he has taken on nothing less than the myth—and myths—of Wynton Marsalis.

Part 3

There never, in all history, has been as effective a myth-making apparatus as modern press agentry.

In the early 1980s, Columbia Records (now Sony) decided to put the weight of their promotional and publicity departments behind Wynton Marsalis. On October 22, 1990, a cover story on the trumpeter was published by *Time*. The magazine's reporter wrote: "Columbia made sure that its star stayed visible. The company assigned him to high-powered publicist Marilyn Laverty, who represented rock star Bruce Springsteen, and she soon generated reams of press clips." Including, of course, the selfsame *Time* article.

The campaign was enormously successful. Marsalis became the most visible figure in jazz, and his power steadily increased. In 1987 he was appointed artistic director of the newly founded Classical Jazz Summer Series at Lincoln Center. By 1991, this had evolved into the year-round Jazz at Lincoln Center program. By 1994, the three men who write about jazz for the *New York Times*, Tom Piazza, Jon Pareles, and Peter Watrous were treating him with something bordering on obeissance. Watrous wrote: "Wynton Marsalis has further solidified his position as the most important jazz musician working, both politically and musically."

When the Lincoln Center jazz program began giving commissions of new compositions, Marsalis gave the first one to himself, and there was hardly a murmur of astonishment in the press. Since then Marsalis has passed them out to the tight circle of his friends. Not one commission has gone to a white musician; and not one of the artists celebrated by the program is white.

In view of this, it is instructive to consider an incident that occurred while Wynton Marsalis was with Art Blakey, playing an engagement at the New Morning in Paris. Marsalis was vociferously denigrating Phil Woods and Scott LaFaro.

What made the incident almost bizarre was the group of witnesses to it. Backstage to talk to Blakey were Chan Parker and her daughter, Kim, whom Charlie Parker had in part raised. After Parker's death, Chan married Phil Woods, and Phil completed Kim's upbringing. She is now an outstanding singer. Listening to Marsalis put her in tears. Blakey reprimanded Marsalis and made him play ballads to Kim for the rest of the evening.

Kim told me, "The band was on a break. I left the band room and returned to hear Wynton say, '. . . and all those white cats like Phil Woods getting all the press!' I had heard Wynton at the North Sea Festival the previous year and at the Olympia Theatre in Paris prior to the New Morning gig. I was very impressed by his musical maturity, which, I assumed, carried over to his personal maturity. There was no musician that year who had received more press than Wynton.

"I was raised in an exceptional family and didn't discover racism until I was ten or eleven, having grown up in a tolerant neighborhood on the Lower East Side of Manhattan. I thought that jazz music was the one place where racism didn't exist. That night at the New Morning my faith was shattered. That's why I cried—not because Marsalis had maligned Phil Woods. It was a loss of innocence.

"But, you know, the night had its rewards. The old father, Art Blakey, taught him a lesson. And, hey, baby, if you ain't got any soul—it doesn't matter if you're black or white."

The incident was of minor significance when Marsalis was only a young sideman in the Blakey group. But it grew to importance when he assumed his position at Lincoln Center.

In the more than ten years since that incident in Paris, Marsalis has used his position to issue a steady flow of pronunciamentos in letters to editors, magazine articles bearing his name, and interviews in which he seriously misrepresents jazz history in an unwavering attempt to exclude white musicians. His language is habitually scatological; the statements are often shrill.

At twenty-three he told a *JazzTimes* writer that Sonny Rollins and Ornette were "selling out," and that "Bird would roll over in his grave if he knew what was going on." This invocation of the name of a major innovator whom he never knew personally, this presumption of speaking for him, is the sort of thing that inspired some of the young black musicians in New York to call him, behind his back to be sure, Mr. Wisdom. And they stirred the impatience even of some of his friends, including Herbie Hancock, his record producer at the time. Hancock said, "Wynton's very much a thinker—things that come out of his mouth aren't just frivolities. But I've read some things in print that are a little harsh and opinionated—too narrow-minded. Up to a certain point, I'm glad he's saying a lot of things, but then he goes overboard."

The *JazzTimes* interview, with writer Hollie I. West, was published in July 1983. He said:

"We gotta drop some bombs here. Indict some motherfuckers. Talk about the music. I don't want to cut Freddie [Hubbard] down. I'd rather cut Miles [Davis] down than Freddie.

"He ain't doin' nothing. I think Freddie has taken enough heat. He's a great trumpet player. He's a great musician. [Miles] was never my idol. I resent what he's doing because it gives the whole scene such a letdown. . . .

"There's that interview with Miles where he said he didn't hear me and he's not interested in hearing me because we're all imitating Fats Navarro. He imitated the shit out of Fats Navarro the first five years, and Clark Terry and Louis Armstrong and Monk and Dizzy. Then he sits up and talks about how he listens to Journey and Frank Sinatra. He's just co-signing white boys, just tomming."

These pronouncements did not escape the attention of Miles. Miles said, after a speech Marsalis made at the Grammy Awards ceremony of 1984, "He sounded to me like he's supposed to be the savior of jazz. Sometimes people speak as though someone asked them a question. Well, nobody asked him a question."

On another occasion, Miles said, "He's got a lot of technique, but that's about it." And as for Marsalis's statement that Miles was never his idol (the influence is obvious), Miles told him: "Without me, you'd be all *Flight of the Bumble Bee*."

An acerbic confrontation between the two occurred in 1986 at the Vancouver, British Columbia, jazz festival. Miles was in the middle of his set when Marsalis walked on stage, horn in hand, with the clear intention of playing. Miles wrote in his autobiography that Marsalis whispered in his ear, while Miles was in the middle of a solo.

Miles said, "Man, get the fuck off the stage," and repeated it. When Marsalis didn't leave, Miles stopped the band and said it yet again, and finally Marsalis left.

By next afternoon, musicians who were there had spread the story by telephone all through the jazz world. Miles said in the book that Marsalis had "no respect for his elders," which events at Lincoln Center would seem to verify.

In an article for the December 1984 issue of *Keynote*, the magazine of radio station WNCN, Marsalis said that "history is not about pushing the elements you don't like out of the picture," which of course is exactly what he does.

"Especially in America," he said, "our commitment is supposed to be to truth and accuracy. Being black, taking history in school was like a joke to me. Our perspective is never read or heard."

He said that "through much of America's history there has been such a negative racial climate that the contributions of black Americans have been overlooked. . . .

"Jazz was not a popular music—it was not evolved as dance music. . . ." This is nonsense; that's exactly how it began, and even its terminology— slow drag, for example—reflects its origins in dance, not to mention the function of dance in African music.

The *éminence grise* in the career of Wynton Marsalis and the operation of the jazz program at Lincoln Center is Stanley Crouch, whom Marsalis met when the trumpeter was with Art Blakey. Crouch told *Time* he was astounded by how little Marsalis knew of jazz history. He immediately took over his education. He introduced Marsalis to elder author Albert Murray, who is black, and they told him what to read and listen to and generally shaped his thinking. The closeness of the relationship with Crouch is not in question: Marsalis has repeatedly attested to it and quotes Crouch with something approaching reverence. The symbiosis between Crouch and Marsalis is the only known instance in jazz history, and perhaps all musical history, of a musician being controlled by a critic.

James Lincoln Collier's *Jazz: The American Theme Song* contains a chapter on jazz critics that needed to be written but was unlikely to make him friends in that small group. Collier, himself a capable trombonist though by no means a great one (by his own repeated assertion), is one of a handful of persons who has written about jazz who can tell you the key signature of E-flat or spell a G chord. (Another is Leonard Feather, who does not live off his writing about jazz but on his composer's royalties.) Collier writes that Crouch "is unable to make serious musical analysis, and therefore failed to grasp (the) technical dissertations" of Gunther Schuller's book on the swing era, which Crouch reviewed. He groups Crouch in a list of critics of whom he says, "Not one of them has ever produced any significant work that would even remotely qualify as scholarly, if for no other reason than that they never provide the documentation that is essential to scholarship. Their work is simply awash in hunch, guess, dubious assertions that by their nature cannot be documented, and a good deal of outright error. It is clear that very frequently they do not bother to do anything so simple as to pull down a discography from the shelf to check dates and personnel. They seem, often, to take it for granted that what they believe is correct, simply because they believe it."

The response was predictable, immediate, and fierce. After the book received a somewhat favorable notice in the *New York Times Book Review*, the publication received a letter over the signature of Wynton Marsalis, though most persons close to the profession, including musicians, thought it was written by Stanley Crouch, as indeed they do many of the written statements ascribed to Marsalis. Exegetical examination supports this belief, for the two men have different rhythmic patterns. In his interviews, Marsalis speaks in jagged, uneven cadences with limited vocabulary. Crouch has a smoother pattern; and the writings that supposedly come from Marsalis are similar in rhythm and usage to Crouch's work.

Insiders at the *Times* say the Marsalis letter was submitted to the paper's lawyers, who expurgated it, since it was libelous. But even the printed version of his *ad hominem* assault was unusually vitriolic, even by the standards Marsalis has established in assaulting things written about him or his.

He said, "Your reviewer refers to Mr. Collier as 'a stickler for the truth.' That is more than absurd. Among professional musicians and serious scholars of jazz, he is known for what he truly is—a poseur who attempts to elevate himself above his subject. . . . His purpose is not critical, musical or scholarly. As a musician, he is just what he now pretends to be outraged by—a man who cannot seriously analyze music"—one of Collier's books is a textbook on harmony adopted by a number of state boards of education for use in their schools—"but takes advantage of the lay public by using musical terminology. . . .

"Even his research is for camouflage, not illumination. No matter how many footnotes he uses, Mr. Collier is nothing more than a pompous social scientist who for too long has passed as a serious scholar of jazz music. That is why it is unfortunate that he was reviewed by a man apparently unaware of the contempt of all who are seriously engaged in jazz feel for this viper in the bosom of blues and swing."

That was the phrase that convinced everyone familiar with the utterances of Crouch and Marsalis that Crouch wrote the letter: the hyperbole struck many people as funny. And of course the letter did not disprove the content of Collier's footnotes, not one of them. It merely smeared the man, a not uncommon writer's trick.

"In the interest of jazz, men like James Lincoln Collier must be exposed," the letter concluded. "If reviewers aren't capable of doing so, musicians will have to step forward."

One had already stepped forward. And what he wrote was not about James Lincoln Collier, it was about Wynton Marsalis. Anthony Jackson, in a one-page article titled "The New Dark Age," published in the March-April 1991 issue of *Bass Player*, criticized Marsalis for his hostility to some of the current experimentation in jazz, and for his interpretation of The Tradition.

"The apologists, the insecure, and the take-that-jungle-music-off crowd," Jackson wrote, "could not destroy jazz. The innovators, upon whom the music has always depended for its incontrovertible strength, would not destroy it. Why, then, do we now find Mr. Marsalis and his congress of wanna-bes extolling the virtues of 'pure' jazz taking upon themselves the twin mantles of protector and rejuvenator? Inasmuch as the form has shown itself to be more than capable of withstanding the vicissitudes of neglect, corruption, revision, and outright attack, I maintain that this latest crop of 'redeemers' is more artistically bankrupt, morally hypocritical, and historically irrelevant than any that has come before. We are, in my opinion, witnessing no less than a modern cultural parallel to Germany in the 1930s, with a megalomaniacal 'arbiter of good taste' undertaking a redefinition and reclassification of a country's expressive potential, ostensibly to weed out contaminating influences. The underlying purpose is simply the muzzling and suppression of people whose expressive power, originality, and vitality are likely stronger than that of the leaders. . . ."

In an interview published in the August 1993 issue of *Down Beat*, trumpeter Lester Bowie said of Marsalis, "Here's this cat, obviously, obviously—

everybody *knows* this cat ain't got it. But they keep on pressing: 'He's got the technique, and any day he's gonna come up with this astounding new development.' Believe me, it ain't gonna happen. How long did it take Lee Morgan to play something of his own, or Clifford [Brown], or Booker Little? Wynton is a good musician, but he's been totally miscast. No way in the world is he the king of jazz, the king of trumpet. . . ."

The caveats of musicians about the quality of Marsalis's own playing are irrelevant to the central issue, except insofar as they bear on his assumption of the mantle of judgment of all jazz and jazz musicians. Still, it took courage for Jackson and Bowie to speak out. Marsalis now inspires fear, and his letters-to-editors when he is offended, or is even questioned, show why.

On January 24, 1994, the *Detroit Free Press* carried a story on the furor at Lincoln Center under the three-column headline: Lincoln Center Jazz Series Draws Flak. Tom Moon, the writer of the story, syndicated through the Knight-Ridder newspapers, called Marsalis to discuss the criticisms, and he reacted in a way that had become typical.

In what Moon described as "a heated telephone interview," Marsalis said, "I am the artistic director. It's my vision. Because I refuse to commission a work that sounds like European classical music with a little splattering of jazz, I'm somehow guilty?" The comment was an echo of Stanley Crouch's comments on Miles Davis and Gil Evans in his "Sketches of Pain" article in the *New Republic*.

Moon wrote, "Lincoln Center has yet to recognize musicians whose works are considered groundbreaking or of evolutionary significance. . . . And Marsalis is the roadblock."

The file of newspaper and magazine articles on Marsalis at the Institute of Jazz Studies at Rutgers University, and it is by no means complete, is very thick. No jazz musician has ever received as much publicity as he: interviews, reviews, and articles over his own byline, all with the same tone of superiority. Occasionally he tells us how humble he is, and then tells us how good he is, as in a *New Yorker* profile by Whitney Balliett in which he says of his early experience at Tanglewood, "You see, I knew they couldn't believe that a seventeen-year-old who could play the hell out of classical music also knew a lot about jazz."

That race is much on Marsalis's mind is seen in his repeated statements about why he played classical music. At one point he said he got into it because he wanted to prove one of "the brothers" could perform it. "I got into it because I dug the music," he told one interviewer. "Plus, I had always heard that black people couldn't play classical. That's bullshit. Music is music."

Much of what Marsalis says, as Herbie Hancock noted, needs saying. Marsalis said: "The people who really love this country, and realize how great this country is and could really be, are the ones who are responsible for educating our youth correctly. But they seem to have no respect for culture, and that is something that I think will damage our society in the long run. We will end up with culture being replaced by decadence. . . . Just turn on the Friday night videos on television. . . .

"I have been asked by interviewers, 'What do you think about the message in rap records?' Rap records have no message: What you have essentially [are] some rhymes in iambic pentameter"—he is wrong about that—"that have been expressed since the 1950s. So there's rhythm. I'll give them credit for that. But as a contribution to the history of Western music? To hold up the lyrics for comparison with everything else that has been written about man, about the conditions of life in this country? After all the great polemics and poems and pieces of music that have been written? Are we really going to stoop to that level now?

"Standards have become a very unpopular thing to defend in this country. Cultural education is suspect, and brings accusations of elitism. . . .

"Our problem is that we have replaced reality with bullshit. Anything can pass for art."

But then he gets into trouble for, among other things, his recurrent statements that one of the functions of jazz is to improve supposedly inferior popular music, which carries the strong undertone that what makes it inferior is that it was made by whites. For example, in a *Down Beat* interview in 1984, he said, "Jazz is about elevation and improvement. Jazz music always improves pop music. What Louis Armstrong did, singing songs by Gershwin and Irving Berlin, was improve them. Bird improved *I'll Remember April*, just like Beethoven improved folk melodies."

It is abject nonsense. In his whole career, Wynton Marsalis has never produced anything as melodic as any eight bars of Jerome Kern—or George Gershwin or Harold Arlen. As for that Don Raye–Gene De Paul song *I'll Remember April*, it is one of the most gorgeous in the repertoire, and Parker undoubtedly played it because he loved it. McCoy Tyner said:

"There are certain buildings you pass that seem to stand forever because they were built so structurally sound. It's the same with certain songs. They just lend themselves as improvisational vehicles. And they're good learning tools. Monk, Ellington, Cole Porter. I put these people in the category of composers whose music just lives on and on. It's the structure of their compositions that will forever stand the test of time."

It is not coincidence that jazz evolved in tandem with the creation in the

United States, between roughly 1915 and 1955, of an unprecedented body of popular music that was also high art. This body of magnificent songs provided jazz players with an extraordinary pool of familiar material to play on. Had that repertoire not been developed, jazz would not be the art form that it is. Marsalis has it exactly backwards—and because of what seems all too clearly an ethnic agenda. When he talks of tradition, he mentions Stravinsky, Beethoven, Mozart, and Bach, Armstrong, Ellington, and Parker—but never Kern and Youmans and Porter, and even more obviously never Bill Evans or Scott LaFaro, Beiderbecke or Trumbauer. Nowhere, in more than ten years of interviews with and articles by Marsalis, do I find praise for, or for that matter even mention of, one white American musician. The omission of names in Marsalis' invocations of the gods speaks thunderously loud, and when you put that together with the writings of Stanley Crouch, a pattern is evident.

On August 15, 1993, Howard Reich, the arts critic of the *Chicago Tribune*, wrote a piece on the start of the third season of Jazz at Lincoln Center. Reich interviewed Rob Gibson, director (under Crouch and Marsalis) of Jazz at Lincoln Center.

Reich cited the successes of the program, including a performance of Duke Ellington's *Deep South Suite*, which had not been played in forty-seven years.

"Though most of what has been written about us has been positive," Gibson told Reich, "there's one criticism that hurts me. That's when people say we've been racist, that we've honored music by blacks over music by whites.

"Now, I realize I'm a white guy speaking about a music that's played by a lot of African Americans, but I believe that the criticism is not fair.

"I've simply never looked at this music in terms of color. Jazz is an American creation, the most important and most sophisticated American music of this century. And the whole point is that it was made by Americans. It's not about black and white."

Reich wrote that "in these race-conscious times, some critics complain that Jazz at Lincoln Center has not paid homage to such major white artists as Gil Evans and Dave Brubeck.

"From this listener's point of view, the accusation of racism is flimsy at best, disingenuous at worst."

But Reich had apparently not examined the programs of Lincoln Center while reading the writings of Crouch and Marsalis, and given the contempt for Gil Evans that Crouch expressed in his "Sketches of Pain" article for the *New Republic*, it is dead certain that so long as he is associated with Lincoln

Center, Evans's music will never be presented there. No critic in the history of American music has ever had this power: to censor according to his own biases and limitations.

Gene Santoro, in the March 1, 1993, issue of the *Nation*, wrote, "I've complained that Marsalis's attitudes, and to a large extent his music, have been stunted by an overly high-toned moral seriousness based on the politics of exclusion. From my perspective, that stance denied jazz's history of expansion, accretion and appropriation." He was being cautious in the age of politically correct, but the meaning was there.

Other criticisms have arisen, including a furor over, as Gary Giddins wrote in the *Village Voice*, "the debut of Marsalis's *In This House / On This Morning*, an under-rehearsed and apparently unfinished suite that had Lincoln Center's customers fleeing for the exits and journalists pondering the propriety of an institution handing its first commission to its own musical director. . . ."

And then came what New York musicians came to call the Lincoln Center massacre. Rob Gibson sent a letter to every member of the Lincoln Center jazz orchestra older than thirty telling him he was fired. It is inconceivable that Gibson did this without the consent—if he did not indeed do it at the behest—of Crouch and Marsalis. (Crouch does have that much power: Giddins, who writes that he and Crouch have been close for twenty years, notes in his *Voice* article that Crouch vetoed an idea for a concert on music of Don Redman to be conducted by Loren Schoenberg. He also vetoed a commission to composer George Russell, about which Russell is bitter.) Shades of *Logan's Run*. Here was discrimination with a vengeance, not just racism this time but ageism as well. And after all of Marsalis's statements about respect for The Tradition. "As a young person myself," he said in 1984, "I can appreciate the fact that it's hip to be young, but I look to older people for guidance. I expect them to know more than I know, and I don't go around acting as if the reverse were true. Nor do I wish that, as I get older myself, I could go back to being younger. Older people trying to be young look stupid."

He had also said: "The promotion by the media of pop culture has affected our society on several levels." He wrote: "One result is that our culture has become very youth-oriented—we have a terrible hang-up about age in this country."

He had passed thirty when the Lincoln Center massacre occurred. The public response was immediate. Aside from denial of the value of having younger musicians work with veterans, the act contravened U.S. law: job discrimination by age is illegal. And Gibson had to rescind the order, notifying the dismissed musicians that they were rehired. The incident left a bad taste, and called into question the competence of Marsalis, Crouch, and Gibson to run so valuable a program.

Not long after the rehiring, the dismissals began again, and the number of whites (and older musicians) in the orchestra decreased further.

In January 1994 just before the Lincoln Center jazz orchestra was to leave on a five-week tour, Jerry Dodgion, the white and over-thirty lead alto player who had been one of those fired, got a call from Gibson asking him to return, at least for a time. The under-thirty player who had replaced him couldn't cut the part. Dodgion named his price and made the tour.

Reviewing the Lincoln Center jazz program, Whitney Balliett ended an essay on Marsalis in the October 14, 1991, issue of the *New Yorker* by saying:

"It appears that [Marsalis] is reviving not only the older music but also the reverse racism popular among black musicians in the fifties and sixties. Just six of the 54 performers used this week at Lincoln Center were white. Blacks invented jazz, but nobody owns it."

W. Royal Stokes wrote in the winter 1992-93 issue of the quarterly of the National Jazz Service Organization: "A number of musicians, white and black, have in the past several years voiced to me their own displeasure over the tendency of some black musicians, and their supporters, to look at the music as the preserve of the African-American component of our make-up as a society and culture."

Stokes is white, but Willard Jenkins, executive director of the NJSO and editor of the publication, is not. In a long editorial in the same issue, Jenkins addressed the issues at Lincoln Center. After praising the positive accomplishments of Wynton Marsalis and his associates, he said: "All that aside, there is indeed room for spirited discussion and outright criticism of the presentations of Jazz at Lincoln Center. The most cogent quibbles have to do with the sense of narrowcasting which seems to permeate the whole Jazz at Lincoln Center programming philosophy. Point of fact, while we recognize the need for Lincoln Center's jazz program to proceed in slow, incremental steps . . . there is no clear sign . . . that a gradual evolution towards expansion of the program's stylistic vision . . . is even the remotest possibility.

"Case in point is the issue of commissioned new work. Granted, the third season . . . has finally moved a tad beyond the compositional charms of the program's artistic director [Marsalis], who garnered the lion's share of the first two seasons' commissioned concerts. However, the two most recently executed commissions went to two of [his] close musical associates, Terence Blanchard and Roy Hargrove—stylistically remaining within the artistic director's comfort zone—questionably begging nagging questions of cronyism.

"That same issue of cronyism comes into play when one considers the musicians selected to perform repertory works. . . . Marcus Roberts may have been more comfortable with the group of relative jazz youth chosen to play this season's . . . Thelonious Monk big-band re-creation. . . .

"As long as Phil Woods, Johnny Griffin, Steve Lacy, Ben Riley, and Eddie Bert (to name but a handful of big-band Monk mates) still walk the earth, one would think the Lincoln Center faithful . . . deserve the best, most seasoned, most representative re-creation of that repertoire. Fact is the selection of artists from the shallow pool of Marsalis-mates . . . for nearly every tributary concert . . . need not always be . . . his associates."

Jenkins points out that the latest Monk concert featured among the soloists every member of Marsalis's ensemble at that time "and again no Lacy, no Woods, no Larry Ridley or Paul Jeffrey (the latter two having been members of Monk's final quartet)."

Leonard Feather said: "With Marsalis, part of the problem has been the reluctance of the New York media to tackle the issue. I have seen in New York only brief passing mentions of the fact that in the concert celebrating Thelonious Monk, he ignored those white musicians who had taken part in Monk's original concert and replaced them with non-whites."

But, fearful or not of failing to be politically correct, writers in New York were finding it increasingly difficult to ignore what was going on in the Lincoln Center jazz program. In a year-end article published December 23, 1993, in the *Village Voice*, Kevin Whitehead wrote: "Patrons paid $35 to listen to on-the-job training, which raises the larger issue of why jazz at Lincoln Center really exists: to educate the public about it and expose it to quality jazz, or to subsidize Wynton's working groups, whose members are heavily featured . . . ? What's on display at Alice Tully [Hall] is less great jazz than the good life available to musicians who get with the neocon program. . . ."

This time Marsalis sent a letter, fully 1500 words long, to the *Village Voice*. Its tone must have been even more vituperative than that to the *Times* about James Lincoln Collier: the *Voice* declined to print it.

On the issue of cronyism, John Ephland noted in the February 1994 *Down Beat* that excepting Benny Carter, the only recipients of Lincoln Center jazz composition commissions have been Marsalis himself, Geri Allen, Marcus Roberts, Roy Hargrove, and Terence Blanchard, all of them "young African-American artists." Even among black composers, the oversights were conspicuous, George Russell and Hale Smith among them. Both men had reached their sixties, and Russell has reached his seventies. Time was running out for such artists.

Willard Jenkins continued: "As for questions of racism, it's true that none other than African-American artists have been commissioned and in the vast majority of cases, presented. Why are those questions only asked when something appears to be 'too black' for certain folks' comfort zones? While it is provocative to ask such questions—relating to perceived racial imbalance in programming, and certainly valid—one wonders why when the shoe is on the other foot those same questions are not asked from the other side of the coin by those same critics; or why we're still dealing with racial issues nearly 100 years into this supposedly most democratic of musical aesthetics in the first place. Would these same questions be as pointed if someone like Gerry Mulligan or Phil Woods were artistic director of Jazz at Lincoln Center, and . . . utilizing a majority of African-American artists?"

The parallel is improper. First, when things have been too white, critics such as Leonard Feather and Nat Hentoff have indeed raised questions. Questions assuredly would be raised if Woods or Mulligan used an all-white orchestra in such a situation. Sure-footed up to this point, Jenkins suddenly succumbs to his own conditioning.

Lest it seem that Willard Jenkins is one with Stanley Crouch, Herb Boyd, Amiri Baraka, and others of their persuasion, I must note that he is fully as supportive of gifted young white players, including Geoff Keezer and Benny Green, as he is of young blacks such as Marlon Jordan and Roy Hargrove. His writing is not racist. It is, however, racial, which is a different matter. He will, for example, take note of bands that are all white but will make no comment on bands that are all black.

Repeatedly we have heard that jazz is about the black experience. Yet if a black American composer writes a string quartet, there is no reason why he should filter out his personal experience. Art is about personal vision, and no art as much so as jazz. This has been true since Louis Armstrong—and, which is often overlooked, Earl Hines and Sidney Bechet—defined it as the art of the soloist.

The pianist and bassist Don Thompson thinks it is impossible for a player not to have an individual tone. He is probably right. A musician's tone is the consequence not only of his personal experience, emotional makeup, and thought processes but also of physical characteristics. The shape of your fingertip will affect the tone you draw from a guitar. When Eddie Harris asked Lester Young for tips about his embouchure, Prez said, "I can only tell you about my mouthpiece in my mouth. I can't tell you about your mouthpiece in your mouth."

Interestingly, the music of white jazz musicians tends to reflect their national roots. So Irish was the music of Zoot Sims that the late Judy Holliday used to say he played "Barry Fitzgerald tenor." And you can easily observe a Puccini-like lyricism, a truly Italian melodicism, in the playing of many Italian-Americans.

Given the musical character of the two lands of origin, the question "What would an American jazz pianist of mixed Welsh and Russian background sound like?" deserves the answer: Bill Evans. Yet Bill had explored every aspect of jazz. One night late at the Village Vanguard, when the audience was almost all gone, he began to play blues. His gorgeous golden tone was abandoned. He was playing hard and funky, dark Southern blues. After that final set, he said to me with a grin, "I can really play that stuff when I want to." And so he could.

But why should he? It wasn't him. He had assimilated many influences, but the result was what we think of as Bill Evans, one of the most distinctive, original, and finally influential forces in the history of jazz, and one of the most original in the whole history of music.

The black xenophobia in jazz is antithetical to this. But its implications stretch far beyond it. On an overpopulated planet, the strife for turf control is growing ominous. There are countless people who do not want reconciliation of religions, races, nations, even regions.

In the Middle East, extremist Israelis and Palestinians strive to destroy the peace accord that offered a glimpse of possible stability. We have lived through terrorism between militant Catholic and Protestant elements in Northern Ireland. We have watched Czechoslovakia break into separate ethnic units, fortunately without bloodshed. But the most hideous bloodletting has attended the breakup of Yugoslavia. Canada may well break down into two nations, although the indications are that it would do so peacefully, even amiably. In Chiapa, Mayan Indians rebelled against the Mexican government. In Germany, neo-Nazis kill foreign workers. In Sri Lanka, the separatist guerrilla war of the Tamil minority grows more bloody. The Soviet Union has broken down into its component nations, and within them there is new fighting to break these smaller countries into ethnic units. The Armenians war with the Muslims. There has been ghastly internecine warfare in Africa. The Lombardy League presses to separate the north of Italy from the rest of the country. In Los Angeles and other cities, gang-bangers kill to control turf, and there is a deep animosity between blacks and Koreans. Alvin Toffler has pointed out that in the years after World War II, there was an average of thirty wars being waged in the world in any given year. After the breakup of the Soviet Union, the number more than doubled.

What is happening in jazz is an echo of all this. When resources, including space, what the Germans call *Lebensraum*, grow scarce and the ambiance ominous, men and women tend to cluster with their own kind in suspicious and sullen union against the outsiders. This has been exacerbated in jazz by the shrinkage of opportunities. Once there were countless jazz clubs all over the country; there are few now. And there was a great deal of studio work, in New York, Los Angeles, and Chicago to augment the incomes of jazz players and give them a base of operations. This included a great many black musicians, although white musicians formed the preponderance of the studio pool. Nonetheless Clark Terry, Hank Jones, George Duvivier, and others worked regularly at the television networks and on studio recording sessions. In Los Angeles, many jazz players worked in sound-track recording for the movie industry.

But most of that work is gone now. It has been replaced by synthesizers, and a generation of television producers and executives raised on rock music doesn't know good music from bad anyway, or electronic moanings from real music made by real musicians. And there is the ubiquitous Muzak in restaurants, as well as the new computer-driven grand pianos in the lobbies of fancy hotels, producing bland standards while the ghosts of vanished jobs sit at the keyboards. In an increasingly academic jazz world, what remains is a kind of hot-house jazz dwelling on the past, supported artificially by grants and other aid, like the most precious and obscure classical music, and programs to "save" jazz.

In comparing the policies and utterances of Wynton Marsalis to cultural events in 1930s Germany, bassist Anthony Jackson was not being as hyperbolic as it might at first seem. Richard Wagner was a virulent anti-Semite who wrote in a pamphlet published in 1869 that Jews had no place in Germany's artistic or musical life. The pamphlet ended with a statement to an anti-Semitic Jew named Joseph Rubinstein: "Remember that there is only one release from the curse that weighs you down: obliteration." The great musicologist Henry Pleasants, who lived for many years in Germany, said to me, "As to Wagner's contribution to the rise of the Nazis, I would say that they didn't need him, but certainly found him useful." In the search for "purity" in music, the Nazis barred the work of Jewish composers, including Mendelssohn, Schoenberg, and Mahler. They also barred jazz, and in some instances executed Europeans who played it. As Dizzy Gillespie remarked, in a discussion of jazz as "serious" music, "Men have died for this music. You can't get more serious than that." It is this kind of "ethnic cleansing" in jazz to which Anthony Jackson referred.

"Consider this," Jackson wrote. "A well-known pianist was recently discussing a record deal with a major label. The deal was rejected, whereupon the company's representative, either unaware of or unconcerned about the possible consequences of revealing information clearly intended for insiders only, told him why: 'First, you're too old. Second, you're not black.' Does this mean we should dig up Benny Goodman's grave and hack the corpse to pieces? What about Scott LaFaro's?"

Jazz has always had a largely white audience. As Johnny Griffin said in an interview for the Dempsey Travis book *The Autobiography of Black Jazz*, "Let's hope that those faithful white connoisseurs of jazz will hang in there long enough for the people back in the hood to get the message." The continuing insult of whites by Marsalis in his policies and public statements and by Crouch in his writings sooner or later must work to turn that audience off.

Marsalis and Crouch are always invoking the names of the gods, including Count Basie and Duke Ellington. It is instructive to consider what these great men—safe on Parnassus, in the felicitous phrase of a friend of mine— had to say on these issues.

On May 16, 1956, Basie did an interview with Don Freeman (now a syndicated columnist with the *San Diego Union*), printed in the February 1994 *Down Beat*. Basie was discussing what gave him pleasure. High on his list of admired musicians were Duke Ellington and Art Tatum. Basie said: "I'll tell you another listening thrill. Back in the '30s, no matter where we were every Saturday night, we'd have to hear Benny Goodman's band on the old *Camel Caravan* [radio program]. That was a wonderful band. . . .

"I remember one night when I wandered over to Roseland to see Les Brown. I kind of sneaked in, and Les didn't know I was there. Oh, that's a fine dance band.

"And another is Tommy Dorsey's band. If I'm in town, and the Dorseys are there, I won't miss 'em because they got a fine, swinging band too. Tommy is a remarkable musician. Remarkable."

In 1945, Duke Ellington told a reporter from the newspaper *PM*, "Jazz is like the automobile and airplane. It is modern and it is American. . . . The Negro element is still important. But jazz has become part of America. There are as many white musicians playing it as Negro. . . . We are all working together along more or less the same lines. We learn from each other. Jazz is American now. American is the big word."

In 1965, Ellington told Nat Hentoff, "In the 1920s I used to try to convince Fletcher Henderson that we ought to call what we are doing 'Negro music'. But it's too late for that now. The music has become so integrated you can't tell one part from the other so far as color is concerned."

In his 1973 autobiography, Ellington wrote, "Although his background seemed to give the black musician the edge, because environment is intensely important as a shaping factor, jazz was so contagious that many white musicians were infected by it and grew close to the black soul. Today, jazz is international music that is played everywhere in the world."

Kevin Whitehead said in his *Village Voice* article, "Watching Han Bennink, this 51-year-old farmer-looking 'avant-garde' Dutchman, swinging the hell out of Sid Catlett licks at the traps, says more about the triumph of African American culture than the circle-the-wagons programming [at Lincoln Center]."

But there are, clearly, those who do not want to see jazz as an art form celebrating the human spirit. There is an element in jazz that craves retribution and revenge and would use jazz as a weapon of exclusion and insult to get redress. Black America already has had massive retribution. Nat Turner's uprising did not fail if its purpose was retribution rather than revolution. The Virginia legislature, William Styron points out, was on the verge of abolishing slavery. Had Virginia done so, the rest of the South would have followed. The insurrection so terrified Virginia that it tightened the laws of slavery instead. Subsequent events led directly to the Civil War. Nat Turner's retribution was massive: something over 600,000 white dead out of a population that was then quite small.

Wynton Marsalis and Stanley Crouch are only symbols of the deep malaise that divides America. Despite the appearance of black journalists and commentators on television, despite the rise of a large pool of brilliant black actors, despite black achievements in the sciences, in law, and every other area of endeavor, anyone who has any sensitivity whatever to the racial dilemma of the United States has a deep if intuitive awareness that the chasm has grown wider and deeper.

Commented author and cornetist Richard M. Sudhalter: "In some ways the *sina qua non* to understanding the entire matter is the degree to which whites have been and remain complicit in the creation of the lopsided state of affairs. Locked into the white American liberal sensibility there appears to be a powerful machinery, guilt-driven, which inhibits—nay, prohibits—resistance to anything from the black side that can be interpreted, however marginally, as sponsoring redress."

Some surprising figures stand staring across the gap. Two of them are university English teachers. Stanley Fish is at Duke University; Shelby Steele is at San Jose State University and author of *The Content of Our Character: A New Vision of Race in America* (St. Martin's Press, New York, 1993). Fish is white, Steele is black.

In a book titled *There's No Such Thing as Free Speech in America* (Oxford University Press, New York, 1993) Fish says, "In this country whites once set themselves apart from blacks and claimed privileges for themselves they deny to others. Isn't one as bad as the other? The answer is no."

Fish justifies some of the injustices arising out of affirmative action, including the admission to college courses of students of lower academic achievement over whites (or Orientals) with higher grades, and including even his own failure to be given a post he wanted when he was told it could go only to a woman or a member of a minority.

Steele could not disagree with him more. In an essay titled *White Guilt,* he writes: "In 1964, one of the assurances Senator Hubert Humphrey and others had to give Congress to get the landmark Civil Rights Bill passed was that the bill would not in any way require employers to use racial preferences to rectify racial imbalances. But this was before the explosion of black power in the late 1960s, before the hidden paradigm was set in motion. After black power, racial preferences became the order of the day.

"If this paradigm brought blacks entitlements, it also brought the continuation of the most profound problem in American society, the invisibility of blacks as people. The white guilt that this paradigm elicits is the kind of guilt that preoccupies whites with their own innocence and pressures them toward escapism. . . . With this guilt, as opposed to the contained guilt of genuine concern, whites tend to see only their own need for quick redemption. Blacks then become a means to this redemption and, as such, they must be seen as generally 'less than' others. . . . They are seen exclusively along the dimensions of their victimization, so that they become 'different' people with whom whites can negotiate entitlements but never fully see as people like themselves. Guilt that preoccupies people with their own innocence blinds them to those who make them feel guilty. This, of course, is not racism, and yet it has the same effect as racism since it makes blacks something of a separate species for whom normal standards and values do not automatically apply.

"Nowhere is this more evident today than in American universities. At some of America's most elite universities administrators have granted concessions in response to black student demands (black power) that all but sanction racial separatism on campus—black 'theme' dorms, black student unions, black yearbooks, homecoming dances, and so forth. . . . Though blacks have the lowest grade point average of any racial group in American universities, administrators never sit down with them and 'demand' in kind that black students bring their grades up to par. The paradigm of white guilt makes the real problems of black students secondary to the need for white redemption."

Steele concludes the essay:

"Selfish white guilt is really self-importance. It has no humility, and it asks for unreasonable, egotistical innocence. Nothing diminishes a black more than this sort of guilt in a white, which to my mind amounts to a sort of moral colonialism. . . . The selfishly guilty white person is drawn to what blacks least like in themselves—their suffering, victimization, and dependency. This is no good for anyone—black or white."

I would append an anecdote to Professor Steele's observation.

I once had a white Southern friend (he's dead now), a man of eminence and achievement whom I admired. He had many black friends and indeed had grown up close to blacks. One night, after a few too many drinks, he said something with a sort of amiable irony that concealed, I realized, the fact that he meant it. We were talking about the progress in "race relations" that seemed to have been achieved. And he said, "I dunno, I think I liked it better the way things were in the old days. You know, when we kept them and took care of them—like pets."

Ah yes. Like bears riding bicycles and seals tooting horns.

On December 29, 1993, evangelist Billy Graham was asked during a television show what problem he would solve if he could be granted a great boon. Without hesitation he said: "Race. Because it's dividing the world. If I could wave a wand, that would be the thing I would make disappear."

"To be fair," Daisy Sweeney, a noted Montreal music teacher and Oscar Peterson's sister, said to me, "can you name me a race that is without racism? Racism exists among black people with black people. I was discriminated against because I was darker than other girls. . . .

"I remember that even Oliver Jones was discriminated against. Oliver is very dark, like me." Jones is one of the pianists she trained. "I was one of his Sunday school teachers. And I had to fight with one of the leaders because of her wanting to put him in the back. Now this didn't happen in a white church."

Joe Williams too experienced discrimination from other blacks. Dempsey J. Travis in *The Autobiography of Black Jazz* quotes his describing how, during the early phase of his career, black Chicago club owners wouldn't hire him because he was too dark. "My light-skinned black brothers," he said, "really whipped a color game on me."

Throughout history the use of charged vocabulary has served the purpose of demonizing the stranger. The word *barbarous*, for example, descends from a Greek word, *barbaros,* meaning non-Greek and therefore rude. This condescension finds its echo in Gerald Wilson's statement that a certain orchestra was "one of the better non-black bands." It also resounds in the term "un-American," which is offensive to persons of other nationalities. The word *goy* derives from a Hebrew word meaning enemy: anyone who is not a Jew. I have always found it amusing that English terms of condescension toward the French find their exact inversions in French. Going AWOL is to take French leave in English but it's English leave in French; syphilis was once known as the French disease in England but the English disease in France; and so on.

During World War II the Japanese were referred to as Japs and Nips, even in newspaper headlines. In the postwar years, these terms fell into disuse and then were placed on the prohibited list. So too such terms as Krauts and Huns for Germans. They were replaced, as the United States found new enemies, with such terms as gooks and slopes. It might be hard to machine-gun a sensitive young woman; it is not so hard to kill a slope.

At one time in the United States it was seriously postulated that Africans had thicker skulls and could not feel blows to the head the way whites could. An inversion of this is implicit in common black attitudes toward jazz played by white musicians, an attitude present in the work of a good many white writers on the subject. It is curious that whites who would object passionately to the use of the term *nigger* have accepted with equanimity black terms of insult for whites. *Down Beat* at one time commonly used the term *ofay* to mean white, though it is pig Latin for foe. It even turned up in headlines. Its use, of course, connoted that the magazine and its writers were hip, in the know, on the inside of the black world. *Ofay* is by now an almost vanished term. No one much took exception to it, perhaps because white Americans felt secure in power. Jesse Jackson's slip when he referred to New York City as Hymietown may have permanently crippled his ambitions to high political office. Marsalis's reference to "people who read the Torah and stuff" has escaped general notice. So have his references to blacks as "the brothers and sisters"—terms of exclusion.

One of the words most freighted with meaning is *soul*. It is heavy with what actors call under-text, for its use as applied to blacks carries the unmistakable implication that whites do not have souls. Within the world of jazz, its use as a quality that blacks have but whites do not leaves, cumulatively, the impression of whites as subhuman. The attitude, and it is there in comments of Amiri Baraka, Archie Shepp, Wynton Marsalis, and others, is that whites have no feelings of sorrow, joy, reverence, beauty, compassion, laughter, exuberance, and all the other qualities that are the essential materials of art. This is the exact mirror inversion of the white racism that holds that blacks do not feel pain as whites do.

Marsalis would perhaps argue that whites can't get the hang of jazz because they didn't invent it. Indeed he has said that black New Orleans musicians "invented" improvisation. This would come as a shock to the shades of Chopin, Bach, Beethoven, Mozart, the violin and piano virtuosi who were expected to improvise the cadenzas in concerti, the great castrati (who were thoroughly schooled in improvisation), church organists, flamenco guitar players, and gypsy violinists. And, as one musician put it, "It would make anyone who has played baroque figured bass choke with laughter."

Through much of European musical history, improvisation was the norm. The evolution of our notational system took time, and the gradual hardening into a written tradition of music dominated by composers in the nineteenth century is in a sense the aberration.

A few years ago the Detroit Pistons lost a basketball game to the Boston Celtics in a last-minute play by Larry Bird. Sports writers had commonly remarked on how hard Larry Bird worked on basketball, implying that he had to do so because he was not the natural talent black players were. This eventually riled Isaiah Thomas of the Pistons, and in a statement that I believe was widely misunderstood, he said he was tired of seeing black athletes discussed as if they were lions or tigers—animals, in other words, of natural ability. He said that he and his colleagues also worked hard at basketball, just as hard as Larry Bird. In the game in question, he said, at the last minute Larry Bird made his move "and with his God-given gift," as Thomas put it, took the game away from Detroit.

I thought it was a sane statement for human dignity. Thomas nailed it. This is what a coddled separatism invites. His comment and its implications are clear, like that of Dizzy Gillespie in saying that if only blacks can play jazz, then perhaps that could be construed to mean that that is all they can do.

Dizzy said once, with sadness in his eyes, "You can't know what it means to be black in the United States—in any field." He was right of course. Whites can only try to imagine what a life of constant insult, abuse, rejection, and danger must be. But some do try, and in part succeed, particularly those who like jazz, which is why this music, quite aside from its brilliant aesthetic achievements, has been an incomprehensibly powerful force of healing in American life.

Norman Granz put it this way: "This can be a very dogmatic statement, but I stand by it. I don't think anyone gets into jazz—not as players, I'm talking about the public—and understands what it is about, and understands what the musicians are about, without understanding racism."

But sometimes it seems that certain elements in the black world are actively hostile to even the idea of white efforts to understand, as witness the assaults on such works as *The Confessions of Nat Turner*.

In the end, to see Stanley Crouch and Wynton Marsalis and their allies clutching jazz to their collective breast as theirs and theirs alone, the only thing they can claim credit for, is infinitely sad. And it supports the argument of Shelby Steele.

"It saddens me," said Leonard Feather, the dean of jazz critics, who has been documenting the music since 1933, "to observe what Wynton Marsalis is doing to destroy the image of jazz as a truly democratic music."

One of two things is true. Either jazz has evolved into a major art form, and an international one, capable of exploring and inspiring the full range of human experience and emotion. Or it is a small, shriveled, crippled art useful only for the expression of the angers and resentments of an American minority. If the former is true, it is the greatest artistic gift of blacks to America, and America's greatest aesthetic gift to the world.

If the latter is true, it isn't dying. It's already dead.

February 1994